The Politics of Europe

Also by Werner Bonefeld

A MAJOR CRISIS: The Politics of Economic Policy in Britain in the 1990s (*co-author*)

GLOBAL CAPITAL, NATIONAL STATE AND THE POLITICS OF MONEY (*co-editor*)

OPEN MARXISM, Volume I: Theory and Practice (*co-editor*)

OPEN MARXISM, Volume II: Dialectics and History (*co-editor*)

OPEN MARXISM, Volume III: Emancipating Marx (*co-editor*)

POST-FORDISM AND SOCIAL FORM (*co-editor*)

THE POLITICS OF CHANGE (*co-editor*)

THE RECOMPOSITION OF THE BRITISH STATE DURING THE 1980s

The Politics of Europe

Monetary Union and Class

Edited by

Werner Bonefeld
Lecturer in Politics
University of York

palgrave

First published 2001 by
PALGRAVE
Houndmills, Basingstoke, Hampshire RG21 6XS and
175 Fifth Avenue, New York, N. Y. 10010
Companies and representatives throughout the world

PALGRAVE is the new global academic imprint of St. Martin's Press LLC Scholarly and Reference Division and Palgrave Publishers Ltd (formerly Macmillan Press Ltd).

ISBN 0–333–92010–4

This book is printed on paper suitable for recycling and made from fully managed and sustained forest sources.

A catalogue record for this book is available from the British Library.

Library of Congress Cataloging-in-Publication Data
The politics of Europe : monetary union and class / edited by Werner Bonefeld.
p. cm.
Includes bibliographical references and index.
ISBN 0–333–92010–4
1. Monetary unions—Europe. 2. Social class—Europe.
I. Bonefeld, Werner, 1960–

HG3894 .P654 2000
305.5'094—dc21

00–049144

10 9 8 7 6 5 4 3 2 1
10 09 08 07 06 05 04 03 02 01

Printed and bound in Great Britain by
Antony Rowe Ltd, Chippenham, Wiltshire

Contents

List of Tables vii

Notes on the Contributors viii

1 The Politics of Europe: Monetary Union and Class 1
Werner Bonefeld
The chapters 7
Notes 8
Bibliography 9

2 The Contradictions of European Monetary Union 10
Alex Callinicos
Franco-German rivalries and the Maastricht Treaty 12
A monetarist project 16
National tensions 20
Europe versus America? 25
Conclusion 30
Notes 34
Bibliography 35

3 The EMU, Monetary Crises, and the Single Eurpopean Currency 37
Guglielmo Carchedi
Introduction 37
Economic crises, money, and inflation 37
Exchange rates and monetary crises 39
The European monetary union and the single currency 46
The 1994–95 monetary crisis 52
Conclusions 58
Notes 58
Bibliography 62

4 European Monetary Union: Ideology and Class 64
Werner Bonefeld
Preface 64
Introduction 65
European monetary integration in historical context 68
Class and the crisis of capitalist accumulation 74

Neo-liberalism, crisis and institutional reform 79
The politics of EMU 86
Conclusion 97
Notes 102
Bibliography 103

5 The EC's Free Market Agenda and the Myth of Social Europe 107
Bernard H. Moss
Justifications for the EC: peace and prosperity? 108
Academic Europhilia: a sociology of knowledge 111
Treaty foundations: law and history 112
Judicial enforcement: the new liberal order 115
The failure of constructive integration 117
The myth of the social dimension 124
Links of the social to the democratic deficit 128
Conclusion 130
Notes 131
Bibliography 131

6 The European Union and its Periphery: Inclusion and Exclusion 136
Mike Haynes
Rich and poor Europe 136
Economic convergence and divergence 143
Europe and its other 155
Soft security borders and identity 158
Notes 164
Bibliography 166

7 Britain and the Question of Europe 170
Werner Bonefeld
EMU and disarray 171
Monetarism and the search for an anchor 173
Globalization and European integration 180
Conclusion: EMU and employability 184
Notes 187
Bibliography 189

Index 193

List of Tables

6.1 Characteristics of the economies of the European Union 131

6.2 Range of values of regional per capita GDP in PPS for NUTS 2 regions in the EU member states in 1996 139

6.3 Characteristics of selected economies on the border of the European Union 141

6.4 Long run GDP per capita in 1990 international dollars in European Union members and periphery countries, 1820–1992 144

Notes on the Contributors

Werner Bonefeld teaches at the Department of Politics, University of York.

Alex Callinicos is Professor of Politics at the University of York.

Guglielmo Carchedi teaches at the University of Amsterdam, Faculty of Economics and Econometrics.

Mike Haynes teaches at the School of Humanities, Language and Social Sciences, University of Wolverhampton.

Bernard Moss is Professor of History associated with the Institute of European Studies in London.

1
The Politics of Europe: Monetary Union and Class

Werner Bonefeld

Assessments of the politics of European integration in general, and monetary union in particular, are many. In fact, the study of the European Union has become an academic growth industry. This book does not add just another publication. Its theoretical focus and practical perspective are specific. The volume provides a critique of the political economy of European integration. The aim is not just to supply an alternative approach to the study of the politics of Europe but also to contribute to a renewal of Marxist critique of the politics of European integration.[1]

This book does *not* explore the politics of European integration in terms of the well-worn theme of 'pro- or anti-Europeanism'. There is no doubt that the major parties are in broad agreement over most policy questions. This broad agreement corresponds with an uninspiring uniformity that characterizes most aspects of contemporary debate. However, if there is, in Britain, one issue which does divide, not only between the Right and Left but also within the Right and within the Left, it is the issue of European integration. Yet, however heated the debate between Eurosceptics and Europhiles, and whatever 'insights' the claims and counterclaims might offer, it adds little, if anything at all, to the understanding of European integration. In fact, it sheds no light on the reasons for European integration. In this debate even the most elementary question of a critical analysis associated with the great European tradition of the Enlightenment – *cui bono* [who benefits] – is not raised. The debate between Eurosceptics and Europhiles however serves a useful social function. It replaces a critical public debate about the nature of European integration, by a 'discursive' spectacle that serves to hide and conceal the true character of its constitutive process. Friederich Hayek, to his benefit, had not such scruples. In the late 1930s, he advocated 'inter-state federalism' as a solution to the labour question. For him such federalism would keep the bourgeoisie in business and the working class down and busy.[2]

Later in his life, Hayek saw a single currency as a dangerous thing and, instead, prescribed the issue of rival currencies by competing private banks (see Anderson, 1997, p. 131). However one views Hayek's stance, his position in relation to labour was at least clear, unambiguous and principled. The conceptualization of European integration, its constitution, purpose and direction, can not be based on either party political propaganda, widely biased and profoundly ideological accounts, or a 'scientific perspective' whose focus falls on the fine detail of technocratic government and on how the functionality and legitimacy of its operations might be improved.[3] In this technocratic perspective our social world is approached in a tupsy turvy way: it is not the social institutions that need to fulfil human needs; rather it is the human beings who need to be adjusted to the system's functional requirements. Against the technocratic specialists of the common good, the book insists that the focus of the social sciences is the human being, her condition and possibilities. This role of the social sciences was emphasized, long before Marx, by Kant (1868, p. 625, author's translation) who argued that 'only that science is true which helps the common Man to his dignity'. Who, then, benefits from European integration and whose social interests does it serve?

The new European currency, the euro, was launched on 1 January 1999. The preparation for its launch has helped to justify austerity across Europe. Yet, critical publications which develop a sustained assessment of the class-politics of European integration are rare. This is most surprising since most accounts, including the Delors and the Emerson Committees on EMU, recognize that the single currency entails huge adjustment costs and that these, unsurprisingly, are expected to be born by European labour.[4] The question of European integration, and monetary union in particular, appears as if the class conflict between capital and labour has nothing to do with Europe, as if Europe were a world apart from the aspirations and expectations of those upon whose effective and efficient application and docile existence the wealth of Europe rests and depends: the dependent masses, that is those who depend for their livelihood on the sale of their labour power and whose life as a labouring commodity is refered to as a human factor of production. In our so-called globalized world, the talk about the 'dependent masses' appears outdated and is viewed with a certain suspicion regarding the author's political correctness. No such response is offered when the proponents of EMU explain the economic adjustment mechanisms of monetary union. Here the existence of the dependent masses is quietly taken for granted, their compliant and effective application is confidently presupposed, and their readiness to contribute effectively to the stability of EMU is discussed in thoughtful and serious terms. Hix's (1999, pp. 299–300) summary of what is expected of European labour is apt: 'a monetary union should be able to adapt either through labour movement from states in recession to states in high growth, or through labour-market flexibility, with a reduction of wage and labour costs in states in recession to attract capital investment'. Adjustment is not restricted to 'European labour' but includes also, as Haynes makes clear in his contribution to this volume, the policing and criminalization of the so-called third country nationals and refuges, including immigrant labour. According to the *Guardian* (14.3.00), the EU is considering to provide special funds for member states to deal with the repatriation of illegal immigrants, and failed asylum seekers. This merely serves as a reminder that, concerning the dependent masses, their integrity and dignity as human beings is not at the top of the EU's agenda.

Still, mention of the dependent masses is unpopular in an intellectual environment that favours the language of political correctness and whose indifference to the human condition is obscured by its concern for so-called minority interests. How might these minorities be defined against the background of a society which preserves its abstract wealth through the 'sacrifice of "human machines" on the pyramids of accumulation' (Gambino, 1996, p. 55)? While favouring a vocabulary with a progressive ring, such as equality and social inclusion, politically correct approaches engage with our class-divided social world merely in terms of philosophical convictions. It is a well known fact that, in the world of philosophical convictions, unfavourable conditions need not be changed. All that is required is to interpret them more favourably, that is in politically correct terms. This, I suppose, underlies the correspondence between, on the one hand, the language of political correctness and the concern for the minority interests of capital, and the projection of an economically strong and viable Europe based on liberal concerns for abstract equality, on the other hand. The circumstance that every individual is equal before money means that 'the power which each individual exercises over the activity of others or over social wealth exist in him as the owner of *exchange values*, of *money*. The individual carries his social power, as well as his bond with society, in his pocket' (Marx, 1973, p. 157). Moss shows in his contribution that the notion of a social Europe is a myth; and Haynes takes issue with the idea that an economically strong European core will even out levels of socio-economic disparity between the richer regions and their poorer 'partners'.

The term social inclusion is problematic. It accepts that there is an excluded minority and that the division of society is that between the included majority and the excluded minority. Exclusion is thus considered as a problem that obtains at the margin of society. This view fails to appreciate that 'exclusion' is not only constitutive of capitalist society but, also and because of this, the essential characteristic of a society that accumulates wealth by exploiting the social labour power of those who are free from the possession of the means of production and thus free to sell their labour power. For Marx, the dividing line between classic political economy and vulgar economic thought was whether the question of the genesis of surplus value was raised. From the standpoint of 'social inclusion', this question is a non-question since 'capital' is not conceived in terms of an antagonistic social relationship between capital and labour. Rather, capital is treated in terms that defy reason: the answer to the question 'What is "capital"?' is already presupposed: capital is capital and *vice versa*! Capital, in sum, is conceived as an economic mechanism that – if regulated well and competently – discharges useful economic functions. The insight that labour is the substance of value is thus dismissed in favour of a technocratic understanding of capital where, disregarding all logic, capital is defined in relation to itself – as a self-relation. It is disturbing that today's 'third-way' conceptions of liberal thought are unaware of their own theoretical heritage.[5] Adam Smith at least sought to offer a theory of the social constitution of value – however flawed his labour theory of value.

Nevertheless, the understanding of capital in terms of an economic mechanism leads to a conception of the EU as a supranational regulative framework that has been created by its constituent members in order to pool the necessary resources for re-regulation of the globalized economic relations on a regional basis. Integration is here considered merely in terms of its technocratic potentials for protecting the institutional requirements that the free market requires for its smooth operation. Callinicos analyses the integration process as an expression of a dialectical relationship between inter-imperialist rivalry and dependency. Carchedi conceptualizes the foundation of this relationship in terms of the labour theory of value. For Bonefeld (Chapter 4) and Carchedi, the global crisis of capitalist accumulation serves as a useful starting point for assessing the relations of inter-imperialist rivalry in terms of its social constitution.

The perennial question of any critical social theory is 'Why does this content take this form?'. Concerning European integration, this question concerns not only the removal, through Europeanization, of for example monetary policy from mass democratic aspirations and scrutiny. It refers also to the question of the relationship between the political and economic; and that is the question of the creation of extra-economic institutions that safeguard the retention and detention of the dependent masses as a dispossessed, disempowered and thus as an exploitable resource. In this context, we encounter again the Kantian (1979) question about the 'true character of the constitution' to find, beyond the 'deceitful publicity' of the constitutional treaties and beyond the exaltations of its supporters, the reason for the Europeanization of the domestic policy stance of the member states. Is this simply a question of the 'convergence' of the domestic policy choices? There is no doubt, as Anderson (1997) argued in relation to France's acceptance of Germany's tight monetary conditions for EMU, that the 'national' bourgeoisie is ready to operate on a European platform for as long as European labour pays the costs. For the European bourgeoisie, then, European integration is agreeable for as long as labour is kept out of the bargain. Callinicos assesses the rivalry between Germany and France. Carchedi analyses the politics of exchange rates. Moss discusses the neo-liberal foundation of the EC/EU and Bonefeld (Chapter 4) analyses monetary union with reference to the neo-liberal prescriptions for crisis resolution.

What, however, if labour fails to be such a well behaved exploitable resource? How would bourgeois society – and in the context of this book that is the bourgeois society of an integrated 'Europe' – respond if its integration policy is at risk, an integration policy that aimed at keeping the 'mob' away from the centre of power? What in other words will the response be if the supranational political structures of the EU fail to defend the existing class relations? Would the bourgeoisie, as Rosa Luxemburg foresaw in 1899 (in terms of the rise of fascism), push aside its liberal state and call for a police-state?[6] If so, which of the member states will take on this role, or will Europe break up into its constituent parts? The strongest argument in support of European integration is that it has, since Auschwitz, prevented war between Germany and its neighbours. For its proponents, this is the strongest legitimation that can be mustered in support of monetary integration.[7] European integration developed in the shadow of a barbaric past. Yet, the possibility of barbarism continues to exist for as long as the social relations of the past constitute the social relations of the present, that is capitalist social relations.[8] Callinicos concludes his contribution with reference to Luxemburg's dictum that humanity faces the choice between socialism and barbarism. For him, this choice is again posed in most urgent terms.

What then are the benefits of the political economy of European integration and why does Britain find it so difficult to espouse the European idea? The book assesses the political economy of European integration through Marxist lenses. However, the book does not speak with one voice. Indeed, it contains contributions from quite different and distinct Marxist perspectives and traditions, and no individual contributor will necessarily agree with the findings and arguments of the others. Such agreement was neither intended nor sought. The argument of the volume is not only 'external' in terms of its subject-matter but also internal – an intersecting of differing views. The aim is to open a space for a renewed and sustained Marxist critique of the political economy of European integration. Such a task can neither be enunciated monologically, nor can it be based on a narrow and foreclosed theoretical perspective. This book aims to provoke critical debate through a collective effort of reappraisal and determination.

The use of the term 'determination' will upset some readers, and confirm the suspicion of others. Leaving aside the true meaning of 'determination', that is to negate, the *Zeitgeist* does of course not wish to be disturbed. It offeres critical opinions but does not wish to criticize. It differentiates between the good norms and the less than perfect political reality, with a view to making the reality conform with the – good – norms. Concerning the question of 'Europe', the critical dimension of the *Zeitgeist* is characterized, for example, by the painstaking quest for closing the so-called democratic deficit of the EU. The overcoming of this deficit would indeed be a colossal and, *pace* the *Zeitgeist*, a truly revolutionary task. Concerning the book's critique of the political economy of European integration, it will be a disappointment for 'Eurosceptics'. Regardless of the distinct theoretical shades and political perspectives of its contributors, the thrust of the volume is profoundly pro-European. Its critique of the political economy of European integration in no way suggests that it does not anticipate a Europe based on reason, enunciated by Kant's endorsement of the Enlightenment as 'humanity's exodus from its self-imposed immaturity'. In terms of Marx's critique of political economy, this would mean a Europe where humanity, and her human purposeful activity and social practice, no longer exists as an exploitable resource but, rather, as a purpose. It would be well worth to globalize such a Europe.

The chapters

Alex Callinicos locates monetary union in an international context of capitalist crisis. He emphasizes the German–Franco axis as the most important element in the construction of Europe. He shows that hidden behind this axis lies a world of inter-imperialist conflict and rivalry. For him, EMU has arisen from these conflicts and EMU is seen to sustain them. The Europe to come, then, is neither a recovered social-democratic paradise nor a prosperous 'Americanized' consumer society. European monetary union is full of contradictions and is intensively conflict-ridden, giving a new urgency and relevance to the question of socialism or barbarism.

Guglielmo Carchedi provides a value theoretical explanation of currency exchange rates and EMU. The development of EMU is contextualized in terms of inter-imperialist rivalry and global economic and monetary crisis. He examines the relationship between the DM/Euro and the Dollar, and uses the global financial crisis of 1994–95 as an illustration of the instability of monetary relations, and through them, currency relations. Carchedi insists that the class relation between capital and labour is fundamental for the understanding of EMU. The European bourgeoisie is united in EMU because European labour is to pay the costs of monetary union.

Werner Bonefeld surveys the history of European monetary union, especially since the 1970s. He places the creation of EMU in the context of the capitalist crisis of accumulation and asks why, in Europe, the 'political resolution' to the capitalist crisis of reproduction was addressed specifically in terms of the Europeanization of monetary policy. He analyses the politics of EMU's institutional design and argues that EMU reproduces the contradictions it was set out to resolve. While EMU focuses the burden of adjustment on European labour, it transmits regional class conflicts directly throughout Europe.

Bernard Moss scrutinizes the so-called 'social dimension' of Europe and argues that integration has been, from the start, a neo-liberal project. He shows that the big myth of European integration is that of a social Europe. He contrasts his findings with what he calls the 'soft left' and its endorsement of European integration. For Moss, European integration amounts to an attempt by Europe's political elites to secure institutional safeguards for a neo-liberal regulation of the labour question. Moss concludes that the national state remains the most important arena of struggle for the international labour movement.

Mike Haynes challenges conventional economic accounts, according to which strong states at the centre will create powerful equilibrating forces that will benefit the less developed 'nations'. He analyses the politics of immigration controls from so-called third countries and the politics of European enlargement toward these same countries. On the one hand Europe is an ever enlarged and enlarging market and, on the other, a fortress against the free movement of unwanted and criminalized migrant labour. The ideology of Europeaness thus serves to underpin the idea of a Europe as an inclusive core. Yet, within the core sharp divisions of inequality in wealth obtain.

In the final chapter Werner Bonefeld assesses the *raison d'être* of Britain's relation to European integration, especially monetary union. Europe poses an impasse for the British ruling class and this is no better expressed than by Britain's forceful campaign to retain its 'sovereignty' over monetary policy and its – two-third – membership in EMU. The conclusion assesses the politics of Britain's two-third membership in EMU and Labour's policy of 'employability'. The key to the understanding of Britain's relationship to Europe is inter-imperialist rivalry over competitive rates of labour productivity.

Notes

1 There was no Marxist debate on European integration. Instead, there were many distinct Marxist voices, see for example, Holland (1980); Holloway (1976); Holloway and Picciotto (1980); Mandel (1967, 1970); Poulanztas (1974).
2 See Hayek (1939). For comment see Anderson (1997) and the contributions of Bonefeld (chapter 4) and Moss to his volume.
3 On the question of legitimacy in relation to the EU, see Beetham and Lord (1998).
4 Committee (1989, pp. 19–20) and Emerson *et al.* (1992).
5 For an endorsement of third way liberalism see Giddens (1998).
6 See Luxemburg (1974, pp. 398ff).
7 The former German Chancellor Helmut Schmidt argued in 1995 that 'if the common currency does not come about within the next 15 years or so you will see the Deutschmark domineering banks, insurers and other institutions across Europe, and it would inevitably lead to a repetition of what one has already seen twice in this twentieth century' (*International Herald Tribune*, 5.12.1995). Another German former Chancellor, Helmut Kohl, echoed this view and stated that the 'policy of European integration is in reality a question of war and peace in the 21st century' (*Observer*, 4.2.1996). Other

commentators, for example Feldstein (1997), see war as a probable consequence of monetary union.

8 On this see Adorno (1969).

Bibliography

Adorno, T. (1969) 'Erziehung nach Auschwitz', *Stichworte, Kritische Modelle 2* (Frankfurt: Suhrkamp).

Anderson, P. (1997) 'The Europe to Come', in Gowan, P. and Anderson, P. (eds), *The Question of Europe* (London: Verso).

Beetham, D. and Lord C. (1998) *Legitimacy and the EU* (London: Longman).

Committee (1989) Committee for the Study of Economic and Monetary Union in Europe, *Report on Economic and Monetary Union in the European Community* (Luxembourg: Office of Official Publications of the EC).

Emerson, M. *et al.* (1992) *One Market, One Money* (Oxford: Oxford University Press).

Feldstein, M. (1997) 'EMU and International Conflict', *Foreign Affairs*, 76.

Gambino, R. (1996) 'A Critique of the Fordism of the Regulation School', *Common Sense*, 19.

Giddens, A. (1998) *The Third Way* (Cambridge: Polity).

Hayek, F. (1939) 'The Economic Conditions of Interstate Federalism', in Hayek (1949), *Individualism and Economic Order* (London: Routledge and Kegan Paul).

Hix, S. (1999) *The Political System of the European Union* (London: Macmillan).

Holland, S. (1980) *The Uncommon Market* (London: Macmillan).

Holloway, J. (1976) 'Some Issues Raised by Marxist Analysis of European Integration', *CSE Bulletin*, 13.

Holloway, J. and Picciotto, S. (1980) 'Capital, the State and European Integration', *Research in Political Economy*, 3.

Kant, I. (1868) 'Nachlass', in *Sämmtliche Werke*, G. Hartenstein edition, vol. 8 (Leopold Voss: Leipzig).

Kant, I. (1979) *The Conflict of the Faculties*; trans. and intro. Gregor, M. J. (New York: Abaris).

Luxemburg, R. (1974) 'Sozialreform oder Revolution', in *Gesammelte Werke*, vol. 1/1 (Dietz: Berlin).

Mandel, E. (1967) 'International Capital and "Supranationality" ', *Socialist Register* (London: Merlin).

Mandel, E. (1970) *Europe versus America? Contradictions of Imperialism* (London: New Left Book).

Marx, K. (1973) *Grundrisse* (Harmondsworth: Penguin).

Poulantzas, N. (1974) 'Internationalisation of Capitalist Relations and the Nation-state', in *Economy and Society, Classes in Contemporary Capitalism* (London: New Left Book).

2
The Contradictions of European Monetary Union

Alex Callinicos

At the beginning of 1999 the European Union (EU) embarked on what the *Observer* called 'the largest, most complex economic event of the late twentieth century, with no historical precedent' – the introduction of a single European currency, the euro (3 May 1998).[1] Eleven of the 15 EU member states took part in the euro's launch. By common consent, a major step had been taken towards the economic and – because of the impact of monetary decisions on public policy – political integration of the biggest economic zone in the world.

The euro's launch, which completed the process of European economic and monetary union (EMU) initiated by the 1991 Maastricht Treaty, was greeted with near-Messianic expectations. John Palmer, for many years European editor of the *Guardian*, expressed the hopes of many on the social-democratic left:

> In an era of sweeping economic globalization, European monetary union will provide an essential foundation for stable and sustainable growth that generates jobs. A single European currency will weaken power of those who thrive on monetary chaos and financial speculation. It can also help ensure that the overweaning [sic] power of the global market place is better balanced and constrained by democratically decided economic and social priorities
>
> (1997, p. 15).

Precisely the opposite hopes were placed in EMU by many on the free-market right. The following comments by the *Financial Times* (20 April 1998) are typical of this line of thought:

> Replacing European-style capitalism with the Anglo-Saxon variety can hardly have been the aim of the politicians who concocted economic and monetary union in Europe. But that, paradoxically, is just what is likely to happen.
>
> One way in which it will do so is through labour markets. EMU's one-size-fits-all monetary policy will be such a straitjacket that flexibility will be needed elsewhere. That could help freer ('Anglo-Saxon') labour practices spread more widely... The single currency will give birth to a large single capital market. This is likely to smell less like continental Europe's stakeholder capitalism and more like the shareholder capitalism predominant in the US and the UK.

If this were indeed the result of EMU, it would be a paradoxical one. The French businessman and economist Michel Albert summed up the view of many European social-democrats when he challenged Francis Fukuyama's claim that the collapse of the Stalinist states represented the End of History. Albert did not dispute the premiss that there no longer existed any systemic rival to liberal capitalism, but he argued that there existed significantly different, indeed rival variants of *capitalism*, notably the 'Anglo-American' deregulated, free-market version, and 'the Rhine model of capitalism', based on high levels of state intervention, corporate bargaining, and welfare spending, and predominant in continental Europe. History would continue, Albert suggested, as the struggle between these different kinds of capitalism.[2] Social democrats of this way of thinking – François Mitterrand, French President 1981–95, and Jacques Delors, first Mitterrand's Finance Minister and then President of the European Commission – played a leading part in the construction of EMU. It would be a great historical irony if their efforts contributed to the demise of the Rhine model.

The other major architect of the euro was, however, Europe's leading conservative politician, Helmut Kohl, German Chancellor from 1982 to 1998. It was he who most forcefully articulated what is ostensibly the primary political reason for supporting EMU, the belief that European integration represents the transcendence of national interests and conflicts. Thus he warned in February 1996 that its failure might make the outbreak of war in Europe more likely. On the left this belief has sometimes taken the form of the expectation that EMU will lead to the construction of a powerful and integrated bloc of European capital capable of challenging the political and economic hegemony of the United States.

The premiss on which these arguments are based is, however, false. Both the original project of European integration and EMU itself have been an expression of the conflicts between the major European national capitalisms.[3] If anything, the euro is likely to intensify rather than to mollify these antagonisms. To understand this we must consider the origins of EMU.

Franco-German rivalries and the Maastricht Treaty

At the very start of the process of European integration in the early 1950s, the West German Chancellor Konrad Adenauer was asked how many participants were necessary. He replied: 'Two' (Grahl, 1997, p. 236). The critical relationship that has bound together European institutions ever since the Treaty of Rome established the European Economic Community (EEC) in 1957 has been that between France and (West) Germany.[4] After three Franco–German wars in 75 years, and faced with the American drive to rebuild German capitalism as a counterweight to Russian dominance of Eastern Europe, the French ruling class sought to contain German power through a close alliance. General Charles de Gaulle, the French President who concluded the 1963 Franco–German Treaty formalizing this alliance, summed up his view of the relationship: 'The EEC is a horse and carriage: Germany is the horse and France is the coachman' (Connolly, 1996, p. 7).[5]

For his part, Adenauer was, as Alan Milward notes in his major study of the origins of the EEC, 'unswerving in his idea that Western European integration must be the basis of the Federal Republic's security and that it was ultimately the only chance of German reunification' (Milward, 1994, p. 198). The crucial Franco–German deal that made possible the Treaty of Rome required Adenauer to override the opposition of his Economy Minister, Ludwig Erhard, an economic liberal who feared that the Common Market would lead to higher wages and more generous welfare policies in West Germany.[6]

The centrality of the Franco–German axis is the main theme of the Community's history. Institutionally it has reflected an uneasy compromise between quasi-federal bodies such as the European Commission and Parliament, and the politically decisive arenas – above all the intergovernmental Council of Ministers and European Council – through which national interests are asserted. The initial success of the EEC as a customs union was made possible by the rapid growth of trade in manufactured goods among the founding six members (West Germany, France, Italy, and the Benelux countries) from the late 1940s onwards, a process that was itself one of the main elements in the long boom experienced by Western capitalism through the 1950s and 1960s.[7]

Efforts to achieve European monetary integration developed, however, against the background of the period of renewed crises into which the world economy entered at the beginning of the 1970s. The instability in the financial markets that was a major symptom of these crises represented in part a reshuffling of relationships among the major capitalist powers. The political hegemony of the US was undermined by its economic decline relative to West Germany and Japan in particular, a process reflected by the fall of the dollar against the Deutschmark (DM) and yen.

These currency fluctuations stimulated a major attempt at European monetary cooperation. In 1978 the West German Chancellor, Helmut Schmidt, and the French President, Valéry Giscard d'Estaing, proposed the European Monetary System (EMS). The operational part of the system was the Exchange Rate Mechanism (ERM): participating currencies were to fluctuate no more than 2.25 per cent either side of a central parity. Schmidt, the main architect of the ERM, saw it as a way of minimizing destabilizing currency fluctuations. But there were also more straightforward German national interests involved. Tying the weaker European currencies to the DM would prevent it from rising too far against the US dollar, and thus keep German exports competitive.

The reality of German financial predominance on the continent was demonstrated during the early years of François Mitterrand's Socialist Party administration. Elected to the French presidency in May 1981, Mitterrand proceeded to implement a programme of extensive nationalizations and social and economic reforms. Predictably enough these measures were met with considerable resistance on the part of capital – an investment strike, the flight of capital from France, and huge downward pressures on the franc in the currency markets.

The Mitterrand government's response to these pressures from local and international capital focused on its futile efforts to maintain the franc's parity within the ERM. Between October 1981 and March 1983 the French currency was devalued no less than three times. The last of these devaluations represented a decisive victory for Delors, then Mitterrand's Finance Minister. He defeated the left wing of the French cabinet, who were arguing for withdrawal from the EMS, and forced through a programme of austerity measures which amounted to the abandonment of the programme on which Mitterrand had been elected and the effective adoption of Thatcherite free-market economics.

The outcome of the 1981–83 French crisis was that, as Bernard Connolly puts it, 'the ERM...turned into an undeclared DM-zone' (1996, p. 33).[8] Henceforth, other currencies in the ERM fluctuated upwards and downwards against the DM. After March 1983, French governments of both right and left committed themselves to the *franc fort* (strong franc) policy. By effectively binding the franc to the Deutschmark the political elite in Paris hoped both to force French industry to rationalize and become more competitive, and to preserve the crucial political relationship with Bonn (though, as we shall see, they hoped to use EMU to shift that relationship in their favour).

The transformation of the ERM into a DM-zone gave exceptional influence to the West German central bank, the Bundesbank. Thus, when a rise in West German interest rates was followed throughout the rest of Western Europe in autumn 1989, the *Financial Times* commented: 'Europe already has a central bank. It is called the Bundesbank, and it is located in Frankfurt.' (6 October 1989) This financial predominance was a reflection of the relative weight of German capitalism within the EC. By the late 1980s West Germany's manufacturing sector amounted to 68 per cent of those of France, Italy, and Britain combined (*Financial Times*, 30 Nov. 1989).

The East European revolutions of 1989 and the collapse of the Soviet Union seemed likely further to strengthen the trends towards a German hegemony in Europe. The combined effect of the Federal Republic's absorption of the defunct East German state in 1990 and of the eclipse of Russian influence in Eastern and Central Europe was to confirm Germany's re-emergence as a world power. The plans for greater European economic and political integration in the Maastricht Treaty appeared to reflect greater German assertiveness. A Thatcherite British minister, Nicholas Ridley, called EMU 'a German racket designed to take over the whole of Europe' (*Spectator*, 14 July 1990). The reality of the situation was considerably more complex. The Maastricht Treaty, and in particular the proposals for EMU at its heart reflected neither the transcendence of narrow national interests nor a scheme for German hegemony. Rather, they represented a compromise between the conflicting interests of French and German capitalism.

On the German side, Kohl expressed the Federal Republic's longstanding support for European political union. The rationale for this policy had been spelled out by his Social-Democratic predecessor, Helmut Schmidt, in a secret 1976 document known as the 'Marbella paper'. Schmidt warned that West Germany's 'unwanted and dangerous rise to second world power of the West in the consciousness of other governments' could lead to 'a revival of memories not only of Auschwitz and Hitler but also of Wilhelm II and Bismarck... perhaps as much in the West as in the East'. It was consequently 'necessary for us, so far as at all possible, to operate not nationally and independently, but in the framework of the European Community and the [NATO] Alliance. *This attempt to cover [abdecken] our actions multilaterally will only partially* succeed, because we will (necessarily and against our own will) become a leadership factor in both systems' (Ash, 1994, p. 87; emphasis in original).

Greater European political integration was thus essential to provide the necessary multilateral 'cover' for the assertion of German interests internationally. It did not follow, however, that the Germans were enthusiastic about *economic and monetary,* as opposed to political, union. The Bundesbank in particular had always been strongly protective of its own position. It had, for example, initially opposed the creation of the ERM in the late 1970s as a restriction on its autonomy, though the system's evolution into a DM-zone helped allay these concerns.[9] The Bundesbank now feared that the end of the DM would mean both the eclipse of its own power and the replacement of its notoriously restrictive tight-money policies with a more lax approach. Moreover, it argued that EMU to be successful required political union as well.

The initiative for EMU came thus, not from Germany, but from elsewhere. According to the memoirs of the former German Finance Minister Gerhard Stoltenberg, Kohl only gave way to Mitterrand's pressures for a rapid transition to EMU in December 1989 in order to allay French suspicions of German reunification (*Financial Times*, 2 May 1998). David Marsh of the *Financial Times* indeed called EMU 'an attempt, led by France and Italy, to emasculate the Bundesbank by subsuming the D-Mark into a single European currency' (23 September 1992).

EMU was attractive to the French ruling class for two reasons. First, by strengthening the EC as an economic bloc it would allow European governments to act more independently of the US. The same objective lay behind French efforts, bitterly opposed by Washington and London, to encourage Germany in particular and the Community more generally to engage in military cooperation outside the framework of NATO. Secondly, EMU would reverse the shift in the balance of economic power in Germany's favour that had occurred in the early 1980s. The European Central Bank (ECB) created by the Maastricht Treaty would, unlike the Bundesbank, be accountable to European governments, in whose counsels France had an exceptional weight.

German opposition to EMU was overcome thanks to a plan hatched on the eve of the Maastricht summit in December 1991. Its architects were the two craftiest politicians in Europe, François Mitterrand and Giulio Andreotti, the Italian Prime Minister. They proposed to make the establishment of a single currency, by 1 January 1999 at the latest, conditional on the attainment of a significant degree of convergence among the participating economies. Tough criteria were laid down to establish whether the appropriate level of convergence had been attained. Notably no country could participate in the single currency unless its inflation rate did not diverge from those of the three most successful member states by more than 1.5 percentage points, its currency had stayed within the normal ERM fluctuation margins for the previous two years, the budget deficit was no more than 3 per cent of gross national product (GNP), and gross government debt no more than 60 per cent of GNP.

The adoption of these convergence criteria overcame the German objection that EMU would lead to softer monetary policies and therefore a weaker currency than those produced by the Bundesbank. The Treaty also established an independent European Central Bank with the stringent duty 'to maintain price stability' (though the French have persistently disputed the interpretation of these clauses). Kohl could not refuse the offer of such a tough version of EMU. On the front of political union, he gained only limited concessions. Thus the development of common foreign and security and immigration and criminal justice policies was not made the responsibility of transnational institutions such as the European Commission but left to political cooperation between EU governments. The directly elected European Parliament received only a moderate increase in its powers.[10]

A monetarist project

EMU was thus the product of a complex compromise between French and German national interests. It does not follow, however, that the euro's launch would not unleash processes which had their own dynamic. In particular, as John Grahl (1997, p. 129) has argued, '[t]he Maastricht Treaty... inscribed the monetarist project into the EU's agenda for the rest of the century and beyond.'[11] This can be seen along three dimensions.

First, there is the role of the ECB. The ideology of what the American neo-conservative commentator Edward Luttwak (1999, ch. 11) calls 'central bankism' – and in particular the idea that control over monetary policy should be vested in politically idependent central banks – has become an entrenched part of the policy consensus in leading capitalist countries. Monetarism, as it is convenient to call the currently dominant version of neo-liberal economics, has gone through three stages. Underlying all three has been the drive to remove economic decisions likely to have any sort of impact on markets from political control and therefore from anything resembling democratic accountability.

In its first avatar, monetarism, as its name suggests, consisted in the belief that governments should restrict themselves to controlling inflation by keeping the money supply rising at a fixed rate. The experience of the Thatcher government in Britain during the 1980s proved that it was impossible even to identify the relevant variables, let alone to control them. This led to the search for some other way of putting the economy on autopilot. Fixing the exchange-rate to that of some stronger and more stable economy seemed to offer a solution. The commitment of successive French administrations to the *franc fort* policy is one example of such a strategy, as was Britain's entry into the ERM in October 1990. But such an approach is highly vulnerable to the efforts of the financial markets to test fragile exchange-rates, as was shown by the series of currency crises which drove Britain and Italy out of the ERM in September 1992 and led the following August to the decision, aimed at preventing France from suffering a similar fate, to allow participating currencies to fluctuate within widened bands of plus or minus 15 per cent around their parities.[12]

Central bankism represents a third attempt to achieve the aims of monetarism. Here control over monetary policy is vested in a central bank that is required to give priority to reducing inflation. Once again, critical economic decisions are removed from any sort of political accountability, and in this case left to the discretion of unelected bankers. The US Federal Reserve Board and the Bundesbank are the main models on which such a strategy is based. Its influence is shown by the speed with which the Labour government in Britain moved after its election in May 1997 to give operational independence to the Bank of England. The Bank of Japan became the latest major central bank to gain independence in April 1998. The ECB represents a particularly restrictive version of the Bundesbank model, in which it is required to give priority to maintaining price stability, and little consideration is given to the traditional role of central banks as lenders of last resort ready to intervene to prop up the financial system in times of systemic crisis even if the short-term consequences of such interventions may be inflationary.[13]

A second dimension along which to consider the euro's economic consequences concerns the nature of monetary union itself. Fluctuations in exchange-rates – devaluations and revaluations – act as a means through which economies can adjust more easily to the development of imbalances between them. European monetary union deprived a collection of highly diverse national economies of this shock absorber.

The history of the ERM gives an intimation of the consequences. The system's development as a DM-zone meant that the German currency itself became the fixed point around which the other currencies fluctuated. The DM itself could never be devalued relative to the currencies in the system. This meant, in the first place, that interest rates in other EC countries had to be higher than German ones, in order to maintain their parities within the ERM. When German interest rates rose sharply, the effect could be devastating. Thus in December 1991 the Bundesbank increased interest rates, both to slow down the German economy, then experiencing the boom stimulated by the huge increase in public spending to finance reunification, and to demonstrate its distaste with the Maastricht Treaty. The move helped to thrust the entire EU into recession, and to produce the strains in the currency markets that drove Britain and Italy out of the ERM. Second, other currencies could only be devalued, not revalued, against the DM. This deprived these economies of a crucial adjustment mechanism when they were booming. Since revaluation was ruled out as a means of cooling down an overheating economy, inflationary pressures built up till a much more severe *de*valuation became unavoidable.[14]

Of course, existing national states with their own currencies contain considerable uneven development within their borders. In a huge continental economy such as the US, there are enormous contrasts between different parts of the country, yet all are subject to the same federal government and share the same currency. Nation-states, however, have at their disposal certain means of minimizing the impact of these regional differences, notably labour mobility and fiscal transfer. Lawrence Lindsey, a governor of the US Federal Reserve System, describes the first mechanism:

> The US is characterized by a very mobile workforce. The US Census Bureau estimates that roughly 17 per cent of Americans move in a typical year and three per cent of the population, some 7.7m people, change their state of residence.

> This provides a big part of the interregional adjustment in the US economy. For example, during California's economic difficulties between 1990 and 1994, nearly 1.2m left the state. This led to a rapidly expanding workforce for the booming areas of the west. For example, Utah added 200,000 jobs, a 24 per cent increase in the same period and Colorado added 300,000 jobs
>
> (*Financial Times*, 29 November 1996).

The second mechanism, federal government taxation and expenditure, serves to counter-balance the effects of any regional recession. Studies in the 1980s suggested that 40 per cent of any fall in gross state product would be offset through higher benefits received from, or lower taxes paid to, the federal government (*The Economist*, 11 April 1998). Neither of these mechanisms are likely to play a remotely comparable role in the EU when the single currency is introduced. Labour mobility between European nation-states is still very limited. As for fiscal transfers in favour of poorer regions and countries, even a supporter of the euro like the *Financial Times* conceded that '[t]he EU's "federal" budget is much too small to make significant adjustments' (14 October 1996), and the whole direction of European policy is towards further restricting social spending.[15]

In the absence of the mechanisms that existing states possess to even out regional imbalances, the effect of introducing the euro will probably be to trap the poorer and less competitive EU countries in a hard-money regime which will keep their unemployment rates permanently high. This impression is strengthened when we consider the third dimension along which EMU's consequences can be plotted, namely the terms on which the single currency has been introduced. The convergence criteria, as we have seen, require participants in the euro to reduce their budget deficits to 3 per cent of GNP and gross government debt to 60 per cent of GNP. This has necessitated the adoption throughout the EU of large-scale programmes to reduce public spending.

Particularly since they were introduced at a time of recession, the effect of these cuts was to help slow down the continental European economies for most of the 1990s. Moreover, fearful that the participation of heavily indebted southern European states would make the euro significantly weaker than the DM, German Finance Minister Theo Waigel campaigned for a 'Stability Pact'. This would in effect make the convergence criteria a permanent financial regime, policed by the Commission and the ECB, and enforced by fines of up to 0.5 per cent a year of the GDP of defaulters. The 'Stability and Growth Pact' finally agreed at the EU's December 1996 Dublin summit represented a compromise, since the French persuaded the Germans to allow the Council of Ministers to exempt by qualified majority vote countries running an excess deficit which are able to plead the excuse of 'a severe economic downturn'.

Nevertheless, even the strongly neo-liberal *Economist* (11 April 1998) was concerned about the consequences of the pact:

> there remains a serious risk that the stability pact will interfere with automatic stabilizers. After all, EMU will have removed the scope for independent monetary or exchange-rate policies, leaving fiscal policies as one of only a few ways a country can respond to a sharp economic downturn. If that country is running a deficit close to 3 per cent, as most euro members are today, it might not be able to let its automatic stabilizers work. According to OECD estimates, a 1 per cent shortfall in GDP growth normally pushes up the budget deficit by half a percentage point. The stability pact's let-out is far too tightly drawn for this. Had the pact been in force over the past ten years, Germany and France would have had to pay fines . . . respectively in three and four of those years.

National tensions

In no way then has the Maastricht project provided Europe's economies with a hedge against the effects of unrestrained *laissez faire*. On the contrary, it has served as the form in which what the *Financial Times* (9 December 1995) calls 'fiscal correctness' – Western governments' mania for cutting their budget deficits – has been expressed in Europe. The neo-liberal form in which EMU has been introduced is thus liable to counter-act the notional economic benefits of monetary union that some left-wing economists have been keen to stress (see, for example, Weiss, 1999, pp. 130–1). This might seem to support the belief prevalent in one wing of neo-liberalism that EMU will act as an instrument for economic globalization and the world-wide triumph of the Anglo-American model of free-market capitalism.

Thus Peter Martin predicted (*Financial Times*, 28 March 1998) that, as a result of the euro's launch, 'national boundaries, the boundaries of statehood, will be progressively less important. As national economies become integrated within the euro-zone, it will become less and less important to use them as a frame of reference.' The emergence of a pan-European capital market, inaugurated by a wave of major cross-border takeovers and mergers in the late 1990s, was widely heralded as a sign of this process of internationalization.

Yet at the political level, EMU has been marked by an *intensification* of national conflicts within the European Union. The Maastricht Treaty itself provoked major nationalist opposition. This was most intense in Britain. This country's late entry into the EEC in 1973 reflected its ruling class's apparently endemic inability to decide between the necessarily futile effort to maintain Britain as a world imperial power – or, in reality, as junior partner with the US – and whole-hearted participation in the process of European integration. In the late 1980s this uncertainty developed into a bitterly polarized dispute within the ruling Conservative Party, initially over entry into the ERM, and, after sterling's humiliating expulsion from the system in September 1992, over the euro and Britain's continued membership of the EU. These inner-party struggles first destroyed Margaret Thatcher's government and then paralysed that of her successor, John Major. The 1997 general election reduced the Tory party, the dominant party of British capitalism for the previous century, to a rump dominated by xenophobic hostility to the EU.[16]

While Labour under Tony Blair was able to achieve formally more amicable relations with other European states, and indeed declared the characteristically arrogant ambition of establishing 'British leadership' in Europe, the new government effectively continued its predecessors' ambivalent policies towards the EU. During the 1997 election campaign Blair pointedly used Thatcherite rhetoric in attacking any move towards a 'European super-state'. After much dithering and confusion, the Chancellor of the Exchequer, Gordon Brown, announced in October 1997 that the Labour government would exercise Britain's right under the Maastricht Treaty not to take part in the euro-launch, and to defer entry until 2002 at the earliest, when any such decision would be based on a judgement of British national economic interest and subject to approval in a referendum. Behind this announcement lay both divisions with the cabinet and Blair's pathological fear of offending Rupert Murdoch's rabidly anti-European media empire. After the widely derided Tory opposition beat Labour in the 1999 European elections, the Blair government showed signs of further delaying a decision on the euro. The effect has been to ensure that Britain remains marginal in European counsels. As Zbigniew Brzezinski puts it, 'London has largely dealt itself out of the European game' (1997, p. 42).[17]

But if nationalist reservations about Maastricht had the greatest influence over government policy in Britain and in Scandinavia (a referendum in Denmark initially rejected the treaty, while Norway remains outside the Union), they also affected the two core EU powers. In France the treaty was only narrowed approved in a referendum in September 1992. The French Communist Party, and powerful wings of both the Gaullist and the Socialist Parties opposed the euro. When the Gaullist President Jacques Chirac called snap legislative elections in May/June 1997 to win a popular mandate for the austerity measures required to meet the Maastricht criteria, the ruling right-wing coalition suffered a shock defeat. The pro-European Socialist Party leader Lionel Jospin formed a government of the 'plural left' which contained powerful forces (represented, for example, by Interior Minister Jean Chévènement and by the Communists) hostile to the euro.

Bitter opposition to EMU developed also developed within Germany itself. Here, of course, the fear was not (as it was for nationalists elsewhere in Europe) of a German-dominated Europe, but of the loss of economic power and security represented by the abolition of the D-mark and the subordination of the mighty Bundesbank to the ECB. Within the conservative–liberal coalition that ruled Germany 'till 1998 these concerns were expressed in particular by the Bavarian Christian Social Union (CSU). It was as a result of pressure from the CSU that, at the EU intergovernmental conference at Amsterdam in June 1997, Kohl played a key role in blocking any significant extension of qualified majority voting in European decision-making – even though such a revision of the Treaty of Rome is generally seen as a necessary condition of the greater political integration which the German government had in the past strongly advocated, particularly if plans significantly to expand EU membership are implemented.

The backlash against Maastricht within individual countries fuelled a series of national conflicts within the EU. One of the most important concerned the question of which countries would qualify for taking part in the euro by the deadline of May 1998. After the effective collapse of the ERM in 1992–93, the French and German governments pushed hard in the direction of a multispeed Europe. They envisaged a northern 'hard core' launching the single currency while Britain and the southern European states remained on the side-lines. But in 1996–97 new governments in Italy, Spain, and Greece insisted that they would be able to join in the euro's launch in January 1999.

The prospect of Italy in particular joining the euro in the first wave caused great unease in the German government and business circles because it seemed to suggest that the new currency would be weaker than the D-Mark. The Italian deficit and government debt were way above the Maastricht limits, and blatantly cosmetic devices were used to try to massage the figures down – for example, the imposition of a special one-off 'Eurotax' which would be used to reduce the budget deficit and partly repaid in 1999. (They weren't the only ones: France's success in meeting the Maastricht target depended on some creative accounting, for example, a special £4 billion payment from France Télécom.) The CSU prime minister of Bavaria, Eduard Stoiber, demanded strict adherence to the convergence criteria in order to defend Germany's 'stability culture'. 'A weakening of the criteria would have incalculable consequences,' he said. A weak euro would mean 'inflation, higher interest rates, less investment, more unemployment'. Rather than this Stoiber preferred a 'controlled delay' of EMU of one or two years (*Financial Times*, 7 July 1997).

In response to these pressures, Theo Waigel, German Finance Minister and CSU leader, vacillated. On the one hand, he insisted repeatedly that '3 per cent is 3 per cent', and that any country whose deficit overshot this target by the slightest decimal fraction could not participate in the euro. On the other hand, he confronted a situation where it seemed that even Germany would fail to meet this test. Recession forced up social spending and reduced tax revenues, making it harder for governments to hit the Maastricht targets. Germany, anchor of the European economy, was particularly hard hit. In May 1997 Waigel even sought to use creative accounting – the revaluation of the Bundesbank's gold and foreign exchange reserves – to keep the budget deficit within the three per cent limit 'till he was blocked by the Bundesbank.

In the event, the immediate crisis passed. As Larry Elliott and Dan Atkinson (1998, p. 160) put it, 'like an alien being in a cheap science-fiction film, EMU seemed to draw a hideous strength from the attacks and crises that beset it.' This reflected the political priority given to the project, especially by Kohl. Moreover, continental Europe enjoyed a modest economic revival in the late 1990s. The Bundesbank loosened its monetary policy in 1995, allowing the D-Mark and the currencies linked to it through the ERM to drift lower against the dollar, thereby boosting exports. The resulting economic growth, combined with Italian-and French-style creative accounting, and genuine austerity measures allowed the Commission in March 1998 to pass 11 out of the 12 EU states which desired to take part in the euro-launch as having met the convergence criteria. Only Greece failed to pass muster; Britain, Sweden, and Denmark chose for political reasons not to participate.

Yet the actual ratification of these findings at the European Council in May 1998 was overlain by a bitter dispute over the presidency of the European Central Bank. The German government, determined to ensure that the ECB should be a Bundesbank Mark II, was strongly committed to establishing its political independence. Successive French governments nevertheless pushed hard, against fierce German resistance, for the ECB to be subject to political control. Achieving this was, after all, a central part of the French rationale for EMU – to replace the Bundesbank as the effective European central bank, not with a Bundesbank Mark II, but with a bank over whose decisions Paris would exercise a significant influence. Thus the Gaullist Prime Minister Alain Juppé (*Financial Times*, 9 December 1996) declared:

> The basis of the French position is that we don't want all decisions on economic, budgetary, fiscal and monetary policy to be shaped by a technocratic system. That is not our concept of democracy... There needs to be an *interlocuteur*, a political power, the government leaders of the euro-zone, who would meet periodically to fix broad lines of economic policy, dialogue with the central bank, and give their opinion.

The French right was defeated in the legislative elections of May/June 1997, but Jospin's new coalition pressed for the ECB to subordinated to a European 'economic government'. It argued that the new informal Euro-X council of countries participating in the euro should take responsibility for coordinating their macroeconomic policies – a proposal which irritated the Blair government because it would make ECOFIN, the council of European finance ministers, a largely ceremonial body, and thereby exclude Britain from the real centre of economic decision-making.

But what brought the issue into focus was the question of who should head the new bank. Europe's central bankers, led by Bundesbank president Hans Tietmeyer, lined up their Dutch colleague Wim Duisenberg for the job. Infuriated by what Jacques Santer, President of the European Commission, called a bankers' 'coup d'état', and seeking to gain a political advantage over his uneasy cohabitee Jospin, Chirac in November 1997 nominated Jean-Claude Trichet, governor of the Banque de France, for the presidency of the ECB. After chaotic scenes over the weekend of 2–3 May 1998, a Brussels summit negligently chaired by Blair reached the compromise that Duisenberg would informally agree to step down about halfway through his eight-year term and be replaced by Trichet for a full term. The French demand that an actual date be set for Duisenberg's retirement was blocked after the German delegation overruled a weakened and declining Kohl.

Lionel Barber (*Financial Times*, 5 May 1998) commented that the affair 'reveals the tensions between elected politicians and unelected central bankers whose power has expanded exponentially in a world of monetary orthodoxy and liberalized capital'. It also suggested that the Kohl government had failed to create a Bundesbank Mark II. Tietmeyer conceded: 'Not everything that happened last week in Brussels contributed to the necessary expectation that the euro will be a really supranational and depoliticized currency' (*Financial Times*, 6 May 1998). The 'Wim–Claude Trichenberg' compromise showed, as the *Financial Times* (4 May 1998) put it, that 'national politics extends far into the monetary realm.' This judgement is confirmed by Oskar Lafontaine's short-lived campaign, after he became Finance Minister in Germany's new Red–Green government in October 1998, to force the Bundesbank and the ECB to cut interest rates. Duisenberg pointedly delayed a rate-cut till after Lafontaine had been driven from office in March 1999 by a ferocious campaign by German big business.[18]

Nor is there any reason to believe that once EMU beds in, national tensions will become weaker. On the contrary, the next European recession will present right-wing politicians with the irresistible temptation to blame unemployment on the unelected bankers in Frankfurt. The 1990s saw the parties of the fascist right gain considerable electoral support throughout the EU. Their impact on bourgeois conservative parties is already visible – for example in the deals made by some French right-wing politicians with the Front National, in the adoption by the Bavarian CSU of racist policies (including the slogan 'Germany is not a country for immigrants') to prevent a fascist electoral challenge, and in the decision of the Austrian People's Party to form a coalition with the far-right, and anti-EU Freedom Party. Opposition to the EU is already a staple of right-wing propaganda. The tone of their attacks is hardly likely to become more muted in coming years.

Europe versus America?

A major reason why many on the left persist in believing that European integration will alleviate national tensions is the hope that a strong EU will be able to challenge and at least partially to tame global American power.[19] Often this is associated with the idea, which assumed the status of a cliché in the early 1990s, that the post-Cold War era would see the world divided into three regional blocs – the Americas, dominated by the US, the European Union, and East Asia under either Japanese leadership or a Sino–Japanese condominium.

Once again, these beliefs are held in defiance of the evidence. Far from Washington regarding European integration as a threat to its interests, the very establishment of the EEC represented the culmination of consistent efforts by the US. At the time when the Marshall Plan for European reconstruction was launched in 1947–48, the US administration advanced the idea of a European customs union. The proposal had, as Milward (1994, p. 122) puts it,

> an essentially political rationale, the creation of a strategic political bloc in western Europe of which West Germany would be a member as part of America's security system. But underlying this was also an economic argument. A larger market, it was argued, by increasing the productivity of European manufacturing would reduce the prices of European manufactured goods so that Europe would become less dependent on American aid.

From Washington's perspective, European integration would provide the economic underpinning of the NATO military alliance formed in 1949. The political benefits this would produce outweighed the damaging impact that US policy-makers feared the formation of the Common Market, and the filip this might give to European protectionism, would have on American economic interests. Thus, for example, the US Department of Agriculture's complaints about the lost exports the Treaty of Rome would cause American farmers were overriden. The State Department explained in 1955: 'In this United States approach [of support for European integration] other problems including the admittedly serious commercial ones which might arise as a result of the development of the common market, were necessarily subordinate' (Milward, 1994, p. 427).

Washington has maintained this general stance of political support for European integration in the subsequent 40 years. Thus, once it became clear that EMU was a going concern, the Clinton administration became increasingly explicit in backing the process. Bill Clinton himself declared: 'An integrated Europe is America's natural best partner for the twenty-first century.' Deputy US Treasury Secretary Lawrence Summers has repeatedly asserted: 'If EMU is good for Europe it will be good for us' (*Financial Times* 5 May 1998). Clinton sought unsuccessfully to nudge his close political ally Tony Blair into taking Britain into the euro-launch.

This apparent harmony of political objectives does not imply any simple convergence of interests between American and European capital. On the contrary, a crucial factor in US relative economic decline was the rapid growth during the long postwar boom of the EEC in general and West Germany in particular. The resulting intensification of international competition played an essential role in destabilizing the world economy at the end of the 1960s and the beginning of the 1970s.[20] Indeed, by the 1990s, *economic* conflict between Europe and America had become institutionalized. Aggressive bargaining over issues such as genetically modified foods, the Common Agricultural Policy, and the American blockades of Cuba and Iran have become a routine feature of transatlantic relations.

What the EU has signally failed to develop is the capacity to pursue an independent *political* strategy. Achieving this ability has been a prime objective of every French government since De Gaulle took power in 1958. But it was a Germany emboldened by reunification that made the most determined effort to flex Europe's political muscles. At the beginning of the 1990s Kohl undertook a series of foreign-policy initiatives independently of Washington. The most important of these was the effective sabotage of the Bush administration's efforts to hold Yugoslavia together.

But the Balkan wars proved a cruel demonstration of the EU's failure to achieve the common foreign and security policy laid down in the Maastricht Treaty. The German government succeeded in forcing through European recognition of Croatia and Slovenia as independent states soon after the Treaty was signed. But the Community was unable to impose any solution on the Bosnian war that was the inevitable consequence of the break-up of Yugoslavia. Divided counsels prevented the development of a coherent European policy. The Germans remained strongly pro-Croatian, while the French and British, with troops on the ground as part of a United Nations force, were much more cautious.

In the end, it was the US that brought the war at least temporarily to an end. After a period of initial confusion, the Clinton administration provided the Croatian and Bosnian government forces with massive military assistance and deployed NATO air and sea power against the Bosnian Serbs. American diplomatic pressure secured the 1995 Dayton peace agreement, which a US-dominated NATO army enforced.[21] This outcome did not simply reflect Washington's overwhelming military superiority over any other power in the world. For all its notorious faults, the US governmental apparatus provided a much more effective decision-making and command structure that the bizarre European amalgam of supranational institutions and intergovernmental cooperation.

The political balance was further shifted by the fact the US economy grew strongly after 1992 while continental Europe stagnated for most of the decade. Associated with this was a recovery, in some industries at least, of US competitiveness compared to the low-point American capitalism had reached in the early 1980s.[22] European firms felt the resulting pressure in various sectors. For example, the *Financial Times* reported (19 April 1994) that 'US investment banks are increasingly dominant in European financial markets.' Meanwhile, the Pentagon responded to the reduction in arms expenditure following the end of the Cold War by encouraging a ruthless process of rationalization and mergers in the US defence industry. The surviving American arms firms emerged with their competitiveness enhanced, while their European counterparts struggled to sustain themselves on the hopelessly inadequate basis of national investments and markets.

The long American boom of the 1990s fed a mood of triumphalism that was reinforced by the 1997 East Asian crash. Even Alan Greenspan, the normally cautious chairman of the US Federal Reserve, declared: 'My sense is that one consequence of this Asian crisis is an increasing awareness in the region that market capitalism, as practised in the West, especially in the US, is the superior model, that is, it provides greater promise of producing rising standards of living and continuous growth.' (*Financial Times*, 19 April 1998) The more gung-ho American commentators announced the discovery of a 'New Economic Paradigm' in which deregulation and new technology allowed uninterrupted non-inflationary growth. Similar predictions have accompanied every major American boom since the 1920s, and have always been rapidly refuted by events: there is no reason to doubt that present claims will suffer the same fate.[23]

Nevertheless, the boom in the US, contrasted as it was to stagnation in continental Europe and by the long Japanese economic slump, allowed Washington to re-assert American political and military leadership. Some developments seemed to point towards the formation of regional blocs, but the US regards itself as a member of all these blocs – thus, not just the North American Free Trade Agreement (NAFTA), but also the Asia-Pacific Economic Co-operation Forum (APEC).[24] In Europe, the key means for the assertion of US power was NATO. The alliance's rationale as a counterweight to Soviet military power implied that it should have been wound up after the Cold War, but by the late 1990s its role had been extended to such tasks as military intervention in the Balkans. A key Clinton foreign-policy initiative – the dangerous gamble of expanding NATO eastwards to the borders of the old Soviet Union – served both to incorporate Moscow's former East European clients within the Western bloc and to re-assert US primacy within that bloc.

NATO's disastrous 1999 bombing campaign against Serbia over Kosovo more than anything else represented an assertion by the US of its claim to be the dominant power on the Eurasian continent (Callinicos, 2000). Even France, normally the most independent-minded of European governments, followed the American lead over Kosovo (Rouleau, 1999). Nor did the initiative, agreed by Blair and Jospin at St Malo in December 1998 and confirmed by the NATO summit the following April, to launch a European Security and Defence Identity (ESDI), necessarily threaten US hegemony in Europe. Greater European military cooperation would free the Pentagon of the burden of mounting messy and dangerous ground operations in the EU's backyard while leaving strategic control in Washington's hands. The American political leadership is, however, insisting that such initiatives take place within a NATO framework: in October 1999 the US Senate resolved that the EU should undertake an 'autonomous' operation 'only after NATO had declined to take on that mission' (*Financial Times*, 25 November 1999).[25]

None of this should be taken to imply that we now live in a 'unipolar' world dominated by American 'ultra-imperialism'. On the contrary, the end of the Cold War has ushered in a period of much more fluid competition among the Great Powers than was characteristic of the postwar era, when all conflicts could ultimately be contained within the framework of the confrontation between the two superpower blocs. Thus the development of Central Asia's oil and gas reserves has opened up a new zone of intense economic and political competition where once Moscow's suzerainty reigned unchallenged. US military strategy is intelligible only on the assumption that it regards Russia and China as major potential rivals.[26]

In this global context, the conflicts of national interest among the European ruling classes make it extremely difficult for the EU to pursue a coherent political strategy. The Anglo-American bombing campaign initiated against Iraq in December 1998 illustrated the problem: Britain, consistent with London's traditional policy of trailing along behind Washington, was the only power willing to participate in a unilateral military attack on Iraq; France has consistently sought an accommodation with Baghdad; Germany and the rest of the EU adopted an equivocal policy. If, as I have suggested above, national antagonisms persist and are maybe even strengthened under EMU, the construction of an effective European political actor is unlikely to become any easier.

It is not, in any case, obvious why the emergence of the EU as a rival to the US would be a welcome development. Such a process would require both greater political centralization within the Union and much higher levels of European defence expenditure in order to give the EU the military capacity to operate independently of Washington. But, quite aside from the regressive social effects of such measures in the present economic climate, how would the emergence of another global power benefit the peoples of Europe or of the rest of the world? The belief that it would can only rest on the assumption that our present ills are a consequence of American hegemony. This ignores the structural tendencies, inherent in the capitalist mode of production, leading to economic slump, environmental degradation, and mass poverty. These tendencies would be just as powerful if a United States of Europe were to step onto the world stage as they are at present.

Conclusion

The approach of EMU was accompanied by many dire predictions. The Harvard economist Martin Feldstein, chairman of the Council of Economic Advisers under Ronald Reagan, even warned that the national conflicts it provoked could lead to a European war (1997). Most critics are less apocalyptic, but, particularly in Britain, many leading business figures continue to express serious reservations. Despite his paper's support for the euro, Richard Lambert, the editor of the *Financial Times*, probably spoke for many when he wrote *Financial Times*, 19 November 1997) that 'it is difficult not to shake off this sneaking feeling: if it were not for the fact that the Europeans who oppose EMU are mostly so frightful, you would begin to harbour a few doubts yourself.'

These doubts became more muted around the time of the euro's launch, but they did not disappear. Indeed, they were reinforced by the euro's subsequent poor performance on the foreign exchange markets: by the end of January 2000 the euro had fallen by 17 per cent against the dollar, taking it below parity. Despite the continental economy recovery of the late 1990s (particularly pronounced in France, where the Jospin government allowed public spending to rise in order to stimulate growth), capital poured out of Europe, attracted by the speculative boom across the Atlantic: in the first eleven months of 1999, there was a net outflow from the euro-zone of 120 billion euros in direct investment and 28 billion in portfolio investment (*Financial Times*, 5 February 2000). This naturally encouraged the neo-liberal cheerleaders of Anglo-American capitalism – among whom Tony Blair played a leading role – to redouble their denunciations of 'Eurosclerosis'.

Nevertheless, the EMU project's capacity to survive a series of major setbacks makes it wiser to avoid short-term predictions. It is best to emphasize its broader context. Two main elements stand out. First, European integration has, since its inception, been part of the global process of inter-imperialist competition – both that between the two superpower-blocs and that between the major European states, notably France, Germany, and Britain. Europe's eclipse during the first half of the twentieth century by the US and the Soviet Union undoubtedly provided an important incentive for integration, but the conflicts of interest between national capitalisms have traversed and disarticulated the resulting institutions. As I have tried to show, EMU arose from these conflicts, and will help to sustain them.

Belief to the contrary rests on, aside from the illusions analysed above, on the fashionable idea that, in the era of 'globalization', the nation-state is becoming an irrelevance. The remarkable success of American capital in securing political interventions favourable to its interests gives the lie to any such notion. Political power remains an indispensable instrument for the advancement of economic interests. It is indeed crucial to the French case for EMU that it will permit the emergence of a European 'economic government' capable of, among other things, dealing with Washington on equal terms. But there is considerable evidence that multinational corporations tend to concentrate their trade and investments in their 'home' markets.[27] European firms have access to nation-states retaining considerable powers (including, in the case of France and Britain, nuclear weapons). To maximize their bargaining position against their rivals, they are likely to use their influence on their own national government to increase their leverage in Brussels. These structural factors will continue to undermine the coherence of European policy-making.[28]

EMU also reflects the commitment of the Western ruling classes to neo-liberal economic policies. In the European case, as we have seen, this has meant the institutionalization of deficit-cutting and the transfer of monetary policy to the judgement of unelected central bankers. This cannot be explained simply on the basis of the ideological influence of *laissez-faire* economics. The official mania for deficit cutting in particular had deeper causes that must be traced back to the era of global economic crisis that opened up at the end of the 1960s. Three global recessions – in the mid-1970s, the early 1980s, and the early

1990s – and the uneven and unstable recoveries from them sharply reduced average growth rates. This affected public finances in two ways. In the first place, stagnation and slump reduce tax revenues and pushes up social spending, forcing governments to borrow more heavily.

In 1993 Martin Wolf (*Financial Times*, 12 July 1993) pointed to '[t]he accumulation of public sector debt by the governments of the industrial countries':

> Over the past quarter century, the ratio of aggregate gross public debt to gross domestic products has risen from a little under 40 per cent to 68 per cent... In only two brief periods has the ratio fallen: during the inflationary economic expansion of the early 1970s and again during the expansion of the second half of the 1980s.
>
> Unfortunately, the rise in the debt ratio during recessions has more than offset the paltry declines during expansions.

A second feature of the economic crises of the 1970s and 1980s was stagflation – that is, the tendency for the rates of unemployment and of inflation to rise together. Eventually economic slump would force up unemployment to levels high enough to cause a reduction in inflation, but the subsequent periods of recovery were haunted by fears that price increases would take off again. From governments' point of view, one advantage of inflation is that it reduces the value of their debts. Many investors who lent money to governments by buying their bonds saw the value of their assets more or less wiped out by the inflations of the 1970s and 1980s. Financial markets, reflecting the bondholders' concerns, now closely monitor government policies to make sure they do nothing which might stoke up inflation.

The *Financial Times* (23 December 1996) summed up the resulting state of affairs:

> From the 1970s onwards the developed world has seen persistent structural deficits and an associated increase in government debt to levels previously only experienced after wars. At the same time bond investors who were burned by high inflation now punish governments by imposing a high risk premium. This combination has reduced the potency of fiscal policy as a reflationary weapon. Hence the slow recovery from the recession of the 1990s, which caught many forecasters on the wrong foot.

> In effect, we have returned to the pattern of the nineteenth century, where the public sector was too small to permit active fiscal management and monetary policy was dictated by the requirements of the gold standard. As in the nineteenth century, cyclical turning points now seem to be dictated by banking crises and market collapses. Recessions are exacerbated by credit contraction and debt deflation.

This analysis is somewhat overstated. The public sector today, despite the privatization and deregulation of the past 20 years, still represents a far larger proportion of economic activity than it did in the nineteenth century, averaging around 50 per cent of national income in the EU. The constraints of the financial markets did not prevent the US government helping to stimulate and sustain a relatively strong and prolonged recovery from the slump of the early 1990s. Nevertheless, in the rest of the advanced capitalist world, the 1990s saw, not stagflation, but strongly deflationary tendencies (most pronounced in the second biggest economy, Japan). The Maastricht convergence criteria are the particular form in which these tendencies are expressed in the EU. Inasmuch as they have contributed to sharp reductions in welfare spending and high levels of unemployment, they have helped to create the climate of social polarization that developed in continental Europe during the 1990s. The initial introduction of neo-liberal policies in the previous decade produced a glum and demoralized atmosphere in the European working class. But the past few years have seen a striking escalation of social conflict. The most spectacular example to date has been the French mass strikes of November/December 1995, which smashed the austerity programme of the Chirac–Juppé government and laid the basis for the left's electoral victory 18 months later. Germany, moreover, has experienced the most intense class polarization in the history of the Federal Republic.[29]

The general deflationary thrust of EMU is likely to feed rather than to attenuate these social conflicts. Of course, these developments do not automatically favour the left. The fascist right has, as I have already noted, grown considerably in Europe during the 1990s. In the paradigm case of the Front National in France, the fascists' first electoral breakthrough was made possible by the disillusionment produced by the experience of the Mitterrand government in 1981–88. Social-democratic governments now rule Germany, France, Britain, and Italy. Yet the case of the Blair government in Britain suggests that contemporary social democracy is unwilling to break with neo-liberal orthodoxy. A situation where centre-left mirrors free-market right is likely to offer more opportunities for the fascists.

The Europe of EMU will therefore not be either the recovered social-democratic paradise anticipated by some of its supporters, or the continent of prosperous Americanized consumers predicted by others. It is likely to be polarized between the kind of collective organization and action which, for example, the French mass strikes revived, and the regressive racial Utopias evoked by the fascists. In these circumstances, Rosa Luxemburg's dictum that the choice facing humankind is socialism or barbarism will gain a new relevance and urgency.

Notes

1 This chapter draws on Callinicos, 1997. An earlier version was published in *Economic and Political Weekly*, 29 August 1998.
2 Albert, 1993. A similar analysis was put forward by the leading British social-democratic theorist Will Hutton: see Hutton, 1995.
3 For a prescient analysis of the predominance of national interests in the European integration process, see Harman, 1971.
4 In 1986 the EEC was renamed the European Community, while the Maastricht Treaty expanded it for certain purposes into the European Union.
5 For a lucid analysis of the driving forces behind the formation of the EEC, see Anderson, 1996.
6 See Milward, 1994, pp. 196–226.
7 Milward, 1994, ch. 4.
8 Connolly's history of the ERM is wildly biased: its author is a fanatically Eurosceptic Thatcherite who was sacked from his senior post in the European Commission for writing it. Nevertheless, the book's combination of inside information and rigorous economic analysis makes it required reading for those who want to understand the real workings of the EU.
9 Connolly, 1996, chs 1 and 2.
10 See the discussion of the Maastricht deal in Marsh, 1993, ch. 9.
11 Grahl's book is an excellent critical analysis of EMU from a left-Keynesian view, which seeks to relate the process of monetary integration to theoretical debates among orthodox and Marxist economists.
12 See, on the ERM crisis, Connolly, 1996, esp. chs 7 and 12, and Grahl, 1997, ch. 6.
13 See Grahl, 1997, ch. 8.
14 Connolly, 1996, analyses these and other perverse effects on the ERM.
15 A recent study suggests that regional earnings inequalities in the EU are markedly greater than those in the US, partly in consequence of federal social provision: Galbraith *et al.*, 1999, pp. 47–51.
16 For a detailed account, see Stephens, 1997.
17 For a more detailed discussion of the British debates, see Callinicos, 1997, pp. 33–44.
18 See, on Lafontaine's fall, Callinicos, 1999, pp. 13–16.

19 See, for example, Palmer, 1988.
20 See Mandel, 1972.
21 See German, 1995, and Petras and Vieux, 1996.
22 See Callinicos, 1994a, pp. 56–9.
23 For a sense of the issues involved, see Zuckerman, 1997, and Krugman, 1998, and, for contrasting Marxist analyses, Geier and Shawki, 1997, and Brenner, 1998.
24 I am grateful to Joel Geier for this *bon mot*.
25 For a lucid analysis of US strategic interest in a strong but subordinate EU expanding into Central and Eastern Europe, see Brzezkinski, 1997, ch. 3.
26 See Achcar, 1998, and for a broader analysis, Callinicos, 1994b.
27 See, for example, Hirst and Thompson, 1996.
28 For broader theoretical discussion of these issues, see Harman, 1991 and 1996.
29 See Callinicos, 1994 and 1999, and Wolfreys, 1999.

Bibliography

Achcar, G. (1998) 'The Strategic Triad: the United States, Russia, and China', *New Left Review*, 228.
Albert, M. (1993) *Capitalism against Capitalism* (London: Whurr).
Anderson, P. (1996) 'Under the Sign of the Interim', *London Review of Books*, 4 Jan. 1996.
Ash, T. G. (1994) *In Europe's Name* (London: Vintage).
Brenner, R. (1998) 'Uneven Development and the Long Downturn', *New Left Review*, 229.
Brzezinski, Z. (1997) *The Grand Chessboard* (New York: Basic Books).
Callinicos, A. (1994a) 'Marxism and Imperialism Today', in Callinicos *et al.*, *Marxism and the New Imperialism* (London: Bookmarks).
Callinicos, A. (1994b) 'Crisis and Class Struggle in Europe Today', *International Socialism*, 2, 63.
Callinicos, A. (1997) 'Europe: the Mounting Crisis', *International Socialism*, 2, 75.
Callinicos, A. (1999), 'Reformism and Class Polarization in Europe', *International Socialism*, 2, 85.
Callinicos, A. (2000), 'Barbarity and Hypocrisy: the Ideology of Humanitarian Intervention', forthcoming in a reader on the Balkan war edited by Tariq Ali.
Connolly, G. (1996) *The Rotten Heart of Europe* (London: Faber).
Elliott, L. and Atkinson, D. (1998) *The Age of Insecurity* (London: Verso).
Feldstein, M. (1997) 'The Euro and War', *Foreign Affairs*, November/December.
Galbraith, J. *et al.* (1999) 'Inequality and Unemployment in Europe: the American Cure', *New Left Review*, 237.
Geier, J. and Shawki, A. (1997) 'Contradictions of the Miracle Economy', *International Socialist Review*, 2.
German, L. (1995) 'The Balkan War', *International Socialism*, 2, 69.
Grahl, J. (1997) *After Maastricht* (London: Lawrence & Wishart).
Harman, C. (1971) 'The Common Market', *International Socialism*, 49.
Harman, C. (1991) 'The State and Capitalism Today', *International Socialism*, 2, 51.

Harman, C. (1996) 'Globalization: a Critique of a New Orthodoxy', *International Socialism*, 2, 73.
Hirst, P. and Thompson, G. (1996) *Globalization in Question* (Cambridge: Polity).
Hutton, W. (1995) *The State We're In* (London: Jonathan Cape).
Krugman, P. (1998) 'America the Boastful', *Foreign Affairs*, May/June.
Luttwak, E. (1999) *Turbo-Capitalism* (London: Orion).
Mandel, E. (1972) *Europe vs. America* (New York: Monthly Review Press).
Marsh, D. (1993) *The Bundesbank* (London: Mandarin).
Milward, A. (1994) *The European Rescue of the Nation State* (London: Routledge).
Palmer, J. (1988) *Europe Without America?* (Oxford: Oxford University Press).
Palmer, J. (1997) 'The Case for Joining', in M. Kettle *et al.*, *The Single Currency: Should Britain Join?* (London: Guardian).
Petras, J. and Vieux, S. (1996) 'Bosnia and the Revival of US Hegemony', *New Left Review*, 218.
Rouleau, E. (1999) 'Errements de la diplomatie francaise au Kosovo', *Le Monde diplomatique*, December.
Stephens, P. (1997) *Politics and the Pound* (London: Macmillan).
Weiss, L. (1999) 'Managed Openness: Beyond Neoliberal Globalism', *New Left Review*, 238.
Wolfreys, J. (1999) 'Class Struggles in France', *International Socialism*, 2, 84.
Zuckerman, M. B. (1997) 'The Second American Century', *Foreign Affairs*, May/June.

3

The EMU, Monetary Crises, and the Single European Currency[1]

Guglielmo Carchedi

Introduction

Europe's economic integration will reach a higher stage with the creation of the Economic and Monetary Union (EMU). Daily, the media bombard us with reports and analyses which, due to their ideological and apologetic nature, are unable to uncover the contradictions marking this process. Thus, the sudden eruption of monetary crises, the last one having occurred in 1994–95, is ascribed to purely speculative capital movements; the inability by some (at the time of writing, almost all) member states to achieve the EMU convergence criteria seems to be caused only by lack of fiscal discipline; and the introduction of the single currency, the euro, is seen purely as a monetary operation. Analyses based on the labour theory of value, i.e. on the production and distribution of value, even though potentially much more fruitful, are few and far between. The purpose of this chapter is to contribute to the development of such an alternative view.

Economic crises, money, and inflation

The bumpy road to the EMU should be placed within a theory of economic and monetary crises based on value production and distribution. It is impossible, within the limits of this chapter, to submit even the rudiments of such a theory. Only a few scanty remarks will have to suffice (for the theoretical underpinnings and relevant literature of this section, see Carchedi, 1991a).[2] The cardinal point is that technological competition is the basic force behind capitalism's dynamic nature. Through it, greater productivity (defined as units of output per unit of capital invested) is achieved. However, technological innovations cause the replacement of people by means of production and thus, due to the nature of capitalist production, unemployment. It follows that, more products are made with less people and that less purchasing power is available for the purchase of those products. The same point can be made from the point of view of value theory. Value is human labour (a) carried out under capitalist production relations, (b) transforming use values (both material and mental), and (c) realized through purchase/sale, that is, as money.[3] Thus, while the quantity of products increases, the value contained in them decreases. Lower purchasing power is the consequence of the fact that less value has been produced – that less living labour has been employed for the production of that higher output. Realization (sale) difficulties ensue. These are followed by profitability crises, and by business failures.

While there is simply no solution to this inner contradiction, a number of palliatives have been devised to postpone production and realization crises. One of these is the increase in the quantity of money in order to 'create' the needed purchasing power. This, however, inasmuch as money is not hoarded, cannot but lead to inflation (whether in the real sector or in the financial one it does not matter here), in other words the reduction in money's purchasing power. There is thus a direct relation between increased productivity, unemployment,[4] and inflation. But not all enterprises benefit equally from the increase in the quantity of money. Those goods whose price rises at a higher rate appropriate value from those whose prices rise more slowly. This redistributes value among capitals. In addition, value is redistributed between capital and labour if the rate of change of wage goods' prices diverges from wages' rate of change. In both cases, there is a redistribution, rather than creation, of less purchasing power.[5] This can temporarily alleviate realization and profitability difficulties for some (or even for all) capitals but eventually a crisis will erupt (as empirical observation clearly shows). Both monetarist and neo-Keynesian policies are impotent against the inevitability of crises (See Carchedi, 1991a, ch. 5).

Consider now a different type of value redistribution, that associated with technological competition. Given that, within each sector, products are sold approximately for the same price, this latter is an average of the value contained in each of those products. Moreover, given that in each sector there operate producers with different levels of productivity, the more efficient enterprises realize higher profits while the less efficient ones realize lower profits, or perhaps even losses.

Even in the absence of inflation, price formation implies value redistribution according to productivity differential.[6] The same mechanism operates at the international level, if we consider the producers of a certain good worldwide. If the most advanced producers are situated in a country and the less competitive producers in another, the former, and by extension the country in which they operate, realize more value (higher profit rates) at the expense of the latter which might be unable even to sell (part of) their products. Given that prices are expressed in different currencies, the production of and distribution of (international) value, or price formation, is inextricably bound with the mechanism of exchange rates. From the point of view of the labour theory of value, this mechanism is a redistribution of international value rewarding higher productivity. In spite of its importance, this analysis is still in its infancy (See Carchedi, 1991a, b). The next section aims at filling this lacuna.

Exchange rates and monetary crises

Nowadays, the production and realization of value is an international process. Capital crosses national borders: a) to acquire foreign means of production (including raw materials); b) to set up abroad either the whole production process of parts of it; and c) to purchase foreign labour power and either 'import' it or use it abroad. Moreover, the value thus produced is realized not only at home but also on foreign markets. Finally, capital roams the world (including the world's financial markets) in a constant search for the highest profit rates. The economic units responsible for all of this are not so much small enterprises but rather large oligopolies, which operate and compete on a global scale, the transnational corporations. As a rule, it is these latter which, due to their higher productivity levels, realize greater quantities of value (in other words, higher profits) at the cost of their less efficient competitors. Moreover, if the demand for their products is large enough, they appropriate value also from other (producers in other) sectors. Since these sectors are international, the optical illusion arises that it is countries, rather than capitals, which appropriate value. Given that products are sold for different currencies, the mechanism of exchange rates, far from being only a conscious institutional arrangement for the exchange of the different currencies, is also an objective system of appropriation of international value. National capitals, then, appropriate international value in its foreign currencies form. Let us dwell on this a little longer.

The *rate of exchange* is the rate at which foreign currencies, including the international one, are converted into one unit of the national currency.[7] If the mechanism of the exchange rates implies appropriation of value, then movements in the rate of exchange affect that appropriation. The revaluation of a currency, for example the Japanese yen, against another currency, for example the German mark, gives right to the holders of yen to a greater quantity of DM and thus to a greater aliquot part of use values priced in DM (but not necessarily produced in Germany). A greater appropriation of international value by yen holders follows. Similarly for the devaluation of the yen and the revaluation and devaluation of the DM. Let us assume at first that capitalists in the productive sphere are the sole holders of foreign currency. Then, revaluation implies the appropriation of value by the (producers in the) country whose currency has been revalued and devaluation implies the appropriation of value from the (producers in the) country whose currency has been devalued. This, as we shall see shortly, is the tendency. This argument must now be articulated by considering changes in productivity levels, in exchange rates, and in value appropriation.

Consider first the effects of technological competition on the production and redistribution of international value, holding exchange rates constant. We have seen that a capital's increased productivity boosts the quantity of use values per unit of capital invested while decreasing the value produced (inasmuch as labour power has been replaced by means of production). If that capital sells the increased output on the foreign market it appropriates a greater quantity of foreign currency which, upon exchange against the national currency, results in a higher profit rate.[8] The innovative capital has increased its profit rate while causing the production of less (international) value.

Suppose the innovative capital is Japanese. How can the other Japanese producers react? The best alternative for them is to introduce new and yet more advanced technologies so that it is they who now acquire a competitive edge. If they succeed, they appropriate extra value which they perceive (and this is all that matters to them) as higher profit rates. So long as this process is restricted, the rates of exchange are not affected. However, if one or more sectors in the Japanese economy experience a continuous and generalized productivity increase, the demand by other countries for yen increase, thus generating an upwards pressure on, and eventually a revaluation of, the yen. Consider now the effects on imports and exports. Due to yen revaluation, yen priced Japanese exports exchange for more foreign currency. Japanese exporters appropriate more international value in its foreign currency form for each commodity exported. As for Japanese importers, they pay less value in its national (yen) money form for each unit of commodity imported priced in foreign currencies. While greater appropriation of international value due to increased efficiency benefits only the innovative capitals, revaluation benefits all exporters (innovative and not) and importers.

Thus, due to *revaluation* caused by technological advance and concomitant higher productivity with shedding of labour by the innovative exporters, the *tendency* is the appropriation of a greater relative share of a decreased mass of international value both by the exporters (with an extra advantage for the innovative exporters) and by the importers. But revaluation affects also the quantities imported and exported. The dearer yen encourages imports (assuming that the imports' prices in foreign currencies remain unchanged) so that the share of international value appropriated on this account increases. This too belongs to the tendency. But, on the other hand, exports are discouraged (the foreign importers need more foreign currencies to buy the same quantity of yen and thus of goods priced in yen), so that the share of international value appropriated on this account is checked. The *counter-tendency*, then, is the restraint imposed upon the greater share of the decreased mass of international value appropriated by the revaluating country due to the negative effect revaluation has on the quantity exported. While technological innovations diminish the quantity of value produced, revaluation does not. It only redistributes that quantity, whether it has been decreased by technological innovations or not.

Empirically, the revaluing country's net appropriation of value (a greater share of a decreased quantity checked by lower exports) can be either positive or negative. But in terms of the functioning of the system, it is important to distinguish the tendency from the counter-tendency. It is the tendency which explains the dynamism of the system. The country (in this simplified example, both the importers and the importers) of the innovative capitals is rewarded for their increased productivity through the appropriation of international value following revaluation. But, since countries do not act and think, only people do, this reward takes the form of higher profit rates for the innovative producers and both for the exporters (greater international value as more foreign currency received) and for the importers (greater international value as less national currency paid). In the pursuance of higher profit rates the innovators cause the currency's revaluation and thus the greater appropriation of value on this account for the country as a whole and for all the holders of that currency. This movement is checked by the counter-tendency, the slowing down of exports due to revaluation and thus of the international value appropriated.

What strategies are there for the technological laggards in other countries (say, Germany)? They too can try and increase their productivity. In this case, they improve their own economic position (appropriation of value and thus a higher profit rate) while further contributing to the aggravation of the general situation (lower international total value produced and thus lower international average rate of profit). If higher efficiency is not viable, the option is open for competitive devaluations in order to foster exports. A greater quantity exported can increase the mass of profits in national currency for the exporters even if less national currency is exchanged for the foreign currency received for each commodity exported. Similarly to revaluation, devaluation affects the redistribution of the diminished quantity of international value but does not bring about that decrease (which is caused by the Japanese innovators). The difference is that now the *mass of profits increases* with greater exports (but the rate of profit computed in the national currency does not, *ceteris paribus*) while the *value lost* to other countries *increases too*. Suppose, for example, that DM1 = Y300 and that the price of a German good *X* is DM1. Upon export, the German exporter realizes an international value corresponding to Y300. Now Germany devalues to DM2 = Y300. The German exporter sells *X* for DM1 = Y150. To realize the same international value as before, 2*X* must be exported. That exporter has retained its level of profits but it has ceded twice as much of the value produced in Germany. As for German importers, they pay more DM for each unit imported priced in yen, get less value contained in Japanese goods per unit of national currency and realize less international value.

Given the loss of value on each unit of output traded internationally and thus the smaller share of international value realized, why, should Germany devalue? The reason is that devaluation makes the realization of the value produced in Germany possible thus making possible the realization of a higher mass of profit. Only, given that Germany has become a technological laggard, less value is realized by German exporters as well as by German importers. Germany's loss of value is the price she has to pay for having been left behind in the technological race. This conforms to the rules of capitalist functioning which reward technological innovators and punishes the technological laggards. This loss of value is then the tendency. But a DM devaluation cheapens exports priced in DM and can cause their increase. The share of international value lost by Germany augments on this account too. This too is part of the tendency. Since total international value has decreased due to Japan's technological change, this smaller share is also a smaller absolute quantity of international value appropriated (contrary to Japan, whose absolute share can increase). On the other hand, devaluation makes German imports dearer, so that less might be imported and less value lost. This is the counter-tendency.

Thus, due to *devaluation*, the *tendency* is a loss of value, that is the realization of a smaller share of a smaller mass of international value. This loss is increased if exports increase. The *counter-tendency* is a reduction of this loss due to the negative effect devaluation has on imports. Orthodox economics, in assessing the effects of devaluation sees only the advantages for exporters and disadvantages for importers in terms of the money they realize.[9] Orthodox economics does not see the tendential loss of value taking place both through exports and through imports and increased by the positive effect devaluation has on exports. This tendency is checked by the counter-tendency, a reduction of this loss due to the reduced quantity of imports.[10]

To sum up these first results, increased efficiency leads to the creation of less value but to the appropriation of more value by the innovators. Their rate of profit increases too, at the cost of that of their competitors and perhaps of those of the rest of the economy. This can lead to a revaluation and thus to the appropriation of more value both by the other exporters and by the importers. This is the tendency. Revaluation does not increase the value produced but affects only its distribution. The same holds for devaluation. The difference is that the exporters increase their mass of profit proportionally with the increase in exports but lose value on each unit of export and that the importers lose value and see their (rate of) profit fall. This too is the tendency. The tendency is what explains the functioning of the system. The working of the exchange rates is, in spite of its specific characteristics, just another way tendentially to reward technological innovations within the international capitalist context at the expense of those who have been left behind in the technological race.[11]

Up to here, the focus has been on international value redistribution among capitals (and thus nations) following modifications in exchange rates. These results can now be used to inquire into the redistribution of value between capital and labour within the context first of the relations between the centre and the dominated block of the imperialist system (in this section) and then of the relations among the EU's member countries (in the next section).

First of all, the analysis above presupposes that all countries are unrestrained in their capacity to compete technologically. In reality, capitals in the *dominated block* are often unable to compete with the technologically advanced (enterprises in the) imperialist *centre*.[12] Given that the dominated block cannot achieve productivity levels as high as those in the imperialist centre,[13] the former must resort to forcing labourers to work longer and/or more intensively to compete with advanced technologies in the centre.[14] At the same time, this higher production (both of value and of use values) must not be rewarded by higher real wages, or the rate of profit will not rise. The result is an increased rate of surplus value.[15] But the working day, as well as people's physical endurance, are limited. Then, real wages must also be lowered through inflation. It follows that higher prices in national currency must be offset by lower international prices. Hence, devaluation. Consequently, countries whose exporters have a competitive advantage due to higher efficiency tend to appreciate their currency. Their technologically inferior competitors, inasmuch as they try to avoid a loss of foreign markets and thus of profitability through inflation, tend to depreciate their currency.[16]

But devaluation in its turn calls for inflation. In fact, devaluation hits import prices in the national currency thus decreasing importers' profits. Inasmuch as imports are means of production, their higher prices decrease capitalists' profits. A tendency towards inflation follows. Inasmuch as imports are wage goods, their higher prices decrease labour's purchasing power (wages) thus increasing profits. However, labour might resist lower real wages and capital might resort to inflation, on condition that the rate of increase of wage goods prices rises more than that of wages. But inflation, a shift of purchasing power from labour to capital, while initially beneficial to capital, creates realization difficulties in the wage goods sector which can be alleviated through exports and thus through a further round of devaluation and inflation. This downward spiral results in labour's increasing impoverishment with all the social tensions and problems associated with it. Moreover, if this process goes on far enough a country might be left with a worthless currency. This is what happened in many Latin American countries in the 1970s and 1980s. The combination of technological lag, inflation, and devaluation has led to the well-known incredible conditions of misery in those countries as well as to the military dictatorships and authoritarian regimes which are often needed to impose these conditions (in case the neo-liberalist ideology fails to convince people that it is in their interest to tighten their own belt even more).

To end this section, one more aspect should be mentioned: the country whose currency is the international one enjoys a very peculiar privilege, international '*seigniorage*'. This is the appropriation of value by the country issuing the international means of payment simply because it issues that currency. It is equal to, for each note, the difference between the nominal value and the cost of production of that note. Since the postwar period, this is the case of the US dollar. By simply printing dollars, the US can pay for real commodities, and thus for value, with practically worthless paper. But this is not enough for the US to appropriate international value. The other countries, which have earned those notes by exporting to the US, must not use those dollars to import goods from the US. This is the case if those dollars either are frozen as those countries international reserves or circulate only within those economies. In this way, the US imports goods without exporting goods in exchange. Of course, there are limits to this process. The greater quantity of dollars diminishes their purchasing power[17] as well as the willingness of foreigners to hold them both as a means of payment and as a reserve currency. This erodes the status of the dollar as the international money and thus the possibility to profit from seigniorage. Moreover, money creation can be inflationary. This can lead to devaluation and to further erosion of the dollar's status as international money.[18]

After World War II, in the period of absolute US economic domination, both the 'First World' and the 'Third World' not only did not object to receive, but actually wanted, US dollars both because the dollar was covered by great gold reserves and because dollars allowed the purchase of cheaper and better quality US goods. This was possible because of the unscathed and more productive US economy. This is why the dollar was 'as good as gold'. The international monetary system agreed upon at Bretton Woods in 1944, in which the dollar was given a fixed gold value and the other currencies were anchored to the dollar in a system of fixed exchange rates, reflected this state of affairs. But this system could function smoothly only inasmuch as it reflected the technological superiority of the US. Once the US began to lose its absolute competitive advantage, the system of fixed exchange rates began to crack. On the one hand, the dollar was not allowed to devalue by The Bretton Woods system and its devaluation would have dented its role as international currency and its seigniorage. On the other hand, devaluation was needed as a measure to prop up US international competitiveness (in 1950, the percentage share of world industrial production was 47.8 for the US and 1.6 for Japan; in 1985 it was 39.3 and 11.5 respectively).

The US was caught in a dilemma. The solution was found in the 'soft landing' of the dollar, that is, in a gradual devaluation of the dollar in order to avoid undermining international confidence in it. But this implied a change from fixed to flexible exchange rates and the suspension of the dollar's gold convertibility which took place in 1971. This dented the dollar's status as international money. Gradually, two rivals have begun to emerge as international currencies, the DM and the yen. The dollar has not lost its seigniorage but its position of privilege is being increasingly threatened.[19]

Monetary crises are the immediate result of speculative capital movements but are caused by changed long-term relations of economic and technical power. This holds also for the dollar. Since the 1970s, the US has increasingly lost its absolute technological lead and economic power. Consequently, the dollar has become increasingly unstable and prone to speculative attacks. But speculative movements are due to, and reveal, deeper structural laws of movement. This is revealed by the fact that after each monetary storm the new exchange rates settle down around the new parities rather than returning to the old levels. Any suggestion that the exchange rates of the DM, the US dollar and the Yen be fixed, fails to see the structural reasons for the volatility of these rates. The single European currency, when it will have replaced the national currencies, will abolish monetary crises within the European Community. But this result will abolish neither wider monetary crises nor unequal development within Europe. Crises are inherent in the capitalist system. Attempts to rid capitalism of them can only change their form of manifestation.

The European monetary union and the single currency

The previous discussion can now be used to inquire into the European Monetary Union (EMU). To this end it is necessary to begin with an analysis of the precursor of the EMU, the European Monetary System (EMS).

The two basic features of the EMS were the *Exchange Rate Mechanism*, or *ERM*, and the *European Currency Unit*, or *Ecu*.[20] The Ecu was a composite currency in which all member states' currencies were represented in different quantities (weights). Through this fixed value relative to the Ecu, national currencies had a fixed value relative to each other. For example, according to the *Financial Times* of 7 March 1995, Ecu 1 was equal to Fl.2.152 and to FFr.6.406. These were the bilateral central rates against the Ecu or *central rates* for short. They implied that FL.2.152 =

FFr.6.406. Or, FFr.1 = 2.152/6.406F1 = Fl.0.3359 and F1.1 = 6.406/2.152FFr = FFr.2.976. These were the cross bilateral central rates, or *cross rates* for short. Up to 1992, the member states undertook to keep their currencies' fluctuations within relatively narrow limits – 2.25 per cent above or below the cross rates (Italy was allowed a ± 6 per cent band but adopted the ±2.25 per cent band in 1990). These limits of fluctuations were the *bands* or *bilateral limits*. After the 1993 crisis, these bands were widened to ±15 per cent (except for Germany and the Netherlands which retained the ±2.25 per cent band).

Consider by way of example the maximum fluctuation of the FFr and the F1 relative to each other. Suppose the FFr loses value relative to the F1 (that is, the F1 gains value relative to the FFr). Either the FFr devalues by a maximum of 15 per cent or the F1 revalues by a maximum of 15 per cent. Politically, there is a difference between Holland revaluing relative to France or France devaluing relative to Holland. France will prefer the former option in order to avoid devaluation and the concomitant negative image associated with it. Computationally too these two outcomes are not the same. Then, the average is taken. For example, if the FFr devalues by 15 per cent, it falls to (6.406 + 15 per cent of 6.406) = FFr.7.3669 relative to F1.2.152. This means that if F1.2.152 = FFr.7.3669, F1.1 = 7.3669/2.152 = FFr.3.423. If the F1 revalues by 15 per cent, it rises to (2.152 – 15 per cent of 2.152) = Fl.1.8292 relative to FFr. 6.406. This means that Fl.1.8292 = FFr.6.406, so that Fl.1 = 6.406/1.8293 = FFr.3.5021. If the average is taken, (3.5021 + 3.423) /2 = FFr.3.457. This gives the maximum devaluation of the FFr relative to the F1 (in other words, the maximum revaluation of the F1 relative to the FFr). Or, given that the cross rate is F1.1 = FFr.2.976, the FFr is allowed to devalue relative to the Fl (that is, the Fl can revalue relative to the FFr) up to a maximum of Fl.1 = FFr.3.457. Similarly for the case in which the FFr revalues relative to the Fl (in other words the Fl devalues relative to the FFr).

To keep currencies within their bilateral limits, central banks and governments had to intervene. In the case of a weak currency, they resorted to a rise in interest rates, support operations using a diversity of currencies, or a tightening of fiscal policy. The opposite in case of a strong currency. However, central banks did not wait until the bilateral limits had been reached before intervening. Once a country's currency had diverged by three quarters of its permissible margin above or below its Ecu central rate, the *divergence indicator* was reached. Then, there was a presumption that a government would take remedial action. Notice that a currency, inasmuch as it was a part of the Ecu, could not fluctuate around itself. Thus, for example, if the DM formed 30.2 per cent of the value of the Ecu, it could only fluctuate by 100 – 30.2, i.e. 69.8, around the Ecu, in other words against the other currencies forming the Ecu. Then, the maximum fluctuation against the Ecu was $0.698 \times 15 = \pm 10.47$.

We can now see how the bilateral bands limited the technological laggards' possibility to use anti-cyclical measures, thus tying them to the dominant country's policy. Consider the example of Germany (higher productivity) and Italy (lower productivity). Germany, given her higher productivity, was more competitive on foreign markets. Also, greater productivity allowed German labour greater material welfare.[21] Germany's pursuance of higher profits, then, was relatively independent from high inflation. Moreover, inflation would dent price competitivity thus requiring devaluation, something Germany was reluctant to use because, as we shall see shortly, this would have checked Germany's aim to make of the DM an international currency. Inflation, then, was (and still is) enemy number one in Germany. Italy's situation was the opposite. Lower productivity levels created the conditions for inflationary policies as a means to reduce the level of real wages (that is, to increase the rate of surplus value and thus the rate of profit). To safeguard her international competitiveness, Italy had to resort to devaluation. But this escape route was limited, given the relative fixity of exchange rates within the ERM.

Suppose for example that the Italian government would decide to resort to money creation to stimulate the economy. This might have generated inflationary pressures and might have called for a devaluation of the lira. However, the bilateral bands ruled out large exchange rate fluctuations. Consequently, if Italy did not want to devalue by modifying its central rate, it either had to accept a deterioration of its balance of trade or reduce the rate of inflation. In this indirect way, i.e. through the ERM, Germany set a limit to the Italian rate of inflation thus restricting the (limited) effectiveness of this anti-cyclical measure in Italy. Or, suppose that Germany lowered her interest rate in order to check inflationary pressures. Inasmuch as interest rate differentials play a role in financial capital movements, financial operators would sell DM and buy lire. This tended to revalue the lira and devalue the DM. If this process threatened to send the lira through the upper limit of the band, Italy had to lower her interest rate in order to relieve the pressure on the lira. But this might have had unwanted inflationary effects.

In this way a seemingly neutral mechanism fostered specific economic policies and interests, those of the dominant country – Germany

– and within it of the German oligopolies. While Germany can compete through greater efficiency (relative surplus value), technological laggards have to compete by extracting more absolute surplus value. This can be done either at the point of production, through longer working days and higher intensity of labour (nowadays called labour flexibility) or through redistribution (inflation). *The ERM* limited the latter option and stimulateed the former. It checked the ability of the weaker countries to hold back, through inflationary policies, the loss of value they suffer due to the stronger countries' higher efficiency and *forces technological laggards to extract more (absolute) surplus value at the point of production* rather than through redistribution mechanisms (inflation). This, then, was the economic significance of the ERM for labour. At the same time, this system seemed to be imposed by a distant bureaucracy whereas it was the result of conscious anti-labour economic policies.[22]

Incidentally, the above highlights the reason, which was (and is) the member states' unequal development, why exchange rates within the ERM could not be stable. But there is also a second reason. Investors, when moving out of dollar positions for fear of a fall in its value, seek a safe currency. Usually, they did not purchase other European currencies but preferred the DM, which was in no (or less) danger of being devalued. This extra demand for DM affected the exchange rate between the DM and the other European currencies putting the bilateral bands under strain and possibly forcing a realignment. In this way, a large influx of dollars threatened the working of the ERM, whose aim was to avoid realignments.

It has been pointed out that technological leaders tend to revalue their currencies and that technological laggards tend to devalue theirs. This law is stronger than the conscious attempts to check it. In fact, during the existence of the EMS, the DM only appreciated (from 1979 to 1990, the DM was revalued six times) and the Italian lira was only devalued, six times (Swann, 1992, p. 211). As for inflation, if 1980 = 100, consumer prices in Germany rose to 121 by 1987 but to 214 in Italy. Moreover, when the weight of the ERM became intolerable for the weaker countries in terms of unemployment, loss of foreign markets and foreign currency, popular discontent, or simply speculative movements, only one solution was left: leaving the ERM. This is indeed what happened to Italy and the UK in September, 1992.[23]

We can now look into the reasons behind the EMU and the single currency. The ERM was important because it was the first step in the transformation of the DM into the euro and this into a world currency.

Before the euro, the DM was only a potential contender for the role of international money. Its economic basis was too restricted. To become a truly international currency, it had to become the currency used in the whole Community, in a market comparable to that of the US, served by an efficient and technologically advanced production system. This would propel a volume of euro-denominated international transactions such that the demand for the euro would be equal to or surpass that for the dollar. This, in its turn, would facilitate the placing of Euro-denominated financial instruments on non-EMU markets, thus increasing the demand for the currency. Inasmuch as this process would be successful, the world's central banks and institutional investors would adjust their portfolios from dollar-denominated to euro-denominated instruments, thus reinforcing this virtuous circle.

But this was not sufficient for the euro to become the new form taken by the DM. This would have been the case only inasmuch as the euro could be managed according to an economic policy reflecting and fostering the interests of German capital (even though in a mediated and negotiated way),[24] that is, according to a strict interpretation and application of the Maastricht convergence criteria (at least, as long as Germany retained its dominant position within the EU).[25] It is through these criteria that the other member countries' interests were subordinated to those of Germany. The single currency will erase even the restricted possibility offered by the ERM to resort to devaluation (realignments) while the stability criteria will tie even more the weaker countries' economic policies to that of Germany. Within the EMU, the ERM has not disappeared but ties non-EMU members to the euro. The difference is that the euro has replaced the Ecu as the pivot of the central rates of non-euro currencies (European Council, 1996). This ties the economic policy of the non-euro members to that of the euro area and thus of its dominant country, Germany. In this way, *the introduction of the EMU and of the euro, a further step towards not only European integration but also towards a strengthening of Germany's dominant position, will be paid by labour both in the euro area and outside it.*

But the EMU rests also on fiscal policies which lead to austerity measures and thus to redistribution of surplus value from labour to capital, even though not through inflation.[26] *The more the EU countries are tied to Germany, the greater the expropriation of value from labour.* This all under a double deception. First, an anti-labour policy wanted by national governments (and by the multinationals) is disguised as if it were an economic policy imposed by some distant bureaucracy, for which the member states are not responsible, and reflecting some socially neutral rationality. Second, an economic policy ultimately in the interest of industrial capital appears as if it were imposed by (German) financial capital. In reality, financial capital forces industrial capital to renounce the competitive instruments of the poor countries (inflation and devaluation), it calls industrial capital to task, and thus is functional for the greater creation of (surplus) value rather than simply for a more favourable redistribution of the (surplus) value created. Supra-national financial capital (the European Central bank) enjoys a measure of relative autonomy in the interest of the expanded reproduction of industrial capital. But, of course, this will not be sufficient to hold back future crises.

Official ideology stresses the euro's common advantages, like better trade conditions deriving from savings on exchange rate costs and hedging. However, this is not the hart of the matter. Neither is it of decisive importance to know that the computer industry will gain from a greatly increased demand while the car industry will suffer from reduced demand. The real advantage for Europe's capital is that the EMU is a continuation of the ERM in that it ties even more the economic, monetary, and fiscal policies of the other EMU countries to that of Germany (better: to the interests of European oligopolies under the leadership of German oligopolies) while at the same time imposing on labour the burden of this process. *The euro, and thus German leadership, is accepted because the bill is paid by labour.* At the same time, *these policies appear as if they were dictated by 'Europe'* in the interest of the 'common good'.

As for the less competitive countries, by adhering to the EMU and to the euro, they renounce definitely inflation and devaluation as independent instrument of anti-conjunctural policy and international competition. But they gain an institutional framework within which it becomes easier, and an ideology through which it becomes obvious, to increase absolute surplus value at the point of production, that is, to force labour to work longer, more intensively, and generally more 'flexibly'. In this way, the total (surplus) value produced, and thus total purchasing power, is increased, whereas inflation only redistributes an unchanged purchasing power. According to official economic doctrine, the EMU is supposed to create a zone of monetary stability and this in its turn is supposed to contribute to the achievement of a stable, equilibrium, and crises-free economy. This, of course, bears no relation to reality which obstinately continues to be in an unstable disequilibrium, and crises-prone state. Also, official economics submit that the discipline imposed by the EMU will induce greater competitiveness through the introduction of technological innovations. But, as shown above, both the ERM and the EMU force laggard countries to extract more absolute surplus value at the point of production, something which if anything slows down the introduction of technological innovations.

The 1994–95 monetary crisis

The third section of this chapter provided some elements for a theory of monetary crises. This section will consider a concrete example, the last monetary crisis before the first version of this chapter was writen. Its specific aspect is its relation to huge quantities of speculative capital. To begin with, therefore, we must understand the causes and origin of this capital. This, in its turn, must be placed within the frame of the crises theory summarily submitted above.

We suggested earlier that crises manifest themselves as unemployment figures. From this angle, it is clear that, notwithstanding GDP figures, the world capitalist system is far from having exited the long-term crisis that started towards the beginning of the 1970s. Since then, periods of recovery, interrupted by depressions and crises, do little to alleviate the joblessness afflicting the Western World, not to mention the so-called Third World. Neo-liberalist policies can only exacerbate this problem. From the collective labourer's point of view, it is employment figures which are the real indicators of an economy's state of health.

But there is also another aspect which reveals that the system is still in a deep crisis. When the general rate of profit starts its long descent, large amounts of money leave the sphere of productive investment and look for profitable outlets in the financial and speculative sphere. A first, traditional, outlet for this financial capital is the stock exchange. This aspect will not be dealt with here.[27] A second outlet is the *foreign exchange market*, which has assumed major proportions in recent years. Huge quantities of financial capital are invested in (very) short term speculations on exchange rates. Great profits (and great losses) can be made overnight, even if exchange rate differentials are small, due to the sheer size of the currencies exchanged. These capital movements can bring about wide fluctuations in the rates of exchange. This aspect has been amply underlined by financial publications as a new element in the monetary crises: 'Global investors become increasingly able to switch from economy to economy at the tap of a computer key... with more than $1 trillion looking for a home in the foreign exchange market every day, even a slight deviation from the straight and narrow can invite a savaging' (*Business Week*, 16 January 1995, p. 20). What has not been evidenced in these writings is the origin of these massive quantities of currencies looking for instant profits. There is thus a clear link between the present still unresolved profitability crisis and this new form of monetary turbulences.[28]

Particularly important is the question of the source of the huge quantity of dollars available for speculative aims. As an article in the *International Herald Tribune* of 18/19 March 1995, reported, 'Over the past five years, the current account deficit totalled $246 billion-dollars that flowed out of the country and into the hands of foreigners.' About half of these dollars have been invested by their foreign owners back in the US, in the form of both direct and portfolio investments. But the other half (half trillion dollars) is now in the hands of foreign central banks. These latter are practically forced to keep these reserves since any massive dollar sale would provoke a sudden fall in the value of the dollar and thus a plunge in the value of foreign-owned dollar denominated assets 'with the risk that the losses could trigger a financial panic back home' (ibid). Moreover, a dollar devaluation would increase the competitiveness of US exports. 'For better or for worse, then, the stability of the world financial system is tied, at least in part, to the stability of the dollar' (ibid). This is the US point of view, which defends the dollars' seigniorage – the usefulness of large trade deficits for the stability of the world financial markets and for the smooth running of international trade. The appropriation of value inherent in this system, however, is lost sight of. In any case, it is the economic crisis in the imperialist centre that originates massive quantities of speculative capital.

We have now all the elements for an analysis of the 1994–95 monetary crisis. Its conjunctural catalyst can be sought in Mexico's financial difficulties. In the 1970s and 1980s, Latin American countries used high rates of inflation as a tool to increase their rate of exploitation and international competitivity. This called for a policy of constant devaluation of their currencies. But extremely high rates of inflation made those currencies practically worthless for internal purposes and constant devaluations made those currencies worthless for external purposes. This caused the 'dollarization' of those countries. Those countries' central banks were left managing a currency, their own, which had become worthless and thus unwanted both by other countries and by their own citizens. In its turn, this entailed complete dependence on foreign capital to spur investments and growth.

To redress this situation, Mexico reversed its economic and monetary policy and decided to anchor its currency to the dollar: one peso was set equal to one dollar. This required a policy of high interest rates, given that this was needed to encourage foreign investors to buy and keep pesos. High interest rates, together with a 'voluntary' income and wage policy, kept the rate of inflation down and this latter, in its turn, was the reason adduced for a policy of wage restraint. The tying of the peso to the dollar, then, was just another means to contain wages and increase profits with a relatively low level of inflation.[29] A high value of the peso relative to the dollar was dependent upon dollar reserves to support the peso. These reserve came from a massive programme of privatization of state assets, especially electricity and petrochemical plants, which were sold for dollars (*Financial Times*, 24/25 December 1995) originating in the massive US trade deficit.

But there are limits to the extent policy makers can hold back the objective laws of capitalist movement. To begin with, high interest rates slowed down not only inflation but the economy as well. Second, due to the artificially high value of the peso and thus to only moderate devaluation, Mexican exports became uncompetitive. 'By 1993, Mexican producer prices expressed in dollars had risen by more than 45 per cent compared with prices in the US' (*Business Week*, 15 January 1995). The Mexican current account deficit climbed in 1994 to $28bn, or 8 per cent of GDP (*Financial Times*, 21 December 1994). The government did not seem to be worried, given that foreign investors (attracted by high interest rates) kept buying bonds and stocks. Also, the government pinned its hopes on NAFTA and on the direct investments and trade opportunities which it would bring. Nevertheless, foreign investors became increasingly wary that the economic slowdown and the size of the deficit might eventually force Mexico to give in and devalue the peso.

International investors, worried about the possibility of losing money through devaluation, and international speculators, anxious to gain money by betting upon devaluation (by selling that currency and buying it again after devaluation) keep an anxious eye both on the budget deficit and on the concomitant public debt. High debt and deficit levels can be financed through inflation, and this, can lead to devaluation. But they can also be financed through international borrowing. This, besides raising the spectre of default, can also lead to devaluation through high levels of debt servicing, expected increases in interest rates (needed to induce investors to buy government bonds to raise the necessary money), the sale of existing bonds with fixed interest rates, the sale of the currency thus gained, and finally the devaluation of that currency. High debt and deficit levels might spur the investors' flight from the national currency. This is magnified by the massive selling by speculators betting on devaluation. The level of foreign reserves needed to support the national currency is thus of significant importance for the 'sentiments' of international money operators. What interests the international money managers is not the real economic state of a nation but the possibility to make a quick buck on exchange rate fluctuations (which they themselves increasingly manipulate).

The use of high interest rates and of foreign reserves to prop up the peso had disastrous consequences. Interest rate shot up to about 35 per cent to 45 per cent annually (*Financial Times*, 28 December 1994). The concern was that, strangled by these interest rates, many companies would stop borrowing from banks, thus depriving the latter of a source of income. But even more important, most company loans carried variable interest rates. Extremely high interest rates could have caused company failures. These, in their turn, would have generated loan defaults which could have provoked banks failures. But the collapse of the bank system was not the only worry. Doubts about the government's ability to service debt arose when, in December 1994, investors bought only a fraction of the $27bn in *tesobonos* – short-term dollar denominated securities issued by the government – offered by the central bank. Mexico had another $26.5bn coming due in the next months. 'Some 80 per cent of these are held by foreign investors, many by US funds' (*Financial Times*, 29 December 1994). The risks involved for foreign investors spurred a massive capital outflow.

On 20 December 1994, the Mexican government finally devalued the peso first by 15 per cent and then to 40 per cent of its pre-crisis level, following ten months of capital outflows and the fall of foreign reserves to $7bn, down from $24.5bn at the beginning of the year and from $10bn from 1 November. (One of the reasons given for this capital outflow was the Zapatistas' insurgence in Chiapas; this point will be taken up briefly below.) This devaluation forced the Mexican government effectively to float the peso, thus 'abandoning a long-held policy in which the currency was kept within a specific target zone' (*Financial Times*, 23 December 1994). As a result, investors who held Mexican assets lost billions of dollars in a couple of days (ibid.)

Thus, the new economic policy, centred on low inflation and relative exchange rate stability through the pegging of the peso to the dollar, failed. Such a policy could have succeeded only if Mexico had been able to generate a capital inflow such that it could have switched from a technologically dependent to a technologically advanced country. This would have required in its turn massive productive investments (modernization) as well as autonomous investments in science and technology. In this case, pegging the currency to the dollar would have fostered foreign capitalists' trust in that currency. But 'Mexico proved more successful at attracting portfolio investments from mutual and pension funds than at garnering direct investment in factories' (*Business Week*, 9 January 1995, p. 15). Or, the Mexican crisis 'stemmed largely from Mexico's dependence on short-term debt to finance investments' (*International Herald Tribune*, 23 March 1995).

Not surprisingly, Mexico's authorities went back to the type of policy, based on inflation and devaluation, which is more suited to countries belonging to the dependent block.[30] This demanded the trade unions' cooperation. But it was feared that this would not be forthcoming, in spite of their traditional subserviency,[31] given that real wages had only begun to recover in 1993 after a ten-year fall (*Financial Times* 31 December 1994/1 January 1995). This explains why a peasant insurgence (in Chiapas) could worry international investors. This uprising could have been the catalyst of a much greater movement of discontent, given the potential restlessness of the Mexican working class. But not only the international banks, the American government was also deeply interested in the fate of the Mexican peso. First, the peso's devaluation meant cheaper imports of Mexican goods in the US and less US exports to Mexico. As *Business Week* (16 January 1995) anticipated, 'Overnight, the 30 per cent devaluation wipes out a US trade surplus with Mexico and creates chronic deficits for the foreseeable future'. Second, a likely recession (and a possible concomitant social turmoil) might have induced higher Mexican immigration in the US, which, especially in California and Texas, is a politically sensitive issue.

For these reasons the US took the lead in the creation of a $53bn peso-stabilization fund.[32] For internal political reasons, the US share ($20 billion) had to come from the Exchange Stabilization Fund which is meant to support the dollar against devaluation pressures. This provoked fears in international investors that the US might have not been able to withstand a raid on the dollar. This came at a time at which a large supply of dollars was available due to both the long-running US current account deficit (see above) and to the diversification of pension and mutual funds (which had been investing in overseas equities and bonds thus selling dollars to buy assets denominated in foreign currencies). Moreover, overseas holding of dollars were in short-term deposits and thus very volatile. Finally, there was also the expectation of higher German interests rates. The outcome was a massive flight from the dollar into the DM.

To try to redress the situation, the US would have had to raise her interest rates (something the international speculators felt the Fed did not want because of the poor state of the US economy) while Germany would have had to lower hers (something the speculators thought the Bundesbank did not want because of Germany's fears of inflation). Finally, on 31 March 1995, Germany cut its interest rate by 50 points. This gave the dollar a reprieve, but only a temporary one.[33] The dollar devaluation and the DM revaluation gained momentum. The DM revaluation put pressure on the weaker EMS currencies and forced their governments to raise their interest rates, something which, for example, France, Belgium and Denmark did on 8 March 1995. The economic policy imposed objectively by the imperialist centre upon Mexico had emerged as the EMS monetary storm through the inherent instability of the dollar.

As for Mexico, two years after the crisis, its peso denominated economy continued to shrink in terms of jobs and purchasing power while the dollar-based *maquiladora* industries – duty free assembly plants which export their output – were steadily growing. Every day, two new *maquiladora* plants opened while two Mexican-owned plants operating in the internal peso economy closed down, due among other things to high interest rates (needed to finance the large foreign debt and chronic current account deficit) and heavy taxes (imposed at the behest of the IMF). On the other hand, the 'success' in the dollar-based industries, highly praised by the US Treasury, does little for the Mexicans themselves. Not only does domestic consumption shrink, due to the export of an increasing share of total production, but also wages and other incomes count for a fraction of the *maquiladora* output (less than 5 per cent of the $26bn in *maquiladora* output in the first nine months of 1996). As for the enthusiasm showed by the US Treasury, it is not difficult to understand its reasons: the US was paid $10bn of the $13.5bn ahead of time, but Mexico achieved this by borrowing $7bn on the eurobond market. This is a recipe for a new economic and monetary crisis (Whalen, 1997).

In discussing the 1994–95 monetary crisis (as well as all other crises) commentators point out that the so-called austerity measures can provoke a recession. In reality, these measures are only the catalyst which brings about a recession which would have manifested itself in any case. This is a constant in the history of capitalism. There are indeed new elements to the 1994–95 monetary crisis but exclusive emphasis on them hides an element common to all crises: it is labour which bears the brunt of crises. If Mexican labour is too recalcitrant, brute force could be resorted to. A return to dictatorial regimes (to restore 'law and order') in Latin America could then be in the making. But even in Europe's more democratic regimes, the brute force of neo-liberalist economic policies is resorted to in order to compel labour to accept its lot. For labour, neo-liberalism is a synonym of poverty, oppression and, especially in the dominated countries, inhuman conditions of life. Not by chance has the Zapatista movement recently held a 'First Intercontinental Meeting for Humanity and Against Neo-Liberalism'.[34]

Conclusions

Since this chapter appeared in 1997, the EMU and the euro have become a reality. But this project has not and will not remain unchallenged. On the one hand, the future form of the Community will continue to be shaped by inter-capitalist rivalries (centring upon the relations among Germany, France and the United Kingdom) and on the power relations within member states. On the other, the consciousness that the process of economic and monetary integration is being paid by the European working class begins to reach wide social strata. Hopefully, Europe's labour will gain a more active role in shaping labour's Europe.

Notes

1 This is a revised version of the article first published in *Capital and Class*, Autumn 1997, No. 63, pp. 85–113.
2 This section is a drastically reduced version of a longer version and is therefore quite incomplete. It disregards, for example, the role of credit.
3 Robinson (1962) identifies five supposedly problematic areas concerning the notion of value. First, there is the problem of distinguishing between productive and unproductive labour. This has been tackled and solved in Carchedi (1991a), both for material and for mental labour. Second, there is the reduction of skilled to unskilled labour. This, together with the reduction of more intensive to less intensive labour, has been solved by Carchedi and de Haan (1995). Third, there are supposedly in Marx two different notions of value. This is, according to Robinson, irrational and inconsistent. But, as Carchedi (1991a) shows, the notions of value contained and value realized are perfectly consistent. Fourth, there is the (in)famous 'transformation problem'. As Carchedi (1984, 1991a) and Carchedi and de Haan (1995) argue, the application of Marx's method disposes both of the infinite regression and of the circularity critique. Fifth, Robinson argues that value is a metaphysical concept because it cannot be measured, so that no empirically testable hypothesis can be formulated about it. Carchedi and de Haan (1995) submit a method for measuring value, that is, the labour both contained in, and realized by, each commodity.

4 The increase in the quantity of outputs per unit of capital invested can be achieved through the introduction of new and more efficient production techniques, machinery, etc, i.e. by shedding labour power, and/or by intensifying the intensity of labour, the length of the working day, etc. In this section, I am concerned only with the former method (which, contrary to the latter, decreases the production of value).

5 This is why the word create at the beginning of this paragraph has been put within quotation marks.

6 This applies to price formation within sectors. Among sectors, the process of price formation is influenced by the movement of capital from the sectors where the rate of profit is lower to those in which it is higher and thus by the concomitant tendential equalization of the profit rates on an international scale. The thesis that international capital mobility warrants the assumption of a tendential equalization of profit rates across borders has not yet been incorporated in value analysis. Interesting work has been carried out in the 1970s by Altvater *et al.*, 1971; Busch *et al.*, 1971; Senf, 1978; for an assessment, see Deubner *et al.*, 1979; Siegel, 1984. A fair assessment is beyond the space constraints of this work. Suffice it to say that the above mentioned authors accept the thesis of international capital immobility and thus reject the thesis of an international tendential equalization of profit rates.

More recently, it has been pointed out that such an equalization does take place but only within the imperialist centre, given that by far the greatest share of foreign direct investments (FDI) is accounted for by the OECD countries. This view, however, disregards portfolio and speculative flows. To focus only on the latter, daily, 1200 bn dollars are invested in the foreign exchange markets (twice the G7 foreign exchange reserves) and 1000bn dollars in the futures markets. These huge flows cannot but tendentially equalize profit rates. Another possibility is that two tendential profit rate emerge, one for the monopolistic and the other for the non-monopolistic sector. This view is not pursued here, given that it would modify but not invalidate the thesis submitted in this work.

7 This is the British convention, or indirect quotation. The direct quotation is the ratio of the quantity of national currency to one unit of the foreign currency.

There is no space here for an analysis of the formation of rates of exchange. Suffice it to mention that, just as the market prices tend towards the production prices, ie the prices at which the average productivity capitals tendentially realize the average rate of profit, in the same way, given sufficient international capital mobility, the international market prices tend towards international prices of production, i.e. those prices at which all average productivity producers on a global scale tendentially realize the international average rate of profit. See Carchedi, 1991a, ch. 7, and Carchedi, 1991b. The same works introduce the concept of tendential rate of exchange which converts the international prices of production expressed in international money into national prices of production expressed in national money so that all average productivity capitals tendentially realize that quantity of international value expressed in their national currencies corresponding to the average rate of profit. The actual rates of exchange tend towards the tendential one. This theory relates exchange rates to productivity and thus to trade.

Speculative movements are ultimately determined by these fundamental factors, as the following sections will argue.

8 Of course, funds can be kept in foreign currencies, but this case is disregarded here because it does not affect the argument.

9 I disregard here the advantage for those engaging in import substitution because this is outside the scope of this paper.

10 Devaluation and revaluation might work towards redressing the balance of payments. But this implies neither equal exchange nor a tendency towards equilibrium. The ideological fallacy that the capitalist economy tends towards equilibrium (or, even worse, is in a state of equilibrium) cannot be dealt with here. See Freeman and Carchedi, 1996.

11 Lack of technological innovation might weigh more heavily on exports than competitive devaluation. For example, the *Financial Times* (1 November 1995), reports that between 1987 and 1994, Italy's EU market share declined from 13.22 to 12.28 per cent, in spite of the lira's heavy devaluation.

12 Of course, there are great differences within both the centre and the dominated block just as well as there are countries (the NIC) which are in a category apart. However, this rough distinction is sufficient for the present purposes.

13 I disregard here multinationals investing in the dominated block. In spite of their geographical location, they belong to the imperialist centre.

14 In the example above, if two German *X* must be sold instead of one in order to realise Y300, labourers will have to produce 2*X* in the same time or with the same intensity needed to produce 1*X*.

15 This does not imply that the rate of exploitation is higher in the laggard than in the leader countries. The point is that this rate, whatever its level, must be increased in the laggards as a means to counter their relative technological backwardness. Due to this backwardness, relatively low rates of surplus value can appear as great poverty and deprivation.

16 Between the two paradigmatic cases of technologically advanced countries whose currencies revalue and technologically backward countries whose currencies devalue, there are many intermediate cases. Moreover, even countries like Japan compete not only through the application of advanced technologies but also through very high exploitation rates. But these general remarks should be sufficient for the present purposes.

17 Hoarding and savings are disregarded here for sake of brevity.

18 Thus, the massive US trade deficit represents at the same time a massive appropriation of international value through seigniorage. It is for this reason that the US deficit, while signalling an economic malaise, ie. the relative (as opposed to absolute) decline of US productivity, is at the same time beneficial for the US economy.

19 'On foreign-exchange markets, the dollar is involved in one way or the other in 85 per cent of the transactions. Often the only way to exchange Mexican pesos for British pounds is to convert pesos into dollars and then into pounds' (*Financial Times*, 9 March 1995).

20 I use the past tense to discuss the ERM even though it is still applicable to those countries which have not adhered to the EMU. See below.

21 This does not necessarily mean that Germany's rate of surplus value is lower than that of the other less advanced countries.

22 For a lucid analysis, complementary to the present one, of this and related points concerning Britain's membership of the ERM, see Bonefeld and Burnham, 1996.

23 Italy was re-admitted to the ERM in August, 1996. The asymmetry in terms of value appropriation is mystified by terms such as 'symmetric adjustments', which refer to equal obligations to intervene by the central banks of both the weak and the strong currencies. But even in this limited meaning, adjustments are asymmetric because they are caused by an economic policy predominantly influenced by the strong country.

24 Contrary to some commentators' opinion (eg Bladen-Hovell, 1994, p. 337), the 'German leadership hypothesis' does not imply Germany's absolute power to impose its policies.

25 These are: deficit must not be greater than 3 per cent of GDP, debt must not be greater than 60 per cent of GDP, inflation cannot be higher than 1.5 per cent of the average of the inflation rates of the three countries with the lowest rates, long-term interest rates cannot be higher than 2 per cent of the rates of the three countries with the lowest rates, and the exchange rates must be within the ERM. While these criteria were meant to transform the future euro into the new form of the DM, it has been pointed out repeatedly that, quantitatively, they are arbitrary (why 3 per cent and not any other figure?) and irrational: Japan would not have been allowed membership in the EMU due to its high level of debt.

Notice that these criteria are not limited to the accession to the EMU. They are meant to continue to play a role also after its inception. On 8 November 1995, the German minister of finance Waigel spelled out his proposal for a 'Stability Pact'. This was approved at the Dublin summit of 13 and 14 December 1996. Basically, after joining the EMU, member countries have to aim at a budget deficit of 1 per cent in normal times and of no more than 3 per cent in difficult times. Countries failing these requirements will have to pay a deposit (of between 0.2 per cent and 0.5 per cent of GDP) which, in case the deficit will not be corrected within two years, will be turned into a fine. There are also escape clauses (Bureau van de Europese Commissie in Nederland, 1996).

26 Within labour, some strata, such as women, children, foreign workers, racial and other minorities are penalized more than others. This important point cannot be pursued here. See Gill, 1997.

27 See Carchedi, 1991a, ch. 5; Coakley, 1988; Evans, 1988; Freeman, 1988; Glyn, 1988; Grahl, 1988.

28 The absurd rationality of this system becomes evident as capital unable to offer employment (because unable to find investment outlets outside the speculative sphere) on the one hand and a swelling reserve army of labour looking for employment on the other. The depth of the crisis is revealed both by unemployment figures (approaching for some countries those of the Great Depression) and by the sheer size of financial capital on the speculative markets.

29 But the Mexican authorities, not surprisingly, argued for this policy as if it were the only way out of economic difficulties.

30 High profits require low wages. There are two ways to keep wages down. One is associated with devaluation and thus inflation (see above). The other is

associated with revaluation through higher interest rates (and low inflation), business difficulties, unemployment, lower wages, and thus higher profits. Notice that in the neo-classical synthesis, to revalue (ie for capital to appropriate international value), inflation must be kept down and this requires that wages be contained. Wage containment becomes a consequence of a 'sound' monetary (and thus economic) policy rather than the main target in order to increase profits.

31 'Labor laws allow firms to fire striking workers', *Business Week*, 30 January 1995, p. 19.

32 Mexico's bailout 'will go down in the recent books as the largest socialization of international market risk in monetary history' (*Business Week*, 13 February 1995). It involved the US Treasury, the Fed, other major industrial countries, the IMF and the BIS. Notice that the US loan guarantees were backed by oil-export revenues to be held by the Federal Reserve bank of New York as collateral.

33 The German move responded to: a) a rocketing DM (and thus to the monetary turmoil within the EU and to the negative effects on German exports); b) a sluggish economy; and c) a slower growth in German money supply. Germany's cut was followed by Switzerland, the Netherlands, Belgium and Austria. Thus, in the contest between the US, which did not want to raise her interest rate, and Germany, which did not want to cut hers, the US won.

34 News and announcements from the Zapatista movement can be obtained from: http://www.peak.org/~justin/ezln.html

Bibliography

Altvater, E., Blanke, B., Neusüss, Chr. (1971) 'Kapitalistischer Weltmarkt und Weltwährungskrise', *Probleme des Klassenkampfs*, 1.

Artis, M. and Lee, N. (1994) *The Economics of the European Union* (Oxford: Oxford University Press).

Bladen-Hovell, R. (1994) 'The European Monetary System', in Artis, M. and Lee N.

Bonefeld, W. and Burnham, P. (1996) 'Britain and the Politics of the European Exchange Rate Mechanism 1990–92', *Capital and Class*, 60.

Bureau van de Europese Commissie in Nederland (1996) *Europa van Morgen*, 26e jaargang, 20.

Busch, K., Schöller, W., Seelow, W. (1971) *Weltmarkt und Weltwährungskrise* (Bremen: Kuhlman).

Carchedi, G. (1984) 'The Logic of Prices as Value', *Economy and Society*, 13, 4.

Carchedi, G. (1991a) *Frontiers of Political Economy* (London: Verso).

Carchedi, G. (1991b) 'Technological Innovations, International Production Prices and Exchange Rates', *Cambridge Journal of Economics*, 15, 1.

Carchedi, G. (1995) 'Non-Equilibrium Market Prices', in Freeman, A. and Carchedi, G.

Carchedi, G. and De Haan, W. (1995) 'The Transformation Procedure: A Non-Equilibrium Approach', in Freeman, A. and Carchedi, G.

Coakley, J. (1988) 'International Dimensions of the Stock Market Crash', *Capital and Class*, 34.

Deubner, Chr., Rehfeldt, U., Schlupp, F. and Ziebura, G. (1979) *Die Internationalisierung des Kapitals. Neue Theorien in der Internationalen Diskussion* (Frankfurt: Campus Verlag).
European Council (1996) *Conclusies van het voorzitterschap,* Annex 2 to Annex I, in Bureau van de Europresse Commissie in Nederland.
Evans, T. (1988) 'Dollar is Likely to Rise, Fall or Stay Steady, Experts Agree', *Capital and Class,* 34.
Freeman, A. (1988) 'The Crash', *Capital and Class,* 34.
Freeman, A. and Carchedi, G. (eds) (1995) *Marx and Non-Equilibrium Economics* (Cheltenham: Edward Elgar).
Gaveau, G. (1982) 'Turmoil in the International Monetary System', *World View, 1983,* (London: Pluto Press).
Gill, S. (1997) 'The Global Political Economy and the European Union: EMU and Alternatives to Neo-liberalism, unpublished paper.
Glyn, A. (1988) 'The Crash and Real Capital Accumulation', *Capital and Class,* 34.
Grahl, J. (1988) 'The Stock Market Crash and the Role of the Dollar', *Capital and Class,* 34.
Robinson, J. (1962) *Economic Philosophy* (Harmondsworth: Penguin Books).
Senf, B. (1978) 'Politische Ökonomie des Kapitalismus', *Mehrwert,* 18.
Siegel, T. (1980) 'Wertgesetz und Weltmarkt. Eine Kritik am Theorem der modifizierten Wirkungsweise der Wertgesetzes auf dem Weltmarkt', *Mehrwert,* 21.
Siegel, T. (1984) 'Politics and Economics in the Capitalist World Market', *International Journal of Sociology,* XIV, 1.
Swann, D. (1992) *The Economics of the Common Market* (Harmondsworth: Penguin Books).
Whalen, C. (1997) 'Divided Economy', *Financial Times,* 14 January.

4

European Monetary Union: Ideology and Class*

Werner Bonefeld

Preface

European Economic and Monetary Union (EMU) amounts to more than just an exchange rate mechanism. It substitutes participating currencies with a single currency or, in other words, replaces several decision making authorities by a single one: the European Central Bank (ECB). Participating countries lose control over monetary policy and are no longer able to use exchange rate devaluation for adjusting productivity growth to globally competitive levels. The ECB is charged with maintaining price stability across the European Union (EU). Macroeconomic adjustment in member states will have to be based on greater labour flexibility and that is on the achievement of competitive labour unit costs. Adjustment, in other words, is expected from the European working class through higher labour productivity, wage restraint and 'neo-liberal' welfare reforms.

The preparation for the launch of the new European currency, the euro, has helped to justify austerity across Europe. The Maastricht Treaty adopted tough convergence criteria. It laid down both the timetable and a set of targets for convergence in the field of government expenditure, accumulated public debt, limits on inflation, and limits on long-term interest rates. The criteria for convergence towards EMU were strengthened by the Stability Pact which was negotiated in 1996 to overcome German objections to EMU. The German government was concerned that fiscal expansionism especially in the southern European states would make the euro weaker than the German mark. The Stability Pact toughened the convergence criteria and made them a permanent feature of EMU. It empowered the ECB and the Commission to police member states' fiscal policy; in case of 'fiscal profligacy' member states can be fined. However, the Pact made allowances to exempt by qualified majority vote countries running an excess deficit in cases of compelling evidence of a severe economic downturn.

EMU appears partly defensive in so far as it seeks to protect member states from the risk of floating exchange rates that allow speculative capital to exploit currency differentials. EMU, on this reading, attempts to reduce the vulnerability of the European economy to the whims of short-term globally mobile money capital. At the same time, EMU appears as an offensive device that seeks to make the European working class work harder in the face of deteriorating conditions. EMU encourages greater competitiveness on the basis of disinflation and increased labour productivity. The project of European Monetary Union has, then, to be looked at against the background of the crisis-ridden development of capital accumulation since the late 1960s. It was this crisis that led to the 'emergence' of globally footloose money capital and new forms of financial crisis. There is thus, as Carchedi (1997, pp. 102–3) puts it, 'a clear link between the present still unresolved profitability crisis and this new form of monetary turbulences', on the one hand, and the project of EMU, on the other.

Introduction

Commentators on EMU argue that it is driven by politics rather than economics. Yet, while this claim is made, and rightly so, there is surprisingly little in the literature concerning the politics of EMU. Of course, the political is emphasized in terms of institutional politics and the division of competence between the political institutions at the supranational and national levels; and it is addressed in terms of the so-called democratic deficit, especially the democratic legitimacy of the independent ECB; inter-state bargains and rivalry; and in terms of inter-imperialist rivalry between the EU, the USA and Japan. In short, the conventional view of 'politics' prevails and therewith an understanding that the 'political' and the 'economic' are two distinctly different forms of social organization. Such a view needs to be treated with suspicion. For example, while the economist treats human purposeful activity as a factor of production, the focus of the political scientist falls on the democratic and legal constitution of the social and political rights and duties of the citizen. However, the so-called human factor of production is no less a citizen as a person endowed with equal rights and conversely the citizen is no less a factor of production as a wage-labouring commodity.

In short, conventional accounts of EMU take for granted the bourgeoisie conception of a social world where the social individuals are not divided according class. Rather, they are conceived to be divided within themselves as economic agents, on the one hand, and citizens, on the other. Each of these apparently distinct 'identities' is seen to derive from distinct political and economic structures and each of these structures is perceived to have its own logic of development. Although these 'logics' interact – 'the fundamental objectives of EMU were political, the strategy was economic' (Grahl, 1997, p. 108) – the social world is nevertheless treated as a fragmented thing where human beings do not exist as such. Their being is sharply differentiated between economic actors who follow the logic of economic rationality and citizens who pursue their specific social and political interests within a democratically constituted 'political state'.

From this perspective, the notion that EMU is a politically driven project allows merely for a discussion of the political in terms of either institutional political economy or neo-realist accounts on the cooperation and conflicts between states, or moral and political judgements on the impact of EMU. These judgements which derive, on the whole, from a Keynesian perspective, do not reject EMU as such. What stands rejected is the 'neo-liberal' design of EMU that, for the Keynesians, is seen to increase unemployment and social distress across Europe. However, has the recession of the early 1990s 'in Europe' really been caused by the transition towards monetary union and would a Keynesian design of EMU help to create conditions of full employment across Europe?[1]

This chapter analyses the politics of EMU. Politics is understood, here, as class politics. Conventional accounts deny the importance of class politics through their premiss that the economic and political are two distinct forms of social organization. Yet, their understanding of the 'economic' significance of EMU reveals the class content of monetary union. Thus, as far as the content of the debate is concerned, its focus is entirely on the 're-integration' of labour, the European working class, into the capital relation. EMU focuses the burden of 'adjustment' exclusively on labour. On this issue, the conventional debate on EMU is unmistakably clear. In short, the conventional debate on EMU does indeed raise the question of the political. While it ostensibly adopts an 'institutional' view, its focus is on the subordination of social labour power to the dictate of exploitation.

Conventional accounts on the institutional arrangements of EMU appear to accept the idea that 'politics' has nothing to do with monetary policy. There is no doubt that EMU appears as an arrangement that not only removes any political significance form economic relations but, also, depoliticizes the political itself. In EMU, politics is initiated in the name of Europe, made through European cooperation and, especially monetary policy, is presented as an institutionally anchored device that leaves monetary policy to those who professionally have the insights into, and possess the expert knowledge required for the regulation of apparently impartial economic mechanisms. However, the institutional set-up of, for example, the ECB, is not just 'institutional' in the commonly understood sense. The language of institutional rationality, institutional legitimacy, optimum currency area etc., disguises what amounts in fact to a most important and radical attempt on the part of the European bourgeoisie at providing an institutional 'solution' to the crisis of capitalist accumulation that, since the late 1960s, has beset capitalist reproduction like a cancer.

In sum, the conventional debate on EMU disguises the class content of EMU either by focusing on the formal aspects of monetary union or by providing moral judgements on its negative impact on, for example, the employment of European labour or the European nation state. This chapter analyses the class character of EMU. There is no doubt that EMU is meant to provide institutional channels for the containment of the so-called labour question and, through it, the political guarantee of the bourgeoisie property rights of exploitation. EMU seeks to take 'politics' out of the making of monetary policy and attempts to remove social labour power as an active subject conferring on capital the realization of its impossible dream of exploiting labour uncontested. However, without exploiting labour's productive power, and thus without confronting labour, capital would be no-thing and thus rendered incapable of asserting itself as the 'self-valorizing value' as which it presents itself.[2] The conclusion suggests that EMU institutionalizes the contradictory existence of capital, that is its dependence on labour's value creating power. EMU, then, is not just a mechanism that regulates the monetary conditions of capitalist accumulation in the EU. It is also an arrangement that transmits 'regional' class conflicts across the EU and beyond, so reproducing what EMU is expected to resolve and that is, the labour question.

The following section summarizes the history of European monetary integration especially since the 1970s. There then follows an analysis of the capitalist crisis of accumulation. We then examine why the problem of 'economic' adjustment has been addressed in terms of the Europeanization of specifically monetary policy. This issue will be examined through the lenses of the neo-liberal crisis-conceptions of the 1970s. The next section analyses the politics of EMU. The conclusion summarizes the argument and suggests that EMU is not only a response to the crisis of capitalist accumulation but, also, a preemptive device for the disciplining of labour, a device however that allows 'regional' class conflicts to assert themselves across Europe.

European monetary integration in historical context

The history of European monetary integration since World War II can be schematized into 5 different phases, each corresponding with major developments in the global political economy. During the 1950s, the international financial system of Bretton Woods was not in full operation as European currencies were not readily convertible into the dollar. During this period, the European Payments Union (EPU) supported efforts of European postwar reconstruction. It was mainly a clearing house for balance of payments deficits between participating countries. By 1958, the convertibility of European currencies was restored. The EPU was abandoned and during the 1960s European monetary integration worked through the system of Bretton Woods that tied the exchange rates of European currencies to the dollar. It was by the late 1960s, particularly the early 1970s with the collapse of the Bretton Woods system, that serious attempts at European monetary integration started.

During the late 1960s, the dollar was under increasing pressure particularly due to the resurgence of German and Japanese competitiveness and the financing of the Vietnam war through an inflationary supply of dollars. This supply accelerated the growing spill-over of world money, the dollar, from financing the productive accumulation of capital into financial markets. The inflationary supply of the dollar put pressure on European countries, a pressure that was debated at that time as an export of US-inflation to Europe. Against this background, the then European Economic Community supported the Werner Plan of 1971 that sought to establish a European system of monetary integration within the framework of the Bretton Woods system. However, as soon as the ink had dried on the Werner Plan, the Bretton Woods system broke down between 1971 and 1973. This breakdown meant that the dollar was no longer backed by gold and, more importantly, that currencies rather than being tied to the dollar started to float against each other. The dollar, however, was not dethroned from its position as world currency, allowing the United States to respond, for most of the

1970s, to competitive difficulties and social discontent through exchange rate devaluations and the inflationary erosion of working class income.

The inflationary supply of dollars posed major difficulties for European countries. They too had responded to the tremendous level of discontent in the late 1960s/early 1970s through fiscal expansionism (see Clarke, 1988). Yet, this response intensified the crisis of money and production. This was discussed at the time in terms of the fiscal crisis of the state and stagflation. High rates of inflation, mass unemployment and sluggish economic growth coincided, leading to increasing pressure on state expenditure as the tax base eroded and claims on the welfare state expanded. During the 1970s, European countries established the so-called 'snake', a European exchange rate system. In this system the participating currencies fluctuated within an agreed margin around each other and all fluctuated within a set margin against the dollar. Hence, the description of the snake as a 'snake in the tunnel'.[3]

The snake was a quite unsuccessful device. Participating countries were forced, time and time again, to suspend membership in the face of speculative pressures that responded not just to sluggish economic performance but, through it, to working class resistance to the intensification of exploitation and wage restraint. During much of the 1970s, the US authorities sought to recoup international markets by letting the dollar fall. This reinforced inflationary pressure on European countries and made it harder for them to bolster their reserves through export earnings. European countries found it therefore difficult to fend off speculative pressures. The snake, then, had to cope with domestic conflicts which compelled governments to commit themselves to existing labour market and welfare guarantees. At the same time, financial and economic conditions deteriorated with hyperinflation increasing speculative pressure. The snake failed to provide an anchor for currency stability and, through it, disinflation.

In the late 1970s, the snake was replaced by the European Monetary System (EMS). Its central feature was the European Exchange Rate Mechanism (ERM). The initiative for the EMS came from Germany and France. Against the background of the pound sterling crisis of 1976 and the dollar crisis of 1978, both governments saw it as a way of reducing currency fluctuations and as a means of confronting domestic difficulties. The EMS was to replace the discretionary influence on monetary policy by a rule-based system. For Germany, the EMS was a means of consolidating its economic position in Europe and, through it, its global economic role and political aspirations. The EMS tied the weaker

European currencies to the German mark. However, up until 1983, the EMS was a rather weak system and currency devaluation occurred regularly.

The early 1980s saw conflicting policy responses to the power of the working class to demand conditions. In the US, during the last years of the Carter administration and then under Reagan, class politics through inflation and dollar devaluation were replaced by a politics of austerity. A similar policy of austerity was adopted first by the British Labour government under Callaghan and then reinforced under Thatcher. In France, however, working class discontent had led to a politics of fiscal and monetary expansion under Mitterand. Against the background of the severe crisis of the early 1980s, both the French and the Anglo-saxon responses to the so-called labour question were short-lived. In France, the experiment of Keynesianism in one country led to increasing speculative attacks, with public debt increasing and inflation devaluing profits. In the face of the deteriorating competitive position of its national economy, the Socialist government sought refuge in a much harder EMS. The EMS transformed, from 1983, into a disciplinary device whose purpose was to contain the 'labour question' on the basis of disinflation and fiscal restraint.

In contrast to France, the UK and the US pursued in the early 1980s a politics of austerity. The aim was to disinflate the economy and, importantly, to deregulate entrenched class relations. With monetary policy being tight, working class 'expectations' for wage increases would be moderated by unemployment. Employers, to prevent the risk of bankruptcy, would have to increase labour productivity while the readiness of the working class to accept the intensification of its exploitation would be increased due to the threat of redundancy. However, in the early 1980s, the tightening of particularly the dollar led, on a global scale, to a severe financial crisis. Banks suffered due to a dramatic increase in company failure, public deficits soared due to an increase in unemployment and a decline in the tax base, and high real interest rates increased the cost of credit. The tightening of monetary policy transformed the credit-based economies of many countries into debtor economies, leading to the so-called debtor crisis of the 1980s and beyond. Against this background, and in the face of a potential breakdown of international credit-relations, both the UK and the US abandoned Friedman's recommendation according to which the control of the money supply will encourage the working class to adjust its aspirations to tight market conditions. Instead, Hayek's version of market freedom became more emphasized. Disinflation was, after 1983, to be achieved by deregulating labour markets directly through an attack on the trade unions and, through them, on the entrenched class positions.[4] The aim was to strengthen the relationship between the money supply and labour productivity through measures such as labour market deregulation, labour process flexibilization, privatization; and the reform of the welfare state towards workfare. These 'supply-side' policies, it was hoped, would adjust the relationship between the money supply and productive work through an increase in the rate of exploitation, leading to greater capital profitability and a renewed period of progressive accumulation of productive capital. At the same time, the financial system that had been dangerously exposed by the 'emergence' of the debtor crisis, was refinanced through a huge US budget deficit. This development has variously been described as delinquent or military Keynesianism.[5]

In Britain, the attempt at disinflation through the control of the money supply was abandoned in 1983.[6] For most of the 1980s, the then Channcellor, Mr. Lawson, sought to enter the British pound into the ERM, much against Thatcher's outspoken opposition.[7] Lawson saw the ERM as a device that would support monetarist policies and enable the government to absolve itself from the impact of tight money. The French government endorsed the ERM for similar reasons. After 1983, France embarked upon a policy of a strong French franc (*franc forte*) to secure and retain competitiveness on the basis of austerity anchored by the German mark through the ERM. By sticking to a harder ERM, monetary policy would be protected from speculative pressure and the impact of domestic class conflict on monetary policy would be reduced. Ostensibly, 'austerity' would be imposed by 'Europe' and the social and economic consequences of austerity would be legitimized in terms of international – European – commitments and requirements. For the German government, the hardening of the EMS was precisely what it had been looking for since the late 1970s. It transformed Western Europe into a DM-zone. The EMS subordinated fiscal policy, as well as social and labour-market policies, to the objective of price stability and provided a European monetary anchor for the so-called neo-liberal supply side reforms of deregulation.

The EMS hardened further after the stock-market crash in 1987. Realignments ceased until 1992 when the British pound which had entered the mechanism in 1990, was forced out of the ERM. The EMS had established the German mark as the European anchor currency and, through the EMS, Germany operated as a European hegemonic power. The EMS was clearly asymetrical: member states had to adjust to German conditions. Against German dominance, France sought, in the wake of German unification and at the start of the deep recession of the 1990s, to transform the EMS into a more collective system where German economic power and influence would at least have to take account of, and be responsive to, French interests. France's position was that the power of the German central bank, the Bundesbank, was to be diluted by substituting it with a European central bank. France would thereby gain a policy-making influence over European monetary policy. For Germany, the EMS had worked well but it accepted EMU to secure French support for German unification. Germany's acceptance of EMU was made easier by the strict and tough convergence criteria for monetary union.[8] The Maastricht Treaty was signed in 1991. Yet, it was almost blown apart in 1992 and 1993 when first Britain and then France, as well as Italy and Spain, were forced to devalue in the face of speculative pressure and to adopt wider margins of fluctuations against the German mark. Perhaps the single most important factor which led both to the crisis of the ERM in 1992–93 and the continued and unabated transition to EMU was German unification. Germany tapped the international money markets to finance deficits arising from the cost of unification. This meant that Germany 'privileged the international strength of its currency, thereby jettisoning the EMS system' in 1992–93 (Halevi, 1999, p. 88). Yet, the appreciation of the German mark not only decreased German export competitiveness it, also, brought to the fore the danger of 'competitive devaluations' in Europe (ibid, p. 89). Furthermore, the disruption of the ERM meant that Germany had to face and confront the dollar and the yen without 'having a secure rear in the form of fixed parities of the EMS' (ibid). The absence of this 'secure rear' can not be overestimated in its importance for Germany to accept European monetary union. In short, the strengthening of Maastricht's convergence criteria through the Stability Pact of 1996 reinforced not only German leadership in Europe. It also indicated Bonn's acceptance of the single currency. Germany accepted EMU as an institutional framework that would secure the international drive of 'German capital'. As Halevi (1999, p. 97) comments, 'German priorities moulded, with France's surrender to them, Europe's contractory fiscal stance' and tight monetary conditions.

In conclusion, the breakdown of the system of Bretton Woods, conflict of interest between the US and Europe, and between European countries, especially France and Germany, appears to explain a great deal of the continuous efforts of integrating European monetary relations. However, as the next section will argue, the treatment of the development of European monetary integration through the lenses of the strategic interests of members states fails to understand that its principal feature is the containment of class struggle and that is the integration of social labour power into the capital relations on the basis of progressive productivity growth. Of course, each of the European states involved in the creation of EMU has been and continues to be concerned to obtain a most suitable and favourable arrangement to improve their respective competitive positions. There is no doubt that France, for example, seeks a more flexible interpretation of EMU by the ECB to accommodate the kind of labour unrest that, for Grahl (1997, p. 236), was seen to be capable of delaying the completion of EMU. For Germany, on the other hand, a hard EMU with little flexibility of interpretation would not only allow it to take advantage of France's troubled labour relations[9] but, also, ensure German economic might through its relatively more competitive unit labour costs. A weak euro would mean that Germany readjusts its conditions to those of weaker states; while a strong Euro would force weaker states to adjust to German conditions. Besides, a hard Euro would support Europe's global aspirations.

However, the fundamental question is not what differentiates France and Germany but, rather, what unites their efforts. Their unity derives from common class interests. Here, the ruling classes of not only France and Germany stand united, and have historically been united. As Anderson (1997, p. 135) comments, since 1983, 'the attitude of the French elite has been a Vichy-like subservience to German economic power'. Moreover, as Carchedi (1997, pp. 100–1) argues convincingly, '*the Euro, and thus German leadership, is accepted because the bill is paid by labour.* At the same time, *these policies appear as if they were dictated by "Europe"* in the interest of the "common good".' Furthermore, as Carchedi (p. 100) makes clear, '*the more the EU countries are tied to Germany, the greater the expropriation of value from labour.*' Why should a 'domestic' bourgeoisie not wish that 'its' working class is made to work harder and faster, and to achieve this in a way which makes it appear as if the bourgeoisie is not responsible for the burden placed on labour? In EMU, monetary conditions appear to be dictated by Europe and to derive from expert and impartial judgements concerning the best practice of economic regulation. EMU's potential in the management of class conflict is well recognized by Henning (2000, p. 21): 'Governments can now credibly argue that their macroeconomic hands are tied and that the burden of adjustment rests mainly with private actors.' In short, the conflict of interest between member states is only one of degree.

Class and the crisis of capitalist accumulation

Carchedi reports in his contribution that, in the early 1990s, 'more than $1 trillion [were] looking for a home in the foreign exchange market every day' so that 'even a slight deviation from the straight and narrow can invite a savaging' (*Business Week*, 16 January 1995; quoted in Carchedi, 1997, p. 102). This massive amount of money by far exceeds the 'money' required for global commodity transactions and productive investments.[10] Where does all this money capital come from, a capital that appears to increase by investing into itself (M . . . M′) dissociated from the progressive exploitation of labour through productive accumulation (M . . . P. . . M′)? What is its source of value?

Since the late 1960s, credit-relations have been checked less and less by the expropriation of value in production. Instead, credit expanded to finance the credit-requirements of productive capital and national states at the same time as rates of profits remained depressed. Credit, then, pertained not in the form of boom-lending supporting the progressive accumulation of productive capital but, rather, maintained company liquidity through the recycling of difficulties. In short, capital, in the form of money, started to apply itself more and more in financial markets, seeking higher and quicker returns than those which could be obtained from direct investment in the contested terrain of production. This development started in the 1960s; there was a growth of an international financial market which existed outside the official financial system of Bretton Woods and alongside the national, regulated markets. Although the new credit markets, the so-called Euro-dollar markets, operated outside the regulative mechanisms of the Bretton Woods system, all money in the form of credit existed as a claim on the US-gold reserves. Under these circumstances, the system of Bretton Woods was threatened and it was eventually suspended under Nixon between 1971 and 1973. Since then the dissociation of monetary accumulation from productive accumulation has continued unabated and on an increasing scale leading to recurring financial and industrial crises such as, for example, the so-called Asian crisis of 1997–98.[11]

How can one understand this development? Within the limits and context of this discussion, only a brief explanation can be offered. First, the inflationary expansion of credit is an expression of the crisis of containing the productive power of labour within the limits of capital profitability. By the mid-1960s, the capitalist exploitation of labour had led to a situation where the productive power of labour had increased to such an extent that too much capital was produced relative to the capacity of the market to realize, with adequate rates of profit, the surplus value expropriated from labour.[12] At the same time, the exploitation of labour was getting more expensive because of higher wage demands, and importantly, because of technological change. The rise in investment required to increase labour productivity increases the cost of production which, even under conditions of a rising rate of exploitation, tends to decrease the rate of profit. This is because of the rising value of constant capital (means of production) relative to variable capital (labour power). As profits fell and as productive investment costs increased,[13] productive capital, on the one hand, borrowed more money to make up for falling profits so as to overcome difficulties and to invest in new methods of production. On the other hand, earned profits were increasingly placed on money markets, either because of the risk of productive investment or because earned profits were not big enough for instant reconversion into productive investment. Capital was thus suspended from productive accumulation and placed, instead, in financial markets. This capital was used as credit by productive capital and political authorities to support investment or borrowing requirements. Since the late 1960s, depressed rates of productive accumulation and depressed rates of profit have coincided with a rapid monetary accumulation. The growing divorce of monetary accumulation from productive accumulation created a spiral of debt, expressed in an over-expansion of the credit system, speculative runs, bad debt problems, and turbulent financial markets.

Second, the disruptive strength of labour made itself felt, by the end of the 1960s, in resistance to the intensification of exploitation and incomes policies. In the face of falling rates of profit and readily available credit, governments responded to labour discontent by expansionary policies that fuelled inflation and led to budget deficits. In sum, the strength in the relation between monetary accumulation and productive accumulation decreased. Furthermore, the contradiction in this development is not only that the increase in the rate of monetary accumulation is supported by a relative decline in the productive accumulation of capital but, also, that the 'state' accumulates deficits that are the same time guaranteed by the 'state' in its capacity as lender of last resort. In other words, the strength in the relation between the money supply and productive growth weakened progressively.

The dissociation between productive accumulation and monetary accumulation is intensely crisis-ridden. The accumulation of capital in the form of money (M...M′) is an accumulation of capital that is suspended from the direct exploitation of labour (M...P...M′). There is thus the contraction between a sluggish exploitation of labour, and therewith the expropriation of surplus value, relative to the accumulation of money. In short, the accumulation of wealth in the form of money is an accumulation of monetary claims on the surplus value not yet extracted from labour; it is a claim, a mortgage, on future surplus value. The more money accumulates divorced form productive accumulation, the less it is validated by the expropriation of surplus value and the more claims on the future exploitation of labour accumulate. The history of the last 25 years suggests that capital found it increasingly difficult to adjust the relationship between monetary accumulation and productive accumulation through a stronger link between money and exploitation. For over a quarter century, economic recessions and monetary turbulences have occurred at regular intervals and neither has led to a readjustment between productive accumulation and monetary accumulation; if anything the divorce between them has become more and more emphasized. Paul Mattick (1934), in his analysis of a similar situation in the inter-war period, discussed such a development in terms of a permanent crisis of capitalist accumulation.[14]

The credit-sustained reproduction of the capital relation led to a situation where governments were increasingly unable to use inflation as a means of eroding real wages and of devaluing public debt. This is because of the unregulated character of global financial markets with currency exchange rates floating against each other. The global speculation in foreign exchange markets asserts itself like an 'international police force' (cf. Marazzi, 1995) where speculative pressure on currencies, or indeed a run on currencies, responds to 'domestic' difficulties in containing inflation through a closer link between working class consumption and productivity growth. In other words, the ability of the national state to devalue its debt through inflation is severely restricted through the ability of financial markets to withdraw from such a country by selling its currency. Such a withdrawal, or capital flight, renders difficult the attraction of internationally mobile money capital required to finance public deficits, including balance of payments deficits. The guarantee of global debt depends on the effective exploitation of labour's productive power. For financial markets, this guarantee translates into the demand that national states pursue credible monetary policies.

Furthermore, as noted above, national governments responded to the labour unrest of the late 1960s and early 1970s with expansionary policies. The guarantee of this credit rested on the ability of the national state to guarantee its debts through its role as lender of last resort. An inflationary devaluation of state debt was extremely risky because of the policing powers of speculative capital. Again, the disinflation of the money supply and the control of public deficits depended on the ability of the state to adopt restrictive budgetary and monetary policies that redistribute income from the working class to capital. Against this background, the so-called fiscal crisis of the state, the crisis of the welfare state, the shift from a Keynesian legitimating of public policy to the monetarist assertion 'you cannot spend what you have not earned', the ascendancy of the notion that public policy has to be 'credible', the almost missionary espousal of a politics of austerity, and the new language of 'economy', 'efficiency' and 'effectiveness', make sense. They make sense insofar as the containment of the disruptive power of labour through credit-expansion threatens the ability of national states to guarantee their debts and therewith the international value of their currencies. Besides, as each debtor crises makes clear, domestic difficulties in guaranteeing the property rights of money capital on the future exploitation of labour are not just 'domestic': they threaten the global stability of capitalist reproduction through the default of debt.[15]

A politics of austerity, then, seeks to adjust the burden of debt in relation to the productive accumulation of capital and guarantee the property rights of capital through the control of that part of public expenditure that 'puts money into the hand of workers' (cf. Cleaver, 1995). 'Adjustment' is much more than just a technical term which describes the control of public debt. It means a policy of tight money and thus the replacement of an inflationary response to working class struggle by a policy of state austerity which accepts unemployment as a means of containing inflation. Furthermore, adjustment means the eradication of balance of payments deficits through improved export earnings. Thus, 'adjustment' amounts to a policy of replacing deficits with sound finance, containing inflation by forging a stronger link between the expansion of the money supply and productive activity. A growth in deficits which is not matched by productivity growth sooner or later becomes hazardous, leaving investors with only one option and that is to run. Interest charges will absorb a growing proportion of the national product. In addition, the incomes from which interest-charges have to be paid has already diminished as a result of weak capital formation and sluggish productivity growth in relation to the expansion of credit.

In order to adjust consumption to productive work, standards of living have to deteriorate and the efficient use of resources, including labour power in production, has to improve. The guarantee, then, of global credit relations (M . . . M′) goes forward through a policy of austerity which aims at making workers pay for the repayment of credit through wage restraint, intensification of work and deteriorating conditions. To adjust the ratio of debt to GDP, the economy has to generate large surpluses so that a net transfer of resources pays the interest on accumulated borrowing. Failure to achieve real savings in state expenditure and lower unit labour costs, will only exacerbate the burden of debt, and growing inflationary pressure will lead to speculative currency attacks and drains on the reserves.

In short, 'adjustment' entails an attack on the entrenched relations of class power without provoking open class conflict. In response to such conflict, money capital has always fled to more secure nationally delimited spaces – afraid that the uncertain outcome of such conflict might threaten the 'wealth' it represents. The cumulative effect of such flight is usually called financial turmoil where a global credit-crunch exposes the bad debt exposure of banks and companies alike. In short, financial crisis and industrial crisis belong together as two halves of the same walnut: the crisis of the capitalist exploitation of labour. In short, the adjustment of exploitation to the 'credit-superstructure' (M . . . M′) entails not only the risk of company failure but, also, the danger of financial turmoil and crisis. A massive industrial crisis means that the very source that 'validates' money as a claim on future surplus value 'recedes', revealing the bad debt exposure of banks through industrial default.[16]

Concerning European monetary integration, the hardening of the EMS from 1983 onwards supplied a supranational disinflationary anchor that helped to protect national governments from class conflict over the bitter long-term adjustment costs. For a government that found it difficult to impose monetary discipline domestically, the ERM offered a golden opportunity to have it 'implemented from without' (Sandholtz, 1993, p. 38). The government could be shielded from the unpalatable consequences of 'economic adjustment' by shifting responsibility on to an international regime (see Busch, 1994, p. 84) that supported governments' public policy objectives without appearing to be directly responsible for them. There is, of course, no institutional or international 'fix' to the 'problem' of inflation. However, against the background of the global police force of speculative capital, government policy has to appear 'credible' so that financial markets maintain confidence in the 'national' containment of the 'labour question' and so retain trust in the guarantee of security of their investment on the future exploitation of labour. In short, the achievement of counter-inflationary credibility is of utmost importance (Helleiner, 1994). European monetary integration emphasizes the issue of 'credibility' and, throught it, the guarantee of the property rights of capital on the future exploitation of labour.

In sum, national states are not insulated from each other but subsist in and through the world market (Holloway, 1995a). Their capacity to impose austerity upon the working class is 'policed' through speculative capital movements. While governments might have been tempted to inflate the debt away and thereby reduce the burden of debt on many firms as well as eroding real wages and standards of living, speculative runs on currency would have resulted in a liquidity crisis, reinforcing the fiscal crisis of the state and making it more difficult to finance balance of payment deficits. The resolution to financial crisis is a policy of austerity which aims at reducing the ratio of debt to GDP. However, such a policy is likely to provoke class conflict leading to sustained speculative attack. Governments are thus keen to ensure the de-politicization of a politics of austerity through, for example, the replacement of discretionary public policy systems by rule based systems,[17] including institutional reforms such as central bank independence.

Neo-liberalism, crisis and institutional reform

During the 1970s, neo-liberal interpretations of the crisis of capitalist accumulation focused either explicitly or implicitly on the crisis of state authority. These commentators reacted in a direct manner to the explosiveness of the then class conflict and recommended two distinctive solutions. One solution emphasized that the economy was to be freed from political interference to allow the market to self-regulate itself. This view, which is associated with the liberal-economic thoughts of Hayek and Friedman and their critique of Keynesianism, recommended the depoliticization of economic relations; better: the economy was to recover its 'autonomy' *vis-à-vis* the political.[18] In contrast to this, the other solution focused more directly on the 'state' and recommended that it should recover its 'autonomy' from society so as to regain its capacity to make decisions (see, among others, Crozier *et al.*, 1975). This view is rooted in the theoretical tradition associated not only with Schumpeter but also Carl Schmitt, the philosopher of German fascism. Within the tradition of economic and political thought, their concerns are connected with the ordo-liberal tradition of the Freiburg school. This school stresses that the liberty of economic relations should be guaranteed institutionally through a constitutional framework of law. While economic liberalism stresses the self-regulating capacity of unfettered market freedom, ordo-liberalism espouses the idea of an institutionally 'embedded' and constitutionally safeguarded economic liberalism.

For the economic liberals, liberal democracy combined with Keynesian economic convictions poses a danger to the very foundations of bourgeois society. For them, the 'Keynesian' state politicized economic relations and undermined market self-regulation and therewith the relations of liberty. The politicization of economic relations was seen to place a growing burden of demands and expectations on the state, leading to conditions of 'planned chaos' (cf. von Mises, 1944). Politically, then, this view responded to the class conflict by advocating the subordination of social relations to monetary exchange relations, to the market. It recommended the dismantling of the welfare state, the undermining of trade unions and the restoration of relations of economic competition, including the deregulation and flexibilization of the labour market and the labour process.

For those advocating the 're-autonomization' of the state, liberal democracy in an 'open society' involves political parties seeking to outbid each other in their competition for a greater share on the 'electoral market'. This is seen to lead, on the one hand, to the expansion of inflationary expectations on the part of the electorate, and to political conditions of ungovernability, on the other. Furthermore, for them, the class conflict of the 1960s and 1970s had led to the democratization of society and this democratization was seen to pose a serious risk to democracy.[19] In short, the state was seen to have become vulnerable to 'society'. As Brittan (1976) put it, 'excessive expectations are generated by the democratic aspects of the system' (p. 97) and 'the temptation to encourage flase expectations among the electorate becomes overwhelming to politicians' (p. 105). The basic trouble, then, was '*the lack of a budget constraint among voters*' (p. 104). In short, social expectations and demands were seen to have overstreched the welfare state, creating a 'dependency culture'. In addition, social conflicts were no longer confined to the redistribution of wealth, with the trade unions asserting the power of specific social interests against the national interest. There was, then, an 'inappropriate' politicization of social conflicts that endangered the fabric of society. As King (1976, p. 12) saw it, government had come 'to be regarded . . . as a sort of unlimited-liability insurance company, in the business of insuring all persons at all time against every conceivable risk'. In addition, King recognized that the level of non-compliance with the rights of private property had increased. As he put it, 'the man dependent on his wife to drive him to work finds increasingly that she refuses to do so' (p. 23). Regardless of what King's specific problems might have been, the general thrust of the approach was that the political response to the class conflict had created conditions of ungovernability characterized by a disparity between the 'volume' of claims on government's 'sharing out function' and government's steering capacity (cf. Brittan, 1976).

Both schools of thought, then, emphasized the 'economic consequences of democracy' (cf. Brittan, 1977) in terms of a decline in the strength of the relationship between consumption and productive activity. In addition, both stress that the politicization of social relations had led to conditions of ungovernability and recommended solutions that are distinct only as variants of a common theme. Both agreed that the politicization of the class conflict poses a threat to the bourgeois fragmentation of the political and the economic into distinct forms of social organization. In other words, class domination through the differentiation of the political and the economic was seen to be at risk, threatening the property rights of capital. The economic liberals argued for the economy to be liberated from the political to allow the market to self-regulate itself and therewith to safeguard the subordination of social relations to the market. Those emphasizing the crisis of the state recommended the 'autonomization' of 'the political' from 'society' to secure the decision-making power of the 'state' over society. Both, in other words, and in their own way, recommended the 're-autonomization' of the economic and the political from each other, reinforcing and securing their bourgeois fragmentation.

For the economic liberals this was to be achieved by 'rolling back' the state, reconstituting the freedom of market relations. For the others, it was to be achieved by 'rolling back' the state from society through institutional reform. The difference, then, between the two solutions is only one of degree: both stressed the need for the depoliticization of economic relations and the depoliticization of political relations. Both attempts at 'rolling back' depend on the depoliticization of class conflict and that is on the fragmentation of class into an economic factor of production, on the one hand, and a law abiding citizen, on the other. Only on this basis would 'society' again be able to cherish the liberating potential of hard labour.

The ordo-liberal solution goes much deeper than the dogmatic call for market self-regulation on the part of the market liberals. The ordo-liberal suggestions include not only the promotion of values such as self-restraint and discipline but, also, the 'reautonomization' of the state from society, that is, the removal of 'decision-making' from mass democratic influence. The real target of reform was the power of the working class to compel government to commit concessions such as welfare guarantees. In short, discretionary processes of decision-making were to be replaced by rule-based systems. Institutional restructuring, then, was to 'reautonomise' the most vital aspects of the state by transferring them into 'extra-democratic' domains. During the 1970s the focus of 'reautonomisation' fell, concerning the German political agenda, on the Constitutional Court and, also, the Bundesbank. Within the context of EMU, the issue of the 'independence' and 'autonomy' of the ECB is very much emphasized. As Emerson *et al.* (1992, p. 87) see it, 'a stable and credible monetary regime requires an independent central bank with the statutory mandate to guarantee price stability. Otherwise the public might expect that the authorities might be tempted to use surprise inflation to temporarily increase output or temporarily reduce the real interest rate on public debt.' Despite splitting his infinitives, Emerson *et al.* merely confirm that a democratic society and relations of exploitation are incompatible.

The guiding idea for institutional reorganization is that there are, in a market economy, basic values that stand over and above the expectations and aspirations of the majority, that is the 'dependent masses', in other words, all those who depend for their existence on selling their labour power. Thus, the institutional restructuring of the state was intended to reaffirm the limited character of the liberal democratic principle of majority rule. The basic 'values' of liberal democracy, those connected with the rights of private property, constitute the social basis upon which liberal democracy's power of decision-making rests. Liberal democracy is charged with protecting and safeguarding the rights and values of bourgeois society through law (and order). Liberal democratic law-making is thus confined to the rule of (abstract) equality, freedom, property and Bentham, i.e. the constitutional rights of capital (cf. Marx, 1983, p. 172). In other words, the ordo-liberal proposals for institutional reform sought to assert these constitutional rights by insulating them from working class aspirations and demands.[20] In the context of this discussion, the purpose of institutional restructuring was to de-politicize monetary policy by removing it from the contested terrain of class conflict. Central bank independence, in this way, would provide a framework within which social conflict might take place without however posing a risk to the conduct of monetary policy. For its advocates, institutional reform would reduce the vulnerability of the state to mass democratic aspirations and 'moderate' the capacity of the working class to demand improved conditions.

The neo-liberal view of the crisis of the authority of the state was based on the conviction that the 'mob' had entered government. Similar views had been aired during the crisis of the inter-war period at the beginning of last century. Bernard Baruch, a leading Democrat, had protested against Roosevelt's decision to abandon the gold standard in 1933 by stating that 'it can't be defended except as mob rule. Maybe the country doesn't know it yet, but I think that we've been in a revolution more drastic then the French Revolution. The crowd has seized the seat of government and is trying to seize the wealth. Respect for law and order is gone' (quoted in Schlesinger, 1958, p. 202). For Baruch, correctly, the 'dependent masses' are the majority and a liberal-democratic system needs to defend itself against the majority through, for example, extra-democratic decision-making powers particularly in the field of monetary policy so as to preserve and guarantee the existence of bourgeois property rights.[21]

In this context, the work of Carl Schmitt (1932, 1934a) provides useful insights. He perceived the crisis of the inter-war period in terms of a decomposition of social and political, as well as cultural structures. This decomposition was seen to be a consequence of the emergence of mass society and caused by the influence it was able to exert on the structure of 'the political'. Institutionally, parliamentary democracy, for Schmitt, caused and focused the crisis: 'the political' was subjected, on the one hand, to pluralist demands and, on the other, to class specific interests of social equality and emancipation. In short, Schmitt emphasized that the parliamentary system undermined the ability of the state to make decisions because 'society' had transformed 'the political' into an expression of distinct social interests leading to the fragmentation of 'the political' and therewith to the decomposition of the central institution that, for Schmitt, is able to maintain social harmony. The state was thus seen to have become 'socialized' and the class-divided nature of society was seen to be reproduced within 'the political'. The 'socialization of the state', then, undermined the central and principal institution capable of making decisions. Hence Schmitt's call for the restoration of the political, of the state, emphasized that the state had to liberate itself from society and that this liberation had to be based on the elimination of all forms of social conflict, conflict, that is, which is not authorized and conducted by the state. Only on this basis would the national interest and common values be secured and guaranteed. In other words, the working class was not only asked to obey the rule of law, and through it the management of its labour power, but also to love it.

Schmitt's notion of the autonomy of 'the political' outlived, in its importance, fascism. This is not because the 'economy' and the 'state' (the political) are two distinct entities of human organization. Rather, the bourgeois state's historic role of protecting the laws of private property entails the state as a bourgeois form of the social organization of exploitation. Yet, as such a form, it appears to stand outside social relations as an institution in its own right whose distinct purpose is to safeguard, through law, the proper conduct of equal and free exchange relations between property owners. Hence, the attempts of political theory to construe the state as a distinct form of political organization that resides outside social relations and that merely intervenes, from the 'outside', into society to secure and guarantee the foundations upon which the society of burghers rest: the rights of private property. What makes the 1970s debate on ungovernability and institutional reform significant is its reconceptualization of the autonomy of the political against the background of intense class conflict. The proponents of ungovernability perceived the democratization of society or, as they put it, the permissive society, as a threat to the ability of the state to secure the relations of economic liberty and recommended institutional reforms to depoliticize, for example, monetary policy.

In conclusion, the advocates of market liberalism argued for the autonomy of the economic from the state and the proponents of state reform argued for the autonomization of the state from society. Of course, the two proposals overlap. Friedman's notion that the political authorities should conduct monetary policy independent from specific social interests (that is, working class interests) and that these interests would automatically accommodate their bargaining behaviour to restrictive monetary policy, shows the overlap well.

However, in our context, Hayek is much more important. In the 1930s, he advocated that national states should combine to create a federal-state system. Such an arrangement was endorsed as preventing inflationary demands which, for him, were a consequence of the polarization of class relations within independent national states. The establishment of a supranational political framework was endorsed as a means that would encourage competitiveness, against a national politics of economic protectionism; support the depoliticization of economic relations, against the power of 'special interests' (the working class) to subject the national state to a politics of inflationary demand management; and do away with restrictions on the movement of capital, labour and commodities. Furthermore, supranationalism would narrow the scope for the regulation of economic life; discourage the solidarity of the working class through its national fragmentation; and 'render possible the creation of common rules of law, a uniform monetary system, and common control of communications' (Hayek, 1939, p. 255). Supranationalism was thus endorsed as a way of keeping the state out of economic concerns. Better: it was endorsed as a device that would disempower the working class to force governments to moderate its aspirations through welfare and employment guarantees. The power of the 'mob' to distort the relations of liberty would thus be severely restricted allowing the state to administer justice 'impartially' and in tranquillity.

Supranationalism, then, was espoused as 'providing a rational framework within which individual initiative will have the largest possible scope' (ibid, p. 268). Nothing would stand in the way to what, today, is termed the deregulation and flexibilization of the wage relation. As Hayek saw it 'even such legislation as the restriction of child labour or of working hours becomes difficult to carry out for the individual state' (ibid, p. 260). He accorded particular attention to the circumstance that within a supranational union, individual states 'will not be able to pursue an independent monetary policy' (ibid, p. 259). In his view, national governments can not be trusted with monetary policy even if they are committed to a policy of price stability. Politicians, he seems to suggest, are always governing with the next election in mind, perverting even the committed 'monetarists' to give in to 'popular pressure' and leading to a politics of compromise and therewith to an integration of the working class into the capital relation on the basis of material concessions. Furthermore, monetary policy always requires an element of judgement and thus discretion that government might abuse to retain popularity. A supranational operation of monetary policy, with an independent bank removed from domestic considerations, would thus create a space for the making of monetary policy that is rule-based and therewith protected from the 'distorting' influence of working class demands. The removal, then, of the central bank from political influence would accord it a quasi-judicial status independent from the established system of 'democratic government', undermining a 'Keynesian' politics of class-compromise at the national level. In short, a domestic policy of austerity would be anchored in a supranational regime.

Hayek's endorsement of 'supranationalism' appears to support the former British Chancellor, Mr Lawson, who argued during the 1980s against Thatcher in favour of British entry into the ERM. However, by the 1970s, Hayek (1978) had changed his position. He argued against his supranational proposals for market freedom and in favour of the denationalization of, and competition between, currencies. His rejection of supranationalism might well have to do with his distrust of what today, in relation to the EU, is called 'subsidiarity'. In fact, when advocating supranationalism, Hayek provides useful insights into the political economy of subsidiarity by making a strong distinction between those institutions responsible for monetary policy and fiscal policy, with fiscal policy a national responsibility and monetary policy a supranational task (Hayek, 1939, pp. 267–8). His rejection, then, in the 1970s, of supranationalism appears to have been caused by his 'fear' that 'subsidiarity' might develop into a paper tiger with the supranational institutions taking responsibility for fiscal policy, leading to an inflation prone single currency and a supranational system of redistribution associated with Keynesianism.[22]

This section has argued that the neo-liberal debate in the 1970s on the crisis of the state was directly concerned with the then class conflict and that the remedies suggested provide useful insights into the politics of EMU. The debate endorsed the institutional 'autonomization' of the state from society as a means of subordinating the 'disruptive' under the obligation of responsibility. This would secure not only compliance with the law on the part of the citizen but, also, ensure that the law-abiding citizenry constitutes, by virtue of its behaviour, a reliable and flexible human factor of production. As Emerson *et al.* (1992, p. 97) explain in relation to EMU, 'since in democratic societies elected officials are in general free to determine economic policy at their discretion, it is very difficult for political bodies to acquire enough credibility to convince the public that inflation will always stay low. An independent central bank . . . does not face this temptation to create surprise inflation'. EMU, in this view, is a device to exclude the 'mob' from the 'seat of government' (cf. Baruch cited in Schlesinger, 1958).

The politics of EMU

Introduction

Most commentators on EMU raise the importance of the connection between the global instability of capitalist reproduction and the domestic containment of the 'labour question'. For example, Gros and Thygessen (1992, p. 35) report that the accord between France and Germany in the late 1970s on the creation of the EMS considered the strengthening of the domestic conditions to be of utmost importance. The then German Channcellor, Mr Schmidt, appears to have been particularly concerned over the 'dangerous' political developments in Italy where the Italian bourgeoisie sought to contain the class conflict by coopting the Communist Party into positions of government. For Schmidt, the EMS would stabilize economic relations and provide a European framework that would legitimize austerity. During the 1980s, Mr Lawson, the then British Chancellor, while not facing the 'indignity' of having to respond to class conflict by coopting the British left into positions of political responsibility, argued for British membership in the ERM for almost the same reason: a politics of price stability would be institutionally fixed at the same time as the British government would be able to hide behind the ERM absolving itself from the consequences of tight money.

EMU goes much further than the EMS by substituting national currencies with a single one, the euro. Proponents of EMU argue that it is a 'nationally' neutral device in contrast to the EMS which is seen to have been asymmetrical supporting German hegemony in Europe. For Padoa-Schioppa (1994), EMU is based on a collective decision-making mechanism which undercuts national hegemony across Europe in favour of a collective hegemon or, as he puts it, 'a collective prince' (p. 151). His Machiavellian conception of EMU is apt. As he explains, the single currency will involve a union 'based on the transfer to a Community institution of the monetary political powers that are currently exercised by the national central banks' (p. 152). For him, the personification of the Machiavellian prince is the European central bank. Expanding on his metaphor, who is courting the prince and who is the Fourth Estate?

In EMU, member states 'lose the possibility of devaluation' and the 'possibility of revaluation at the centre . . . will cease to exist as an option when and if full EMU is achieved' (Williams *et al.*, 1991, p. 227). Thus, while EMU is, concerning its form, indeed symmetrical, 'the fact that the strong are usually reluctant to revalue while the weaker are often forced into devaluation gives the game away' (ibid). The trajectory of the former GDR since German unification appears to hold the mirror image of what might happen in those European economies that find it difficult to compete with German levels of productivity. However, in distinction to German unification where the new East German Länder receive enormous fiscal transfers, EMU specifically excludes fiscal transfers from the centre to troubled national states while the resources of the Regional Fund have been and are expected to remain limited.

Furthermore, EMU severely limits the fiscal power of member states. While they maintain formal responsibility for fiscal policy, member states will have to show fiscal rectitude to avoid punishment. As Godley (1997, p. 177) sees it, 'if a country or region has no power to devalue, and if it is not the beneficiary of a system of fiscal equalisation, then there is nothing to stop it suffering a process of cumulative and terminal decline leading, in the end, to emigration as the only alternative to poverty and starvation'. While this assessment of the likely consequences of EMU rightly emphasizes the potentially devastating impact of monetary union on less competitive countries, it remains, nevertheless, blinkered. It presumes some sort of 'national interest' on the part of the 'national people', with Germany dictating terms through EMU. What, however, is Germany? Does the notion of a German dictate imply that the German unemployed are dictating? Will the German working class, as indeed it does, not also face pressure to work harder in the face of worsening conditions?

There is, however, no doubt that 'Germany' 'dictates' and that it does so through its on-average more competitive unit labour costs. In other words, Germany's dominant position in Europe is based on the relatively more effective exploitation of labour within its territory. This 'economic' advantage impresses itself upon the working classes of other member states who, in order to remain employed, are forced to adjust to German rates of exploitation (see Carchedi, 1997). With EMU, the currency exchange rate instrument is no longer available as a means of adjusting sluggish competitiveness to global conditions through currency devaluation. Failure by employers to respond to tight monetary conditions through improvements in the exploitation of labour, might well lead to loss of competitiveness and bankruptcy. In other words, a policy of tight money forces employers to adjust the exploitation of labour, might well lead to loss of competitiveness and bankruptcy. In other words, a policy of tight money forces employers to adjust the exploitation of labour to globally competitive standards.[23] The labour policies that EMU encourages and anchors institutionally, are those 'wanted by national governments and capital' and EMU disguises these 'as if it were an economic policy imposed by some distant bureaucracy, for which the member states are not responsible, and reflecting some socially neutral rationality' (ibid, p. 100). In other words, with EMU, class politics is disguised in the language of European integration. In this way, and as Anderson (1997) argues succinctly, the European bourgeoisie is ready to accept EMU as long as the cost of adjustment falls on labour and as long as EMU makes it appear as if it is not responsible for the burden placed on labour. In short, for them 'government' through EMU, and therewith the 'resourceful' exploitation of labour in Germany, is by far more acceptable than the prospect of being subjected to working class demands for improved conditions or indeed revolutionary demands for the transformation of the means of production into means of emancipation.

In sum, Padoa-Schioppa's endorsement of EMU as a collective prince is apt both in terms of the collective interest of the European bourgeoisie and in terms of the centralization of monetary policy at the European level. The name of the prince is austerity, the purpose of the prince is the depoliticization of monetary policy, and the aim of the prince is the achievement of greater '*expropriation of value from labour*' (Carchedi, 1997, p. 100).

In EMU, labour market and welfare policy remain within the remit of national governments. Member states will retain 'distributive options on – necessarily reduced – expenditure within balanced budgets' (Anderson, 1997, p. 130) and according to Union fiscal recommendations. The subsidiarity principle of EMU is hierarchically structured with monetary policy at the supranational level, fiscal policy at the intermediate level, and labour market policies of deregulation, flexibilization and privatization at the national level. Within this troika, the supranational level of monetary policy is decisive. EMU renounces the 'competitive instruments of the poor countries (inflation and devaluation), it calls industrial capital to task, and thus is functional for the greater creation of (surplus) value rather than simply for a more favourable redistribution of the (surplus) value created' (Carchedi, 1997, p. 100). Whether it will be functional remains, of course, to be seen. Nevertheless, EMU makes clear that employers will have to improve competitiveness on the basis of lower labour unit costs and that is through the intensification of the exploitation of labour's productive power. Failure to exploit labour more effectively will carry the risk of competitive erosion and bankruptcy.

The European Central Bank

The sole task of the ECB is to guarantee price stability. The objective of EMU is to achieve sound money and the achievement of this objective is seen to be a credibility problem. 'One way to bolster the credibility of this objective is to assign the responsibility for monetary policy to an institution that is not subjected to political influence' (Padoa-Schioppa, 1994, p. 188). An independent ECB, then, is endorsed as an institutional device that will – ostensibly – take 'politics' out of 'economics', reinforcing the view that politics and economics are not only distinct forms of social organization but, also, that the making of monetary policy is in fact a non-political 'thing'. Moreover, the institutional design of EMU reinforces the view that the economy, if left to its own devices, is self-regulating and that the institution of the market is a class neutral – socially impartial – institution whose sole criteria are efficiency, economy and effectiveness. The ECB, then, is endorsed as an impartial institution whose decisions depend on technical expertise and the rational regulation of 'economic mechanisms'. Thus, by removing the making of monetary policy as far as possible from the contested terrain of class conflict, it is expected that the politics of austerity will be protected from the 'mob'. As the proponents of EMU make clear, 'expectations are at the heart of the inflation process' (ibid, p. 21). Since, according to its advocates, inflation is caused by expectations, and since economic relations are self-regulating and since national governments are no longer responsible for monetary policy, any 'economic failure' under EMU would reflect a lack of accommodation on the part of the human factor of production to the 'limits of the market' or 'the unreasonableness of the actors who get a wage' (Williams *et al.*, 1991, p. 221).

In EMU, the 'central bank cannot be given instructions by *any* democratic body... as if it were a court of law rather than an instrument of public policy' (Grahl, 1997, p. 138). The ECB, following Grahl, 'is specifically excluded from lending directly to government at EU and national level' (p. 121), and it is 'obliged to avoid the monetary finance of public sector deficits' (p. 131). The ECB is not 'involved in any way in the financial position of member states' because 'financial markets must be convinced that neither the central bank nor any other Community institution implicitly guarantees the obligations of national governments' (Padoa-Schioppa, 1994, p. 183). In conclusion, the ECB is institutionally divorced from national concerns and unaccountable to democratic majorities. Its institutional constitution is so structured as to make monetary policy appear as a non-political process and so conceived as to insulate national governments from 'popular pressure'. At the same time, national governments are empowered to argue that they can do no other than pursue a politics of austerity: their hands are – ostensibly – tied by the decisions of the ECB. In short, what governments did not dare to implement, or indeed failed to pursue on their own because of opposition, is now imposed upon them, and this on their own will and initiative.

The proponents of EMU do of course recognize that class conflict might lead to tensions on the labour market and 'excessive wage increases'. Would the ECB, in spite of its statutory duty, accommodate to inflationary wage pressures or would it maintain price stability? Thus, class conflict might threaten the legitimacy of the European project. For this reason, it is argued that the politics of the ECB has to be 'legitimized' through 'a degree of democratic accountability' (Emerson, 1992, *et al.* p. 98). As Emerson *et al.* see it, 'regular reports to the European parliament might therefore actually facilitate the task' of the ECB (ibid.). Padoa-Schioppa (1994, p. 189) provides a more detailed account on the democratic legitimation of the ECB. Yet, longer though the account may be, Emerson's much briefer version is at least less embarrassing.

Nevertheless, the issue raised by the problem of the 'democratic legitimacy' of monetary union is of course most important regarding the politics of class. In this context, the principle of subsidiarity is of importance. While the central aspects of EMU, monetary policy, is located at the supranational level, fiscal policy, while restricted and subjected to supranational surveillance and coordination, is given some degree of flexibility to cope with 'local shocks'. The most 'decentralized' aspect of 'subsidiarity' concerns the retention of labour market policies and welfare policies by the member states. This arrangement retains, or 'offers' to labour, the 'national territory' as the 'framework' for working class conflict. The idea, it seems, is that monetary supranational integration, fiscal coordination, and national responsibility for 'labour' will reinforce the national territorialization and regimentation of the working class, so protecting monetary policy from sustained class conflict. The 'territorialization' of the European working classes would of course be helpful for fragmenting its resistance to austerity across Europe; it would be useful for addressing the requirement of higher labour productivity in terms of the 'national interest'; and it would be supportive to containing discontent with declining conditions on the basis of 'nationalist' sentiments. Whether EMU will be 'functional' in this way, is of course a different question and will be discussed in the concluding section.

Fiscal policy

EMU is robust about the need for fiscal austerity as a corollary of and condition for the stability of monetary union. However, in EMU the ability of national governments to respond to labour conflict through fiscal expansionism is both restricted and increased. It is increased because, as Garret (1994, p. 49) reports, EMU poses a 'strong incentive for member states to free ride on the union running large budget deficits'. There is thus the 'danger' that national fiscal expansionism might pose 'a major threat to the overall monetary stability' of the Union (Emerson, *et al.* 1992, p. 100). In addition, the costs of deficit financing would be shifted on to participating countries (Eichengreen, 1994, p. 188). The crucial question, then, for the stability of EMU is that of fiscal policy, and through it, that of containing class conflict within the permitted public expenditure levels across the EU. As Padoa-Schioppa (1994, p. 127) puts it, the question is 'whether monetary union runs a serious risk of being undermined by independent and possibly uncoordinated budgetary policies by member states'. The risk, then, is one of moral hazard.[24] Should a member state that responds to class conflict with fiscal profligacy be stabilized by fiscal transfers from other member countries or should the ECB, despite its brief not to do so, be allowed to monetize the accrued national debt? Were such responses legitimate, would this not 'invite' member-states to adopt 'unsustainable' fiscal measures to cushion social conflicts?

An important aspect of the debate on EMU focuses on the creation of safeguards to ensure that fiscal profligacy is rendered impossible. Germany favours a hard EMU with no obligation to stabilize or refinance, for example, Italy through fiscal transfers. France, in the face of labour unrest, seeks a more flexible interpretation of Maastricht to allow scope for dealing with social discontent. Besides, a more flexible arrangement, and therewith a softer euro, would of course mean that Germany would adjust to the conditions of labour productivity pertaining in France. However, a softer euro is anathema not only to Germany because 'softening' would question the firmness of monetary union derailing the politics of tight money domestically. Such derailment would have serious consequence at a global level. In short, EMU inscribes in institutional form what capital and its national state(s) have sought in vain over the last two decades. National governments use, as Grahl (1997, p. 228) puts it, 'Maastricht as an alibi for their own projects to establish more restrictive welfare regimes, to intensify market discipline and to favour particular social strata'. The differences, then, between the French and German conceptions are distinct only as variants of a common theme and that is that monetary union needs to be buttressed with fiscal restraint. In EMU, fiscal policy is to support monetary union and not to weaken the value of the euro through the so-called fiscal expansionism that is associated with Keynesianism.

In EMU, fiscal policy resides formally with the member states. At the same time, the Union has the power of coordination and surveillance, and the ability to recommend modifications of fiscal policy and to apply sanctions against governments that have not taken the recommended steps. In short, the Union has the power to enforce fiscal discipline upon member states. A different solution to the ability of member states to adopt expansionary responses to class conflict would have been the transfer of fiscal responsibility to the Union. This would have led, constitutionally, to just that sort of fiscal federalism that Hayek, and with him the proponents of EMU, feared. However, in EMU 'subsidiarity, not the Leviathan, is the catchword for European political union' (Padoa-Schioppa, 1994, p. 191). Yet, subsidiarity might be the catchword, the content of the fiscal policy arrangement is clearly the loss of fiscal demand management as a means of containing labour conflicts in member states.

EMU is seen to require safeguards against 'unsustainable budgetary policies in a member state' because these are seen to lead to either 'default or debt monetization' which would 'be a major threat to the overall monetary stability' (*European Economy*, 1990, p. 100). In this view, and indeed as the convergence criteria of Maastricht make clear, any rise in debt whatever the objectives of the expenditure, is 'unsustainable'. As Emerson *et al.* (1992) put it, 'fiscal discipline is defined as the avoidance of an unsustainable build-up of public debt' (p. 107) and the transition to EMU 'amplifies the domestic effectiveness of national fiscal policy for stabilization purposes' (p. 115), requiring a tight control of member states 'if fiscal expansion were systematically beggar-thy-neighbour in character' (p. 119). In short, 'surveillance will have to correct possible tendencies for budget deficits to become too large' and EMU relies on 'fiscal policy to reduce budget deficits' (p. 100). EMU, then, seeks to render obsolete anti-cyclical fiscal policies associated with Keynesianism and confers on fiscal policy the task of controlling public expenditure. EMU discourages a politics of fiscal equalization from rich to poor member countries.[25] Any fiscal demand management, as the proponents of EMU see it, involves the 'risk of weakening incentives for production activity and creates stable welfare dependency' (*European Economy*, 1990, p. 227). Thus, member states are encouraged to 'modernize' their economies through privatization, deregulation of labour markets, flexibilization of labour processes, and the like, including the containment of welfare state expenditure despite high levels of 'redundant' labour. After all, as one of the members of the inner circle of New Labour put it, 'high unemployment is linked to generous benefits that run on indefinitely and to poor educational standards at the lower end of the labour market' (Giddens, 1998, p. 122)!

The proponents of EMU endorse it as a 'framework of incentives and constraints' that will 'condition national budgetary policies, for which the keywords will be autonomy (to respond to country specific problems), discipline (to avoid excessive deficits), and coordination (to assure an appropriate overall policy-mix in the Community)' (Emerson, *et al.* 1992, p. 11). In sum, the retention of fiscal powers by national states is to an extent merely formal at the same time as the Union has no fiscal responsibilities. Its task is to make sure that member states pursue a politics of fiscal restraint. The Union, then, has the power to discipline fiscally lax member states while member states retain the power to implement a 'responsible' fiscal policy by virtue of their own political sovereignty. Subsidiarity, then, means that the Union decides on what is fiscally permissible while member states retain the power to adopt a responsible fiscal policy that redistributes income from labour to capital. Thus, EMU does explicitly reject fiscal federalism. It merely empowers the Union to police the fiscal stance of its members. This, then, creates a problem for the reformist labour movement in that neither the national government(s) nor the Union appear responsible for fiscal policy. Yet, the complete loss of the possibility of exchange rate adjustment by member states raises the issue of fiscal policy as a supranational concern. However, the existing structure of EMU makes clear that fiscal policy is not available as a supranational policy instrument. This seems to imply, as Eichengreen (2000, p. 88) argues, that 'with neither fiscal nor monetary flexibility, Europe will be helpless in the face of business cycle disturbance'. This might well be so unless, of course, 'adjustment' and 'flexibility' is 'derived' from European labour, improving its productivity in relation to global competitive levels.

For its proponents, EMU means that the working class can no longer expect concessions such 'extensive' and 'generous' welfare support mechanisms. EMU is seen to provide strong incentives for labour to move from areas of unemployment to those where employment might be gained. Increased competition within the EU may also 'result in an increased responsiveness of wages to unemployment', with 'labour market flexibility, and most importantly wage flexibility...the most important adjustment instrument' (Emerson, *et al.* 1992, p. 149). Yet, as Emerson *et al.* and others recognize, such adjustment on the part of the working class, that is its utility as an economic, effective and efficient human resource, might take time. For this reason, the retention of fiscal policy by national states is endorsed as a means of enabling national states to respond to 'local shocks' in order to achieve 'short term stabilization' for the purpose of 'medium term adjustment' (ibid,

p. 100). However, while national governments may use fiscal policy measures to absorb 'local shocks', these have to be coordinated with other member countries. Importantly, the fiscal response to 'shocks' is to ensure the maintenance of price stability and wage discipline. As Emerson *et al.* (ibid, p. 103) see it, the purpose and aim of fiscal policy is to offset increases in domestic demand because price and wage adjustments take time due to a lack of wage discipline on the part of the working class. The aim and purpose, then, of national fiscal policy is to induce real wage adjustments. The stability of EMU depends, then, on the readiness of European labour to support the achievement of price stability across Europe through a much more productive utilization of her productive power.

Adjustment and labour

Advocates of EMU see it as a device that will readjust monetary accumulation to productive accumulation on the basis of a stronger link between working class consumption and productivity growth. The convergence criteria and the Stability Pact subordinate countries with relatively high unit labour costs much more directly to those with low unit labour costs. With national currency devaluations rendered obsolete and fiscal policy disciplined by EMU, the 'wage–price flexibility remains the basic adjustment channel as a substitute for the nominal exchange rate' (ibid, p. 102). In addition, labour migration is expected to adjust the burden of unemployment on national budgets. In short, EMU focuses adjustment on 'two primary [channels]: a) workers can move; b) wages can change' (Currie, 2000, p. 124).

EMU focuses on the politics of deregulation, flexibilization, wage discipline, labour mobility, and particularly lower unit labour costs as the basis through which the European economy will have to adjust. Lower labour costs are 'a condition to the relative price decrease needed to restore the competitive position of [member states] and to bring output and employment back into equilibrium' and 'factor mobility, in particularly labour mobility, may solve the problem through migration' (Emerson, *et al.* 1992, p. 147). The belief is that 'wage bargainers will be affected by a credible monetary union' as they will realize that excessive wage rises will not be underwritten by devaluations (ibid, p. 24). In other words, the cost in terms of output and employment might not be high if the working class submits to wage restraint and if it is willing to let itself be exploited more effectively, efficiently and economically. Advocates of EMU project the mobility of US labour as the future of European labour. European labour mobility is seen as one of the most important stabilizers of EMU. Yet, where should labour go and what happens if she wishes to stay?

In sum, the politics of subsidiarity envisages that the institutionalization of price stability at the supranational level will support national governments in their effort of achieving a full scale 'marketization' of the 'factor labour' and force employers to maintain competitiveness by confronting the working class in the contested terrain of production to increase labour productivity. This is not to say that employers have not confronted their workers in the past. Yet, with the devaluation of exchange rates rendered obsolete and with the ECB seeking price stability at the European level divorced from 'national' concerns, the room for compromise towards and concessions to labour have decreased significantly – just as the Hayek of the 1930s thought it would. As Henning (2000, p. 21) puts it, '[k]nowing that exchange rate policy *vis-à-vis* other members of the union can no longer reverse the deleterious effects on competitiveness of high wage and price increases, firms and unions should act with greater discipline'. EMU then is seen to spur employers and unions on to greater efforts to achieve lower unit labour costs. While EMU amounts to an attempt at making the European working class pay for the containment of inflation and the control of deficits, it appears at the same time as a merely technical device and, importantly, as the realization of European harmony replacing its long history of bloody war and conquest. EMU, it seems, seeks to justify the intensification of exploitation and the deterioration of conditions through the absence of war.

In EMU, the definition of monetary policy as a merely technical device best left to the experts and the elevation of monetary policy to the supranational level seems indeed to vindicate Padoa-Schioppa's view of EMU as resembling a modern version of Machiavelli's prince. Its court is fiscal policy that is located in the twilight zone between the national state and the Union. The subjects of the prince are the European working classes who are territorially regimented in the fiefdoms of their national states. As a citizen, the 'human factor of production' appears in EMU's design in the form that has been visited upon the 'dependent masses' since Roman times. It appears as the *plebes*. The metaphor of the 'prince', then, entails the transformation of the national boat into the European home: the majority rowing, the minority navigating.

Yet, as has been argued, EMU needs to be seen against the background of the crisis of the overaccumulation of capital since the late 1960s. Since then capital and its national state(s) have failed to reintegrate labour into the capital relation as an effective factor of production whose exploitation guarantees the global credit-superstructure in the present and whose consumption is within the limits of productivity growth. EMU has not caused the deep recession of the 1990s nor has it forced governments to deflate their economies. EMU provides an institutional framework for coping with the labour question through the institutionalization of a deflationary regime that imposes, on their own initiative, upon national governments a policy they either failed or did not dare to implement due to fear of labour unrest. There is however neither an institutional fix to the problems of inflation nor an institutional solution to the labour question. Class struggle has to be fought and, of course, the institutional reorganization of political power at a European level is an important aspect of this fight. However, as the conclusion argues, such reorganization reproduces the contradiction it ostensibly sets out to resolve.

Conclusion

The chapter has argued that EMU is politically motivated and that it is as much a response to domestic as to global conditions. Both of these conditions are intrinsically linked in and through the capitalist crisis of exploiting labour on an expanding scale. Since the late 1960s, the growth rates of monetary accumulation have outstripped those of productive accumulation. Monetary accumulation dissociated from productive accumulation presents a claim on surplus value still to be expropriated from labour. As a consequence the strength of the relationship between 'money' and exploitation declined on a global scale. Instead, claims on the future exploitation of labour accumulated and the strength of the relationship between consumption and productivity growth weakened. Moreover, national states lost the ability to erode real wages through inflation because of the speculative threat to currency exchange rates.

In this context the search for counter inflationary credibility is of paramount importance. Counter inflationary credibility, however, is not just some sort of technical thing. It involves the containment of class conflict on the basis of austerity that seeks to strengthen the link between consumption and labour productivity. In short, a politics of austerity means a prolonged period of not only living on less but, also, of working harder, longer, more intensely, and more 'flexibly' in the face of declining conditions. Against this background, the convergence criteria of EMU and the Stability Pact make revealing reading. They institutionalize a politics of austerity by calling for a stronger relationship between consumption and labour productivity through the control of monetary policy (austerity); fiscal restraint (the control of budgets); and the loss of exchange rate devaluations as means of adjusting sluggish domestic competitiveness to international conditions. However, while focusing adjustment on the working class, governments have to be careful not to provoke sustained class conflict to avoid uncertainty and thus to maintain credibility. The attempt, then, at depoliticizing the making of monetary policy is of vital importance. The neo-liberal recommendations for overcoming the crisis of the state focused precisely on this issue.

EMU amounts, then, to an institutional attempt at buttressing domestic policies of austerity with a supranational anchor. Institutionally, social and labour market policies remain 'national in nature, allowing for the labour movements to be fragmented rather than integrated on a pan-European basis' (Gill, 1992, p. 173). EMU provides the institutional framework for a comprehensive restructuring of labour relations and erodes 'the conditions of existence of the welfare-national state' (ibid). Most importantly, it creates a huge integrated market where countries with low productivity rates relative to the major economic powers in the EU, will face intense competitive pressure. It has been argued that the European bourgeoisie is supportive of EMU because the burden of adjustment is carried by labour and it has been suggested that EMU is so structured as to depoliticize the making of monetary policy and to insulate monetary policy from working class demands.

EMU, then, appears to amount to the institutionalization of an anti-inflationary police force that seeks to protect member states from speculative runs by securing the rights of private property internally. Furthermore, EMU not only seeks to depoliticize the attack on the labour movement but, also, to reinforce and exploit its regional and national fragmentation. Hayek, in the 1930s, advocated supranationalism for this very reason. For him, inter-state federalism would dilute class polarization, decompose entrenched positions of class power and depoliticize the class struggle. Instead there would emerge complex and changing relations of conflict between the classes. For Hayek, class conflict would be replaced by competitive pluralist relations, segmenting working class struggle and disempowering sustained resistance to the politics of money at the centre. EMU, it has been argued, is an institutional arrangement 'designed to insulate key economic agencies, especially Central Banks, from interference by elected politicians' (Gill, 1992, p. 168). In qualification to Gill, the most intriguing aspect of EMU is not the insulation of key economic agencies from political interference but, rather, the institutional assertion that the political and economic are two distinct forms of social organization. Central bank monetary 'policy' is directly political in nature and EMU's effort to make it look un-political presents the most important aspect of the depoliticization of the politics of class.[27]

Furthermore, it would be quite wrong to suggest that, before EMU, there had been democratic control over monetary policy conferring influence over its conduct on the labour movement. With EMU, the 'concentration of unaccountable decision-making lies precisely in those areas where the capitalist nation-state itself has always resisted democratic encroachment most trenchantly: monetary policy' (Gowan, 1997, p. 97). The supranational character of EMU, then, is important not because it makes democratically unaccountable what previously had been democratically accountable. The importance is rather that national states, on their own initiative, will no longer be able to accommodate class conflict through credit expansion or currency devaluation. Instead, EMU places binding 'constraints on state power' (Gill, 1992, p. 178), institutionalizing a supranational anchor for the subordination of labour to the discipline of the market. EMU, then, amounts to an arrangement that pre-emptively undercuts expansionary responses to labour conflict and unrest. Maastricht, following Anderson (1997, p. 131), 'leads to an obliteration of what is left of the Keynesian legacy that Hayek deplored, and most of the distinctive gains of the Western European labour movement associated with it'. Maastricht, then, inscribes into the EU the neo-liberal policy of market freedom associated with Hayek and it does so through the creation of constitutional devices associated with ordo-liberalism.

However, despite appearances to the contrary, EMU rather than providing an institutional fix to the labour question might, I would suggest, amplify and transmit 'regional' class conflicts across the EU. What would happen if a member state fails to contain class conflict on the basis of fiscal restraint and would be compelled to adopt fiscal expansionism instead? What power of sanction would the EU have? Suspending the membership of such a state in EMU would undermine EMU, re-financing the member state would reinforce the threat of monetary instability across Europe just in the same way as 'unsustainable' national levels of public debt jeopardize the objective of tight money on a European scale. Should the EU be empowered to call for the resignation of the national government that failed in its task to guarantee the citizenship rights of private property? Of course, a member state cannot simply replace its discontented working class by a more docile one. What effect, then, would sustained working class struggle have on EMU? In the absence of 'macroeconomic' instruments of accommodating working class resistance to austerity and intensification of exploitation through inflation, currency devaluation and fiscal redistribution, how to protect European monetary relations other than by coercive means; and on whose orders? In short, Minford (2000, p. 77) is not too far off the mark when he says that, when going gets rough, 'someone has to stop people running for the door and only a state has that power'. What is the state's name that possesses, in the Schmittian perspective,[26] the sovereignty to declare an 'emergency' so that we all follow the lead of the invisible hand and behave well as mere personifications of the capitalist exchange relations?

This scenario might sound bizarre. Yet, Hayek's abandonment of his earlier endorsement of supranationalism is not without significance for the understanding of working class power in EMU. The European bourgeoisie is, as was argued, united in EMU for as long as labour carries the burden. Whether the working class however territorially fragmented, will carry the burden is quite a different matter. Would, for example, the European bourgeoisie agree to pay the cost for containing class conflict in, for example, Italy through fiscal transfers, stabilizing EMU through fiscal expansionism and therewith an inflationary devaluation of its wealth and a weaker euro? Besides, concerning Germany, despite huge fiscal transfers to the former GDR, East Germany still remains one of the poorest regions in the EU. Would the European bourgeoisie wish to see a transfer of resources to the South of Italy to stabilize relations without making a profit? Surely, such transfers might well sustain a certain level of consumption without however leading to an increase in productive activity. Or should South Italian labour be invited to migrate to more prosperous areas where its skills are in low demand? Or should the South of Italy simply be disregarded in favour of those regions where investments make a return? What impact might this have on the political stability of Italy and, through it, on the international value of the euro? EMU does not by itself guarantee the transformation of social labour power into a productive and profitable resource. Besides, capital does not pose unemployed labour as an exploitable resource but posits it as a reserve army whose mere existence bites into profit margins and the suggestion that, under EMU, unemployed labour should migrate to areas of employment smacks of desperation, however painful the consequences might be. In sum, 'national' shifts in the balance of class power will have immediate effects on all other member states due to its impact on the euro and, through it, on monetary relations across Europe. Quite apart from the impact of 'global shocks' on the EU, EMU transmits and amplifies domestic resistance to austerity and exploitation in member states to all other member states of the Union and beyond.

In short, EMU merely provides a supranational anchor for the pursuance of a politics of austerity. Whether the 'anchor' fulfils its role does not depend on the melody of European integration but on the outcome of class struggle. EMU transmits and amplifies domestic or regional conflicts across Europe and, therefore, makes the European states much more dependent upon each other. Failure to contain the labour question in one member state has direct adverse consequences for all the others. In other words, each national state not only competes with the others for competitive advantages but, also, depends on the others for containing class struggle. In the literature, this issue is addressed in terms of 'moral hazard': should member states, or the EU, support expansionary responses to class conflict by a member state through the fiscal transfers, thereby setting a precedent that would encourage the 'expectation' that a similar response will be repeated in the future? Or should the member state be allowed to default? Whatever the response, each in its own terms will jeopardize European monetary stability and union. This might not only destabilize global financial relations through speculative runs on the euro but, also, deepen the crisis of capitalist accumulation on global scale. There would thus be strong pressure to create a European fiscal competence, a fiscal federalism complementing monetary federalism. Such a development, as Hayek saw clearly, would be painful to profits and render problematic the containment of the European working class through territorial fragmentation.

The stability of EMU depends on the acquiescence of the European working class. Domestic resistance to deteriorating conditions have not only repercussions across Europe but, also, on a global scale through the effect of discontent on the value of the euro. The failure of one member state to contain 'its' working class has costly consequences for all the other member states. The former President of the Bundesbank, Mr Tietmeyer, saw this clearly when he said that 'sustaining the monetary union may need perhaps more solidarity than beginning it' (cited in Eltis, 2000, p. 146). In short, the fabric of EMU appears strong – yet the seam is weak. The seam is all important. EMU, in conclusion, reproduces in different form the very conflicts that it sets out to resolve. The question, then, of Europe is not resolved by EMU. Rather, it is posed.

Notes

* This chapter draws on a talk to the Thursday Seminar, Department of Economis, University of Athens, April 1998. A version of this talk was published in *Economic and Political Weekly*, 29 August 1998.

1 For a critical assessment of the relationship between Keynesianism and full employment, see Glyn (1995) and Matthews (1968).

2 See Marx's analysis of the fetishism of the value form (1983, ch. 1, sect. 4). For commentaries see, Backhaus (1997).

3 On this see Parboni (1981).

4 On this shift from Friedman to Hayek, see Clarke (1987).

5 On this see Mandel (1987) and Kemp (1990).

6 On the politics of austerity in Britain during the 1980s, see Bonefeld (1993) and Clarke (1988).

7 On this see Bonefeld and Burnham (1996), and Bonefeld's (Chapter 7) constitution to this volume.

8 See Collony's (1995) insightful though profoundly ideological account on the inter-imperialist rivalry between the European nation states over monetary integration, especially EMU.

9 As Germany's Chancellor, Mr Schröder, put it: 'the 35-hour week in France is a good thing for employment in Germany' (quoted in *The Economist*, 5 February 2000, p. 43).

10 On this see the collection of articles edited by Bonefeld and Holloway (1995) and Walter (1993).

11 For a detailed discussion of the expansion of debt in the 1990s and the dangers of financial collapse, see Warburton (1999).

12 On Marx's crisis theory see Bell and Cleaver (1982) and Clarke (1994).

13 See Mandel (1975) and Armstrong *et al.* (1984) for documentation.

14 On this in the contemporary context, see Bonefeld and Holloway (1995).

15 This was well recognized by the Director of the Banque of France who is reported to have commented at the time of the Zapatista uprising that 'the international system is now so fragile that a handful of Indians in a corner of Mexico can put it in danger' (quoted in Holloway, 2000, p. 5). On the relationship between financial turmoil and the Zapatista uprising, see Holloway and Peláez (eds) (1998).

16 On this see, for example, de Brunhoff (1978).

17 On this see Burnham (2000).

18 Monetarism and Keynsianism are, of course, very slippery concepts whose distinctive difference is more apparant than real. The capitalist state is fundamentally a liberal state whatever its specific historical form. On this see Agnoli (1997) and Clarke (1992).

19 As one German academic of conservative persuasion put it in the 1950s, 'the democratization of society poses the principal danger to democracy' (Hennis quoted in Agnoli, 1997, p. 136, fn 7). See also Schumpeter's (1992) notion that democracy should amount to no more than a rationalized procedure for the selection of rival elites competing for governmental power.

20 For a systematic discussion on the inter-relation between liberal democracy, constitutionalism, and the relations of exploitation, see Agnoli (2000).

21 On this see Holloway (1995b).

22 For a recent endorsement of Hayek's 1930s view in relation to the EU, see Bernholz (1992).
23 This was well understood by the Bank of England during the membership of the pound sterling in the ERM: 'The Governor has emphasized that henceforth companies can have no grounds for expecting a lower exchange rate to validate any failure to control costs. The greater stability which ERM membership offers sterling against other European currencies should in itself be welcome to business as it will enable firms to plan and invest with greater certainty. If companies recognize that they are now operating under a changed regime the benefits of lower inflation will accrue sooner, and at a lower cost in terms of lost output, than could otherwise be expected. But if they fail to recognize the constraints under which they now operate the outcome will prove painful to them' (quoted in Smith, 1993, p. 187).
24 On 'moral hazard' within the global debtor economy, see Benson (1995).
25 On this see Haynes, in this volume.
26 In his *Political Theology* (1934b), Carl Schmitt defined 'sovereignty' as follows: 'Sovereign is who decides on a state of emergency'.
27 For an account on the role of money in the politics of class, see Ricciardi (1987) and Bonefeld (1995).

Bibliography

Agnoli, J. (2000) 'The State, the Market, and the End of History', in Bonefeld, W. and Pyschopedis, K. (eds).

Agnoli, J. (1997) *Faschismus ohne Revision* (Freiburg: Ça ira).

Anderson, P. (1997) 'The Europe to Come', in Gowan, P. and Anderson, P. (eds).

Armstrong, P., Glyn, A. and Harrison, J. (1984) *Capitalism since World War II* (London: Fontana).

Backhaus, H. G. (1997) *Dialektik der Wertform* (Freiburg: Ça ira).

Baimbridge, M., Burkitt, B. and Whyman, P. (eds) (2000) *The Impact of the Euro* (London: Macmillan).

Bell, P. and Cleaver, H. (1982) 'Marx's Crisis Theory as a Theory of Class Struggle', *Review in Political Economy*, 5.

Benson, G. (1995) 'Saftey Nets and Moral Hazards in Banking', in Sawamoto, K. Nokajima, Z. and Tuguchi, H. (eds), *Financial Stability in a Changing Financial Environment* (London: Macmillan).

Bernholz, P. (1992) 'Constitutional Aspects of the European Integration', in Borner, S. and Grubel, H. (eds), *The European Community after 1992* (London: Macmillan).

Bonefeld, W. (1993) *The Recomposition of the British State during the 1980s* (Aldershot: Dartmouth).

Bonefeld, W. (1995) 'Money, Equality and Exploitation', in Bonefeld, W. and Holloway, J. (eds).

Bonefeld, W. and Burnham, P. (1996) 'Britain and the Politics of the European Exchange Rate Mechanism', *Capital & Class*, 60.

Bonefeld, W. and J. Holloway (1995a) 'Conclusion: Money and Class Struggle', in Bonefeld and Holloway (eds)

Bonefeld, W. and Holloway, J. (eds) (1995b) *Global Capital, National State and the Politics of Money* (London: Macmillan).
Bonefeld, W. and Psychopedis, K. (eds) (2000) *The Politics of Change: Globalization, Ideology and Critique* (London: Macmillan).
Brittan, S. (1976) 'The Economic Contradictions of Democracy', in King, A. (ed).
Brittan, S. (1977) *Economic Consequences of Democracy* (London: Temple Smith).
Burnham, P. (2000) 'Globalisation, Depoliticisation, and Modern Economic Management', in Bonefeld, W. and Psychopedis, K. (eds).
Busch, A. (1994) 'The Crisis of the EMS', *Government & Opposition*, 29, 1.
Carchedi, G. (1997) 'The EMU, Monetary Crises, and the Single European Currency', *Capital & Class*, 63 (reprinted in this volume).
Clarke, S. (1987) 'Capitalist Crisis and the Rise of Monetarism', *Socialist Register 1987* (London: Merlin).
Clarke, S. (1988) *Keynesianism, Monetarism and the Crisis of the State* (Aldershot: Edward Elgar).
Clarke, S. (1992) 'The Global Accumulation of Capital and the Periodisation of the Capitalist State Form', in Bonefeld *et al.* (eds), *Open Marxism vol. I* (London: Pluto).
Clarke, S. (1994) *Marx's Theory of Crisis* (London: Macmillan).
Cleaver, H. (1995) 'The Subversion of Money-as-Command in the Current Crisis', in Bonefeld, W. and Holloway, J. (eds).
Collonny, B. (1995) *The Rotten Heart of Europe* (London: Faber).
Crozier, M. *et al.* (1975) *The Crisis of Democray* (New York: New York University Press).
Currie, D. (2000) 'EMU: Threats and Opportunities for Companies and National Economies', in Baimbridge *et al.* (eds) 2000.
de Brunhoff, S. (1978) *State, Capital and Economic Policy* (London: Pluto).
Eichengreen, B. (1994) 'Fiscal Policy and European Monetary Union', in Eichengreen B. and Frieden J. (eds).
Eichengreen, B. (2000) 'Saving Europe's Stabilizers', in Baimbridge *et al.* (eds) 2000.
Eichengreen, B. and Frieden, J. (eds) (1994) *The Political Economy of European Monetary Integration* (Bolder: Westview).
Eltis, W. (2000) 'British EMU Membership Would Create Instability and Destroy Employment', in Baimbridge *et al.* (eds) 2000.
Emerson, M. *et al.* (1992) *One Market, One Money* (Oxford: Oxford University Press).
European Economy (1990) 'One Market, One Money', 44, October.
Garret, G. (1994) 'The Politics of Maastricht', in Eichengreen, B. and Frieden, J. (eds).
Giddens, A. (1998) *The Third Way* (Cambridge: Polity).
Gill, S. (1992) 'The Emerging World Order and European Change', in *Socialist Register 1992* (London: Merlin).
Glyn, A. (1995) 'Social Democracy and Full Employment', *New Left Review*, 211.
Godley, W. (1997) 'The Hole in the Treaty', in Gowan, P. and Anderson, P. (eds).
Gowan, P. (1997) 'British Euro-solipsism', in Gowan, P. and Anderson, P. (eds).
Gowan, P. and Anderson, P. (eds) (1997) *The Question of Europe* (London: Verso).
Grahl, J. (1997) *After Maastricht* (London: Lawrence & Wishart).

Gros, D. and Thygessen, N. (1992) *European Monetary Integration* (London: Longman).
Halevi, J. (1999) 'The Accumulation Process in Japan and East Asia as Compared with the Role of Germany in European Post-war Growth', in Bellofiore, R. (ed), *Global Money, Capital Restructuring and the Changing Patterns of Labour* (Cheltenham: Edward Elgar).
Hayek, F. (1939) 'The Economic Conditions of Interstate Federalism', in Hayek (1949) *Individualism and Economic Order* (London: Routledge and Kegan Paul).
Hayek, F. (1978) *Denationalization of Money. The Argument Refined,* Hobart Paper 70 (London: Institute of Economic Affairs).
Helleiner, E. (1994) *States and the Re-emergence of global Finance* (Ithaca: Cornell University Press).
Henning, C. R. (2000) 'US–EU Relations after the Inception of the Monetary Union: Cooperation or Rivalry?', in Henning, C. R. and Padoan, T. *Transatlantic Perspective on the Euro* (Washington: Brookings Institute).
Holloway, J. (1995a) 'Global Capital and the National State', in Bonefeld, W. and Holloway, J. (eds).
Holloway, J. (1995b) 'The Abyss Opens: The Rise and Fall of Keynesianism' in Bonefeld, W. and Holloway, J. (eds).
Holloway, J. (2000) 'Zapata at Wallstreet', in Bonefeld, W. and Psychopedis, K. (eds).
Holloway, J. and Peláez, E. (eds) (1998) *Zapatista!* (London: Pluto).
Kemp, T. (1990) *The Climax of Capitalism* (London: Longman).
King, A. (1976a) 'The problem of overload', in King, A. (ed).
King, A. (1976b) *Why is Britain Becoming Harder to Govern* (London: BBC Books).
Mandel, E. (1975) *Late Capitalism* (London: Verso).
Mandel, E. (1987) *Die Krise* (Hamburg: Konkret).
Marazzi, C. (1995) 'Money in the World Crisis', in Bonefeld, W. and Holloway, J. (eds).
Marx, K. (1983) *Capital,* vol. I (London: Lawrence & Wishart).
Matthews, R. (1968) 'Why has Britain had Full Employment since the War?', *Economic Journal,* 78.
Mattick, P. (1934) 'Zur Marxschen Akkumulations- und Zusammenbruchstheorie', *Rätekorrespondenz,* 4.
Minford, P. (2000) 'The Single Currency – Will it work and Should We Join?', in Baimbridge *et al.* (eds).
Padoa-Schioppa, T. (1994) *The Road to Monetary Union* (Oxford: Clarendon Press).
Parboni, R. (1981) *The Dollar and its Rivals* (London: Verso).
Ricciardi, J. (1987) 'Rereading Marx on the Role of Money and Finance', *Research in Political Economy,* 10.
Sandholtz, W. (1993) 'Choosing Union: Monetary Politics and Maastricht', *International Organisation,* 47, 1.
Schlesinger, A. (1958) *The Coming of the New Deal: The Age of Roosevelt* (Boston: Houghton Mifflin).
Schmitt, C. (1932) *Der Begriff des Politischen,* 3rd edn. 1963 (Berlin: Duncker & Humblot).
Schmitt, C. (1934a) *Legalität und Legitimität,* 4th edn 1988 (Berlin: Duncker & Humblot).

Schmitt, C. (1934b) *Politische Theologie, Vier Kapital zur Lehre von der Souveränität*, 5th edn. 1990 (Berlin: Duncker & Humblot).
Schumpter, J. (1992), *Capitalism, Socialism and Democracy* (London: Routledge).
Smith, D. (1993) *From Boom to Bust* (Harmondsworth: Penguin).
von Mises, L. (1944) *Planned Chaos* (New York: The Foundation for Economic Education).
Walter, A. (1993) *World Money and World Power* (London: Harvester Wheatsheaf).
Warburton, P. (1999) *Debt and Delusion* (London: Allen Lane The Penguin Press).
Williams, J., Williams, K. and Haslam, C. (1991) 'Leap before you look', in Amin, A. and Dietrich, A. (eds), *Towards a New Europe?* (Aldershot: Edward Elgar).

5

The EC's Free Market Agenda and the Myth of Social Europe

Bernard H. Moss

The European Community (EC)[1] has always enjoyed great favour in the academic community. Of literally thousands of books on the subject in English practically none offer a critical perspective. The European Left, socialists and Communists, had denounced the EC as a capitalist construction, but scholars never elaborated this criticism with a concrete analysis of its laws, institutions and operation.[2] The reigning narrative was that of the weakening of the nation state and the growth of the EC toward prosperity and ever closer union though Whiggish enthusiasm was tempered at times like the mid-1970s and post-Maastricht when the project appeared to stall.[3] The Economic and Monetary Union (EMU) creating the single currency was at least initially viewed as the last great step toward a supranational government that would assume many of the vital functions of a nation state.

The EC has been justified on two major grounds, peace and prosperity. It is claimed that it kept the peace in Europe since World War II, especially between France and Germany, and that it has brought unprecedented prosperity. Those who feel uncomfortable with its market orientation have argued that it holds great potential for social regulation on a regional level, which has become that much more important as globalization has limited the scope for purely national action.

Most writers argue that the project was politically neutral as between the liberal or socialist tradition or at least adaptable to the preferences of member states (Featherstone, 1988; Kapteyn *et al.*, 1989). They do not see that it constituted, quite apart from changes in the international environment like the growth of currency speculation, a barrier to market intervention and a prophylactic, as in the case of Mitterrand's France, against socialism. The chief supporters of its free trade and monetarist policies, especially the single market initiative and single currency, were exporters and multinationals (cf. Moravcsik, 1998, with Fligstein and Brantley, 1995). The understated aim of the single currency was to put downward pressure on wages and benefits (Verdun, 1996, Moss and Michie, 1998, pp. 20, 22). The failure of the so-called social dimension is patent. The reflective view of EC and member states neglects the autonomous influence that EC laws, institutions and practices have had on national economies, social conditions and domestic politics.

Justifications for the EC: peace and prosperity?

It is claimed that the EC has secured the peace in Western Europe since 1945, but assuredly the main credit belongs to the US and the Cold War. As leader of the capitalist world after the war, the US needed to construct a strong united and prosperous Western Europe based on market principles to serve as a bulwark against both internal and external Communism. From the onset of the Cold War, the US pressed for the creation of a supranational European community based on principles of free trade and private enterprise (Maier, 1991). The decision to rearm Germany necessitated by the outbreak of the Korean War impelled the French to propose a coal and steel community that would pool 'the sinews of war' and thus keep Germany under control (Gillingham, 1991). Though the European Coal and Steel Community (ECSC) failed in its objective of economic and social regulation, it provided the institutional framework for the common market established by the Treaty of Rome in 1957.

There were many ways in which European trade could have been encouraged and regulated – through agreements that were bilateral or multilateral, selective, comprehensive or transitional, free trading or externally protectionist and internally regulatory – but the liberal market formula was chosen by the American patron, employers and governing Socialists and Christian Democrats. The French wanted a more regulatory approach, but their Socialist prime minister, Guy Mollet, was a pro-European who basically trusted the larger American-type market to produce prosperity and rising living standards. One reason the French backed down, aside from the isolation they experienced as a result of their invasion of Suez, was that they had just resolved outstanding security issues, over the Saar and nuclear weapons, with the Germans (Bossuat, 1996). In other words, the EC in 1957 and in its leaps forward in 1978, 1986 and 1991, was as much the result of Franco–German accord as its cause.

The EC doubtless created mutual economic interests among members that lessened the risk of conflict, but it did not prevent General De Gaulle from temporarily withdrawing to seek its subordination to a confederation that would preserve national sovereignty and independence from the US. The single market and currency have further enmeshed the economies of member states, but, touching vital national interests, they have the potential for unleashing conflicts such as over British beef, Kosovo or interest rates that could conceivably lead to war (Feldstein, 1997).

Most writers especially those with little economic knowledge assume that the EC has produced prosperity and an integrated regional economy. This is not the case. Pro-EC free traders generally subscribe to Ricardo's theory of comparative advantage that advises countries to seek specialization in those products in which they enjoy relatively lower factor costs than their trading partners. They base their hopes for growth on the American example where the combination of regional specialization, factor mobility and economies of scale derived from wider markets produced high productivity and growth.

None of these advantages however obtained in the EC. Since the emigration of Italians in the 1950s, there has been practically no migration of EC citizens to other EC countries for work. The growth in intra-EC trade has not increased national specialization for it has been overwhelmingly intra-sectoral, relying on differences in quality and brand appeal, mainly at the upper end of the market, for advantage (Fontagné *et al.*, 1997). Little economy of scale has been realized either because national markets were already optimal or because firms obtained greater efficiency from multi-product plants or plants in several countries or from flexible production methods involving outsourcing, zero defects, and reduced inventories (Cutler *et al.*, 1989).

Free trade in the EC thus produced few efficiency gains and little contribution to growth – at best one per cent per annum in the early years (Belassa, 1975). Intra-EC trade has destroyed some national industries for example that of French refrigerators, which could have learned to survive, as did the British, outside the EC. The low external tariff has resulted in increasing dependency on American and Japanese producers, especially in the field of high technology (Bourry, 1993). This disappointing experience with free trade is consistent with the broader lessons of economic history that show competitiveness and expanded trade arising from protectionist regimes that allow producers to perfect their methods in national markets (Bairoch, 1996).

An integrated European market has not been achieved despite the single market initiative. Manufacturing trade among the original six members has actually declined since the 1970s and stagnated since the 1980s among the others (Lafay, 1997, p. 133). Prices still vary enormously between countries, up to 90 per cent for the same model car. Between 1972 and 1986 the top 100 firms increased market share from 24 to 29.5 per cent. The single market and currency stimulated mergers and fusions, giving advantage to larger firms with transnational plant and outlets, but they were more likely to be national or trans-Atlantic than European (Salesse, 1997, pp. 170–4). There has been no convergence of firm structures, export propensity or unemployment rates among members (Pivetti, 1998). Inflation has been lowered, but there is little convergence of business cycles or long-term interest rates. Economists have long known that the EC was not an 'optimum currency area' (Eichengreen and Frieden, 1994). Regulation is better directed at the national or international level.

The EC regime combines free trade with restrictive monetary and fiscal policies embodied in the famous Maastricht convergence criteria. Interest rates have to be kept relatively high and budgetary deficits low to maintain price stability. But one size interest rate and budgetary deficit cannot fit all economies and they are intended to be deflationary, dampening economic activity. This deflationary pressure, first transmitted from the German Bundesbank to other members through the 1979 Exchange Rate Mechanism, is now institutionalized in the single currency (Moss and Michie, 1998). The convergence criteria dampened growth and increased average unemployment from 9 per cent in 1988 to 12 per cent in the mid-1990s.

The minimal efficiency gains from free trade were almost entirely offset by the losses due to restrictive fiscal and monetary policy. An econometric analysis comparing EC members with OECD non-members from 1951 to 1989 shows a loss of 20 per cent in per capita income for the former – up to 8 per cent of the annual increase of non-members if unemployment and international trade effects are considered – which was especially severe for France, Italy, Denmark and the Netherlands, and an annual 4.7 per cent – even more if indirect effects are included – increment of the unemployment rate (Friedman, Forthcoming). Interest rates in the EC were higher than in the larger OECD. Following the Germans, they were unresponsive to unemployment especially after the linkage with the D-mark in the ERM in 1979. In other words, the economic performance of EC members has been mediocre when compared to that of other OECD or Asian nations (Van Paridon, 1996).

Academic Europhilia: a sociology of knowledge

Why is academic opinion so one-sided on this issue? Perhaps one should begin with a generic analysis of modern academics as a hybrid of Gramsci's organic and traditional intellectuals. They are a stratum that is employed in varying degrees in reproducing capitalist social relations but are only effective insofar as they maintain an independent scientific or even critical stance (cf. Walker, 1979) Though many established academics were initially radicalized in the student movement of the 1960s, they do not generally identify with labour and the working class, and usually prefer the 'soft left' reformist and non-materialistic politics of ecology, feminism, and the EC (cf. Hobsbawm, 1977, pp. 253–65). Their class position and attitude may vary depending on national politics, the paradigms of their discipline (political scientists are usually less market-oriented than economists) and the class position and aspirations of their student and research clients.[4]

In the US where the discipline was founded, EC studies were supportive of efforts to build an integrated regional economy and structure to serve as a bulwark against Communism. The dominant paradigm among political scientists inherited from Progressivism was pluralistic interest group functionalism (Olson, 1965, pp. 111–22). The supranational European state was seen by functionalists – as also by Jean Monnet – arising as 'spillover' from economic groups pursuing their interests in new transnational institutions (Haas, 1959). This interest group model was sometimes supplemented or replaced with the paradigm of classical economics that foresaw market forces destroying remaining national regulations and barriers. There was no real conception of class, politics or the state that might structure interests or markets, transcend them or order their priority (cf. Olson, 1965).

The British – as Monnet used to complain – were more empirical than the Americans, but they became no less apologetic. EC studies became a growth industry once Britain joined in 1973. Students and teachers looking for a more relevant subject abandoned traditional disciplines for 'multidisciplinary' European studies. New positions and research programmes were funded by the European Commission and the Economic and Social Research Council. In the 1980s the 'soft left', discouraged by Mrs Thatcher's successful attack on the welfare state, turned to Jacques Delors and his promise of a social dimension for the EC. Support for the EC could be justified as an internationalist blow against Mrs Thatcher's strident nationalism. In any event, the 'soft left', very influential among teachers of EC studies, had concluded that globalization had destroyed possibilities of obtaining social welfare within the confines of the nation state.

Treaty foundations: law and history

Few writers have underscored the liberal market foundations of the EC. Alan Milward (1992), the leading historian of its commercial origins, concluded that it was designed to meet the mercantilist and welfarist objectives of member states. He exaggerated their commitment to income redistribution in the 1950s and failed to distinguish between the ECSC and prior designs for a common market, which had a strong regulatory component, from the Treaty of Rome, which was very market-oriented. Partners had always assumed that the removal of tariffs would be accompanied by common regulations on wages, employment and social policy (Milward, 1992, pp. 189–98). Even the preliminary Spaak Report on the common market featured funds for reconversion and retraining and warned of the danger of deflation.

The actual treaty represented the triumph of the liberal conceptions of the Dutch and Germans backed by major employer associations and producers in all states over the interventionism of the French. The driving political force were governing Christian Democrats and Socialists for whom Europe served the function of trade-mark, substitution and alibi, a way to justify support for market-oriented policies at home forced by the anti-Communist Cold War with a patina of social reformism and international brotherhood (Moss, forthcoming).

The French originally submitted a memorandum calling for a highly planned and regulated European economy. Many French firms and interest groups feared competition, but the pro-European Mollet could count on the support of Socialists, Christian Democrats and most liberals and radicals. The French employer association wanted to seize the opportunity of competition to undermine national regulations and social protection. Mollet at first posed unacceptable conditions regarding this protection, but backed down after the abortive Suez expedition and Hungarian uprising demonstrated the danger of French isolation from her partners. The turning point came when Mollet conceded to the Germans that social protection would have to depend primarily upon market conditions. Negotiations were hastily concluded. To get parliamentary approval Mollet greatly exaggerated the concessions he had won. He never imagined the treaty would be implemented in detail. The signatories did not realize that they were creating a new liberal economic order with primary jurisdiction limiting the sovereignty of member states (Moss and Michie, 1998, pp. 160–1).

The best way to understand the Community is to begin with a legal analysis of its founding treaties. Article 2 of the Treaty of Rome lists its aims as harmonious and balanced growth, rising living standards and stability. The primary means for achieving these aims is the creation of a single competitive marketplace on the model of the domestic market (Kapteyn *et al.*, 1989, p. 76). The treaty incorporates the economic assumption that free trade leads to a reduction in costs and to increased productivity and wages. Rules are to be interpreted without prejudice to the system of property, but no policies except perhaps those of agriculture must be allowed to distort competition.

The other method stipulated in the treaty to achieve its aims is the progressive approximation of economic and monetary policy among the member states, but this does not authorize the creation of European institutions to regulate the market or promote a single policy. Under article 104 each member state was to pursue the economic policy needed to assure a balance of payments and maintain confidence in the currency while taking care to insure a high level of employment and stable level of prices. Unlike the Spaak Report, which noted the twin dangers of deflation and inflation, the treaty seeks to hold down prices. The emphasis is on the harmonization of economic and monetary policy rather than counter-cyclical policies. The treaty contains provision for neutralizing the trade effects of devaluations, which by lowering interest rates had set up growth cycles in France and Italy. The European Court (ECJ) held in 1977 that floating exchange rates were in breach of the obligation under article 105 to coordinate monetary policy (Snyder, 1996, p. 96). Trade interdependence was expected to limit the effectiveness of national economic and monetary policy. Implicit in the logic of the treaty was the goal of fixed exchange rates leading to a single currency.

The liberalism of the Treaty of Rome was not applied with full force until the single market initiative was made possible by the neo-liberal revolution of the 1980s. Until then the Commission charged with development of the common market had to make accommodations with the neo-mercantilism of member states regarding capital mobility, non-quantitative restrictions on trade, state aids, public procurement and monopolies. Special arrangements were made to allow state aids with France and Italy, which flouted the obligation to notify. Public utilities, the major sector for public procurement, were exempted from new regulations. Article 67 had spoken of ending exchange controls only to the extent necessary for the functioning of the common market. Under the directives of 1960 and 1962, nations could still invoke safeguard measures to control short-term financial flows. Freedom of movement for capital was first adopted as a principle in the 1987 Single European Act (SEA) and implemented by directive in 1990 (Oliver and Baché, 1989).

The SEA aimed to achieve the four freedoms, of goods, services, labour and capital, which, with the exception of the latter, were inscribed in the original treaty. Arising from the liberal turnabout of Mitterrand, the act reflected the collapse of interventionist policies in the major states. Liberalization has been a cumulative process in Europe with the common market forcing deregulation upon member states, which then pressed for more deregulation in the EC. In his shuttle diplomacy Mitterrand found a common denominator in the desire to complete the internal market. The idea was taken up in 1985 by the new president Delors, appointed by Mitterrand, and by Lord Cockfield, a Thatcher appointee to the Commission. Cockfield drafted a white paper that contained 300 specific proposals for eliminating barriers to competition – physical, technical and fiscal. To remove barriers the Commission relied on the principle of the mutual recognition of standards, first announced by the European Court in *Cassis de Dijon* (1978), the setting of technical standards by non-governmental bodies and a minimalist approach – only the 'essential requirements' – to the harmonization of health and safety standards (Cockfield, 1994; Moravcsik, 1991).

The SEA made it possible to harmonize national regulations by qualified majority rather than the previous unanimity. In the absence of harmonization the principle of mutal recognition obtained. Under this principle no state could invoke its own standards to bar goods that were marketable in an exporting member state. This meant that the lowest level of regulation, usually that which imposed the least cost, would prevail. Regulations not notified by the Commission by 1992 were to be subject to mutual recognition; in 1992 the Commission failed to notify. A 'race to the bottom' of national standards presumably occurred in many areas.

The Commission requested two reports from economists on the single market. Both reports predicted that the removal of barriers would reduce cost, which would increase demand, competition, productivity and growth. Both also acknowledged the need for macroeconomic stimulation and for special funds to reduce the regional inequalities caused by the increased competition (Cecchini, 1988; Padoa-Schioppa, 1987). The Cecchini Report attempted to quantify the benefits of market deregulation, predicting five million more jobs, 7 per cent supplementary growth and 'an upward trajectory of growth through the next century' (Cecchini, 1988, p. xviii). Cecchini's figures, which represented the views of leading experts, were wildly overoptimistic, combining static and dynamic gains and ignoring the negative effects of competitive efficiency on protected jobs and wages.

The Maastricht Treaty by establishing a single currency with an independent bank committed to price stability further restricted the economic functions of the EC to those of the liberal state. Article 3 defines its guiding principles as those of stable prices, sound public finances and monetary conditions and a sustainable balance of payments. Article 2 lists among its tasks the promotion of a high level of employment and of social protection, economic and social cohesion and solidarity among member states, which are also presented as aims of national economic policy in article 102a. However, the interventionism implicit in article 2 is severely constrained by EMU convergence criteria on budget deficit, debt and inflation and by the requirements in article 3a that economic and monetary policy be conducted 'in accordance with the principle of an open market economy with free competition' and that price stability be the primary aim of monetary policy.

Judicial enforcement: the new liberal order

EC treaties incorporated capitalist and free market ideology. The ECJ found that the treaties confer fundamental rights to property and enterprise and to equal treatment before the law, rights which limit governmental intervention (Mertens de Wilmar, 1993, II, 13–14). Law is much better at knocking down barriers to free trade than at erecting new protection. It was a main vector of capitalism in doing away with the remnants of the feudal and mercantilist state in early modern Europe. Courts of general jurisdiction as opposed to administrative courts are better designed to establish universal rules and poorly qualified to evaluate individual or collective exceptions that are usually required by social or industrial intervention, measures of constructive integration.

The emphasis in the treaties was on negative integration, the removal of discriminatory barriers in the marketplace – tariffs, monopolies, state aids, and safety and technical standards – rather than the creation of new institutions and enactment of constructive welfare measures (cf. Tinbergen, 1965, pp. 77–7, with Pinder, 1969). Much of the negative integration specified by the treaty was found to be either directly applicable in law, such as the bar against quantitative restrictions, or self-executory by the Commission in matters of competition, state aid, public procurement, and so forth.

Provisions for positive integration such as industrial or employment policy were either absent from the treaty or so vague and undefined as to require specific unanimous action from the Council of Ministers (Council), which was the case for the common policies of agriculture, transport and commerce. Actions under article 175 for the failure of the Community to act were far rarer than actions to overturn state regulation; even where the ECJ found failure it could not command the detail of action to be taken (Hartley, 1994, pp. 340–1, 393–415). In any event, the ECJ held that treaty provisions for industrial, transport or social policy – its upward harmonization by member states under article 117 – were too vague, undefined or unsubstantial to be justiciable (Kapteyn *et al.*, 1989, p. 82; Szyszcak, 1994, pp. 315, 325).

With its doctrine of direct effect, the supremacy of European law, preemption and absorption, the ECJ was a powerful instrument for trade integration and national deregulation (Weiler, 1993). Doubtless, if the Treaty of Rome were to be more than an intergovernmental agreement, the ECJ had to ensure uniform application of the law in the member states. Measures that were clear, precise and self-evident were held to have direct effect in national law. The instrument for achieving this uniformity was the preliminary ruling under 177. *Van Gend en Loos* (1963) found that individuals had the right to challenge national regulations in state court under European law. By enmeshing the state courts in the application of European law, the ECJ made the selective application of EC legislation impossible.

The ECJ held European law to be supreme even as against subsequent state legislation. Under the doctrine of preemption national law was precluded in areas of EC competence even in the absence of specific European law. The most extreme extension of jurisdiction was the doctrine of absorption that prevents national states from exercising their jurisdiction where it impinges upon a area of EC competence. The doctrine of implied powers embodied in article 235 by which the EC can assume powers not provided in the treaty if necessary to attain its objectives is an open-sesame to the expansion of Community power (Weiler, 1991, pp. 2413–17).

This exercise of EC judicial power is not checked by any countervailing doctrine of enumerated powers as in the US constitution. The doctrine of subsidiarity written into Maastricht is not very restrictive of EC jurisdiction. The restriction that the EC shall take action only if the objectives of the action cannot be sufficiently achieved by member states and can by reason of the scale or effects of the action be better achieved by the Community only applied to areas not within its exclusive competence, which is very broad. In any event, article 3b is probably too general and political to be justiciable. For this reason the Commissioner from Britain Leon Brittan (1994, p. 94) proposed a body of national parliamentarians to act as guardians of states' rights. There is an absence of an identifiable jurisprudence of states' rights. Judges appointed to the court drawn from among experts on European law are naturally inclined to expand its frontiers. They have a 'certain idea of Europe' (Judge Pascatore cited in Salesse, 1996, p. 58), which overrides other considerations. The anonymity of decisions and absence of dissenting opinions makes it impossible to identify judicial parties as in the US. This may make the law more magisterial but also more removed and remote from the public.

Judicial activism in the EC may not pose as much danger as it might in the US to states' rights because member states have the power to reverse judicial decisions. The judicial activism of the 1960s and 1970s may have substituted for the inactivity of Council, but nothing was done to limit the scope of judicial power. In any event, there is a tradition of the *acquis communautaire* that makes it very difficult for Council to reverse laws or ECJ decisions. Once the market is deregulated it becomes nearly impossible to reregulate it.

It is not only in the margins of legislation where courts ordinarily decide that the judicial bias against national regulation operates. The ECJ's judgment in *Cassis de Dijon* that Germany could not use its own compositional standard for alcoholic drinks to bar the sale of French cassis and that member states more broadly could not use their own standards to prohibit the sale of goods that were marketable elsewhere in the EC was a policy decision. The ECJ was careful however to qualify it with an even more peremptory ruling that states could prohibit goods that failed to meet 'mandatory requirements' of health, fair trade and consumer protection. The impact of *Cassis de Dijon*, endorsed by the Commission as the principle of mutual recognition, was limited however by Council, which incorporated in its policy the reservations of producer and consumer groups (Alter and Meunier-Aitsahalia, 1994).

The failure of constructive integration

The only constructive policy area of the Treaty of Rome that demanded detailed implementation was agriculture. Contrary to the principle of free competition, the EC subsidized farm prices and exports, protecting them from outside competition. De Gaulle made the establishment of the policy a condition of French membership. Since all members gave some form of assistance to farmers, a common policy was indicated. But it was only achieved after many years with marathon bargaining sessions – stopping the clock on New Years' Eve – and threats of a French walk-out. It raised agricultural productivity and incomes, but also created greater inequalities in the countryside, benefiting the wealthy farmers and yielding huge surpluses. Still, if agriculture and the food industry became the only self-sufficient sector it was because it benefitted from the only truly interventionist policy in the EC (Bourry, 1993; Dinan, 1994, ch. 11).

Other areas of constructive integration were not so fortunate. The treaty did not contain explicit provision for social policy. Under article 117 member states were to promote improved working conditions and standards of living for workers, but this was to follow largely from the functioning of the common market. The protocol for France requiring upward harmonization of over-time pay was forgotten. The sole social prescription of the treaty concerned equal wages for equal work between men and women. The social dimension of the law was largely restricted to cross-border mobility of European citizens, who constitute a tiny minority of migrant workers in the EC; the conferral of equal social rights to such workers did not increase their numbers, which remained at about half of one per cent of the population (*Le Monde*, 21 May 1997, p. iv). The first action programme on social policy by the Commission issued in 1972 called for the upward harmonization of labour standards and new European forms of collective representation. The meager results of this enthusiasm were two minor directives on collective redundances in 1977 and transfers of undertakings in 1979 (Ross, 1993; Streeck, 1995).

The social goals of the EC were confided in article 3 to the European Investment Bank and European Social Fund. The bank was to contribute to the balanced and steady development of the common market, which meant aiding less developed regions and projects of common interest. It played a limited role in the 1960s, making 1.8 billion dollars available for the modernization of transport, chemicals, coal and machine tools, mostly in Italy. Thereafter the bank used its funds almost exclusively for purposes of regional development – 7.8 billion ecu for that purpose in 1987. Aside from references to regional disparities the treaty had not made provision for regional policy. This changed with the creation of the European Regional Development Fund in 1975, a side payment for

British membership. Thereafter it became the token for social justice and redistribution in the EC (Kapteyn *et al.*, 1989, p. 214).

The Social Fund was to contribute to improving employment opportunities and raising the standard of living, specifically by increasing geographical and occupational mobility. Most of its funds went to assist with the re-settlement of Italian workers who were already re-employed. During the years 1972 to 1976 the fund was expanded by 500 per cent and used to assist the hard-core unemployed. The Fund reached its peak relative to the EC budget in 1979. Its focus narrowed. In 1988 75 per cent of its 2.8 billion ecu went to young people under 25 and 45.5 per cent to backward regions. As the problem of unemployment deepended, member states were increasingly reluctant to transfer resources to the EC (Kapteyn *et al.*, 1989, pp. 637–41; Taylor, 1983, pp. 204–13).

The treaty provided for a common transport policy. Transportation was treated as a business governed by commercial principles even though article 77 recognized the legitimacy of state aid to fulfil the obligations of public service. The efforts of the Commission to promote competition ran up against the monopolistic practices of member states, which subsidized transport as a public service (Hallstein, 1972, pp. 277–8). Transport policy was mostly concerned with assuring fair terms of competition, removing barriers to carrying by private hauliers and restricting rates within upper and lower limits, the 'two-pronged fork', to avoid monopoly undercutting or overcharging (Holland, 1980, p. 11; Lindberg and Scheinberg, 1970, pp. 163–81).

Public services do not operate under commercial principles. Under French law a public service has the obligation to provide continuous service to all users at equal and reasonable rates. It is also expected by tradition to provide secure and rewarding jobs for its personnel. Article 90 of the treaty stipulated that public services would be subject to terms of fair competition to the extent that they did not interfere with the performance of their mission, which must not be contrary to Community interest. The Commission reversed the burden of proof, making public services the exception rather than the rule. Services must justify their mission and prove that restrictions on competition are necessary to fulfil it. France has had to abandon state monopolies in the import of tobacco, alcohol, gas, electricity and petroleum and France Télécom its monopoly of communication links. The substitution by the EC and ECJ of the duty of 'universal service' modelled on the divestiture of AT&T does not preserve the integrity of the public service (Cartelier, 1996; Debène and Raymundie, 1996; *Le Monde*, 24 June 1997, p. II; Monnier, 1996).

Directives on competition in the public services threaten the integrity of such motors of growth and innovation as the SNCF, the French railways, and EDF, electricity and gas. Only state investment could have produced the technological and commercial success of the TGV, the high-speed railway, in France. French rail also fulfils an obligation to provide service to peripheral regions at the same rates as it charges on the better travelled lines. It has been forced to separate the management of infrastructure from rolling stock, making it more difficult to fulfil its mission. EDF, which has been perhaps the most socially efficient and innovative electrical and gas utility in Europe, must open up its service to the largest consumers – from 20 to 33 per cent of its market – to competition (*Le Monde*, 12 June 1996).

State aids were a major instrument of national social and industrial policy. Such aid including tax relief and even equity investment under certain conditions insofar as they affect inter-state trade is incompatible with the common market. Article 92 allows for limited exceptions and a wide degree of discretion for the Commission to help poorer and undeveloped regions, to remedy a serious disturbance in the economy of a member state and to facilitate development of certain economic activities or economic areas. States are obligated to notify the Commission about their aid. In the early years there was little enforcement. Special agreements were negotiated for shipbuilding and the South of Italy, which gave up notifying the Commission (Holland, 1980, p. 14).

It is difficult to find coherence in Commission policy on state aids, but it is not sympathetic to long-term industrial projects. It has tended to be harsher on aid to a sector or industry than regional assistance. It has been more favourable to short-term relief that reduces capacity than restructuring programmes that would expand it. It is been ruthless towards state aid for nationalized industries in which social and industrial criteria have been sacrificed for the need to reduce capacity and thus the size of the public sector (Pernin, 1996). On the other hand, since the SEA and Maastricht, it has been compelled to consider needs for research and development, for environmental protection and the promotion of small business (Evans and Martin, 1991).

Enforcement was stepped up in the 1980s. Until then only 20 to 30 plans for state aid were notified annually and only one to three denied. The number rose to 200 notified and 20 rejected in the late 1980s (Padoa-Schioppa, 1987, p. 33). The Commission encouraged other states to make complaints and required refunds from companies that were given aid contrary to law (Goyder, 1988, ch. 21). Many governments, arguing the sanctity of contracts, resisted. In return for the recapitalization of Renault the French government had to promise to impose the same requirements of profitability on the firms it aided as those used in the private sector (Cohen, 1995, p. 42). Structural funds do not compare in importance to state aid; even after the 1988 Delors II Packet they were only one-fifth of the value of state aids (Martin, 1996, p. 89). Constricted in the 1980s, state aid has risen since 1992 to 43 billion ecu with the most coming from Germany and the highest per head from Italy (*Le Monde*, 18 April 1997).

Public procurement of goods and services was an even more important instrument of national economic policy, serving regional, technological, and employment objectives. It constituted 15 per cent of GDP of which only 0.14 per cent went to non-nationals. Directives providing for competitive bidding in public supply and public works in the 1970s did little to alter the situation. New directives passed under the SEA, which included the public utilities left out by the first ones, provided for monitored compliance, review procedures and open awards based on the criteria of the lowest price or most economically advantageous. The Commission negotiated with member states in 1989 to end the use of procurement for regional purposes (Martin, 1996).

The new policy was reinforced by ECJ decisions such as *Ireland* (1989) that held that technical standards could not be set so narrowly as to restrict supply to nationals. In *Du Pont de Namours Italiana* (1990) the ECJ voided an Italian law requiring that public authorities purchase at least 30 per cent of their goods from the Italian South on grounds that it was a quantitative restriction on inter-state trade. This law provided 24 billion ecu in aid to the South compared to only one billion that comes from the European regional fund. Yet, the ECJ ruled that the need for unrestricted competition preempted regional considerations in the award of public contracts (Martin and Stehmann, 1991).

Competitive tendering may be profitable for business but is not necessarily socially efficient. Private contractors usually seek to maximize profits sometimes at the expense of quality and service and almost always at that of wages and working conditions. The competitive tendering of public services in Britain has cost severe job losses and wage cuts (Martin, 1996, p. 89). It is unrealistic to expect that public authorities awarding contracts will not give consideration to proximity and effects on employment and economic development. Even by adopting a competitive approach that makes little allowance for social realities, the EC has made negligible impact on procurement practices (Martin, 1996, pp. 45–8).

The treaty did not provide for industrial policy. The Committee on Medium-Term Economic Policy, set up in 1964 to consider the coordination of national economies, discussed the technological gap with the US, but the Commission under German influence ruled out positive intervention for sectors or nations. The French sought changes in commercial and tax law to facilitate transnational mergers. The Commission responded in 1966 by proposing a European Company Statute on the German model, a proposal that is still on the table after 30 years. In 1970 the Colonna Report urged support for an industrial policy to encourage industrial cooperations and mergers in order to narrow the productivity and technology gap with the US, but it was opposed by Germany. Instead of considering a new French proposal for a voluntarist and protectionist policy in 1983, the Commission approved the privatization programme begun in Britain that would eliminate the motors of industrial investment in Europe (Denton, 1969; Hallstein, 1972, pp. 194–6; Hayward, 1995, pp. 7–8; Holland, 1980, pp. 23, 26, 75; Monnier, 1996).

A main purpose of the SEA was to overcome the technological deficit. A title was introduced to strengthen the scientific and technological base of European industry by encouraging research and development in firms, research centres and universities. This provision ran up against the reluctance of member states to transfer resources to the Community. Only 4 billion ecu went to the framework programme and Eureka, which was actually an inter-governmental programme, as against an estimated 67 billion spent for industry by the member states in 1990. Another estimate puts EC aid to R&D at 4.5 per cent of total R&D aid. Restricted to pre-competitive projects, the policy was vitiated by the bias towards deregulation, a tough mergers policy, and public purchasing controls. The EU lacks the structural pre-requisites for launching its own companies: research networks, public procurement, fiscal intervention, promotion, and public sector ideology and leadership. It was not accidental that more has been accomplished by inter-governmental arrangements like Eureka and Airbus in this domain than under the EC (Cohen, 1995; Saint-Martin, 1996; Sharp, 1993).

The Treaty of Maastricht gave Council power under article 130 to take measures by unanimous vote to enhance the competitiveness of EC industry, to speed up structural adjustment, to assist small and medium-sized firms, and to foster cooperation and the better exploitation of innovation among firms. The EC is supposed to contribute to the achievement of these objectives through the policies it pursues under other provisions of treaty. Since the EC was able to act previously under implied powers, the new article may limit rather than extend its industrial competence. How the EC can assist individual firms without violating principles of fair competition remains to be seen (Bourgeois and Demeret, 1995, pp. 72–3). Industrial policy is bound by the restrictions set in the Bangemann Memorandum approved by Council in 1990, which relied on the private sector to make necessary adjustments and limited EC intervention to the pre-competitive environment – research, training and infrastructure. Industrial policy has been stymied by the unanimity principle and by the anti-interventionism expressed by the Commission in its communication of 14 November 1994.

Delors' 1993 White Paper on *Growth, Competitiveness and Employment* tried to link it with regional policy with an ambitious 400 billion ecu scheme for trans-European networks in transport, energy and telecommunications. The aim was to create fifteen million new jobs by 2000 while improving infrastructure. A new European Investment Fund set up in 1994 was to provide transnational finance, but it was never given more than nominal capitalization. The 24 projects planned by Delors were reduced to 14 and left to wither. Led by the Germans, Council has repeatedly refused to finance even minimalist versions of the trans-European networks (Coates and Santer, 1996; Holland, 1996; *Le Monde*, 16 October 1996).

Under articles 3a and 102a of the Maastricht Treaty the 'open market economy with free competition, favouring an efficient allocation of resources', that is the classical Smithian model, has become the guiding principle, not merely a privileged instrument, of the EU. When combined with the principle of proportionality in article 3b this means that nearly all regulatory polices except perhaps agriculture must give clear indications that exemptions from the principle of undistorted competition are justified (Snyder, 1996, pp. 39–40). Already under the old treaty the ECJ had subjected nearly all intervention to the competitive test. In *Continental Can* (1971) it held that a company cannot abuse its dominant position with commercial arrangements that substantially reduce competition. No attention need be paid to the usefulness of anti-competitive conduct. The Merger Regulation issued in 1989 allowed some consideration for technical and economic progress provided consumers benefit and there is no hindrance to competition. The Commission did not consider competitive efficiency when prohibiting the proposed take-over of a Canadian aircraft maker De Havilland by ATR, a French–Italian consortium (Bourgeois and Demeret, 1995, pp. 70–89).

Industrial development has not been assisted by European commercial policy, which is among the freest in the world. Under article 11 the EC must contribute to the abolition of restrictions on international trade and the lowering of customs barriers. Member states under article 18 agreed to reduce duties below the level which they could expect from a customs union. The assumption was that the free internal market alone would prepare firms to face international competition. In the debates between the protectionist French and Italians and free trade Germans and Benelux, the latter usually won especially after the accession to membership of Britain. The US led the charge to open up the European market in the GATT rounds. The Kennedy Round concluded in 1967 achieved cuts of 32 per cent. By 1972 the average tariff on manufactured items was 8.2 per cent. Member states still retained export credits and there was greater protection for textiles. Today after the liberalizing Uruguay Round the average tariff is about 6 per cent, which is one-half that of the US and one-third that of Japan. The EC still disposes of anti-dumping duties, which are subject to the competitive test, and some voluntary export restraint agreements but not the unilateral system of dealing with unfair trade practices that the US under section 301 enjoys (Hine, 1985).

The myth of the social dimension

Despite the obvious market bias of the treaties social democrats hoped that the existence of common European institutions would give them the power to organize the market (Philip, 1957, pp. 250–4). There was indeed an attempt in the 1960s and 1970s to coordinate national planning, industrial and monetary policy under Robert Marjolin and his Medium-Term Economic policy Committee, but the Germans were opposed to planning and the French to a common currency. The medium-term committee was phased out in 1975.

When François Mitterrand came to power in France in 1981 he concentrated on building socialism in France with nationalizations and increased social benefits and tried to ignore the competitive requirements of the EC. Like social democrats before him he spoke vaguely of obtaining 'a social space' for workers in the EC. As he abandoned his socialist policies under the pressure of Germany and the ERM, he came to look at EC construction as a substitute and alibi for his abandon. In 1984 he fixed upon completion of the single market, removing non-tariff barriers to trade, as the next phase to which the appointment of Delors to head the Commission added a fillip.

Delors was not a social democrat but a pro-European, Christian Democrat, who had helped as finance minister to reverse socialist policies. He valued the market as a guarantor of individual autonomy and responsibility and creator of wealth, without which there could be no social improvement. With his belief in the Catholic doctrine of subsidiarity, he preferred voluntary cooperation and social dialogue to state intervention and qualitative issues, working time and conditions, to conflictual and materialistic wage issues. His vision of social policy contained an adequate level of social protection, rights of information and consultation, professional training and social dialogue, particularly on technology and work organization. But he was more concerned with obtaining consensus than reform and his social policy was undercut by competitive market reforms (cf. Ross, 1993).

The SEA implementing the single market initiative extended EC competence over health and safety, the first industrial sphere to be regulated by the nineteenth-century state and one in which employers had a concern for the standardization of products and machines. It also charged the Commission with fostering a dialogue between management and labour at European level which could lead to formal agreements. Discussions at the Val Duchesse created the illusion of bargaining. Neither employers nor unions were authorized to conclude agreements at a European level. UNICE, the employers' association, opposed in principle to EC social regulation, interrupted the dialogue.

Seeking to rally the British trade unions and Labour Party behind Europe, Delors talked of the need for a basic set of social rights at the trade union conference in 1988. He took up a draft for the Community Charter of Fundamental Social Rights proposed by the European Trade Union Confederation (ETUC) but watered it down to accommodate the British, who then refused to sign (Silvia, 1991). Hedged with a subsidiarity clause that requires the conformity of all measures with national practice, the Charter of Fundamental Rights of Workers was careful not to expand EC competence. It was merely a statement of principles without the legal force promised by Delors and demanded by the European Parliament. Progress on implementation was impeded by the British veto, with only six of 24 legislative proposals, mostly on health and safety, being adopted by 1991 (Ross, 1993, p. 52; Streeck, 1995). At Maastricht ministers tried to extend majority voting to other social matters, but once again the British negotiators eviscerated the legislation and then rejected it.

The social protocol to the treaty of Maastricht extended qualified majority voting to laws on working conditions, information and consultation and equal opportunities, but excluded questions of pay and strikes and limited the new legislation with a subsidiarity clause and a stipulation that they were only to provide minimal protection. This latter limitation is a departure from article 117, which calls for the improvement of conditions by member states, and could be used to undermine national social legislation (Shaw, 1994; Szyszczak, 1994). The negotiators showed their dislike of state intervention by providing for negotiated law, laws resulting from negotiations between labour and management and directives implemented by such agreements. When faced with the Commission's proposal for European Works Councils, the last great campaign of the Delors' presidency, the ETUC and UNICE opted for direct legislation. In eight years there have only been two negotiated directives, one according the right of parental leave, the other giving equal treatment to part-timers, but it is questionable whether the encouragement of part-time employment is in labour's interest.

Proposals for European works councils had been circulating since the 1970s. The draft Fifth Directive in 1972 and European Company Statute of 1975 had provided for employee participation on the supervisory board and European works councils. The Vredeling proposal of 1980, limited to multinationals, offered existing local employee representatives rights of information and consultation on a range of issues. It was defeated in parliament and council by a barrage of employee lobbying (Devos, 1989). The legislation finally approved in 1993 under the social protocol was a weakened version of Vredeling, more European but also less regulatory. Works councils were to be set up by negotiations between employees and employers and by default by national legislation, which had to respect minimal conditions of representation and consultation on management decisions likely to have serious consequences for employees (Hall, 1992; Hall and Gold, 1994).

The legislation made no provision for enforcement, which depends on national law. There is a question whether workers have an effective remedy against a company that has a headquarters in another member state. That was the problem raised when Renault failed to notify and consult workers in Belgium about the closing of their plant in Vilvoorde. Workers in Brussels and Nanterre France were able to sue the company under national law, but they received only nominal satisfaction. The French appeals court held that Renault had to provide effective consultation to its works council before closing the plant (*Le Monde*, 9 May 1997). The fracas caused by Vilvoorde pushed the Commission into strengthening worker consultation provisions of proposals for the ECS and national works councils, which made no progress.

Delors raised the profile of the ETUC and in return obtained its support for the single market and currency. Union leaders in the British TUC, German DGB and French CFDT were resigned to market regulation. Faced with declining membership, political support and bargaining power at home, they reached out to Delors as a kind of 'Jesus rail' – what you grope for when you are falling down the stairs (Verdun, 1996, pp. 72, 79). Their faith – they are only now beginning to realize – was misplaced. They failed to obtain European collective bargaining and binding commitments from the social charter. By strengthening unions at European and enterprise level the Commission may have diverted unions away from the sectoral level where their power to fix wages is greatest. EC labour policy may actually serve the employer strategy, which is to undermine sectoral solidarity and achieve enterprise and individualized wage setting (Martin, 1995).

EC policy since Maastricht has become increasingly market-oriented. Delors' 1993 White Paper, proposing the trans-European networks, endorsed employer demands for labour flexibility, work-sharing, the diminution of social charges and wage reductions relative to productivity. Council in December 1993 recommended to member states policies of pay moderation beginning with the public sector, decentralized bargaining, controlling social expenditure and more flexible forms of work organization. The Commission under Santer has adopted the monetarist logic of EMU, recommending budgets cuts and deflation as the way to stimulate investment and create jobs (Coates and Santer, 1996). The Commission has virtually abandoned the legislative approach to social policy, relying more on non-binding recommendations (Streeck, 1995).

The employment chapter of the 1997 Treaty of Amsterdam revising Maastricht provided for the coordination of national employment policy under pre-existing powers that subordinate it to general economic policy, which is deflationary. In response to French demands to put employment at the top of the agenda, the European Council adopted a resolution based on a British memo that would make job creation depend on market conditions and a reduction of taxes and social charges. The French failed to obtain any extension of EC competence or expenditure for employment (*Le Monde*, 18 June 1997). Under the Amsterdam Treaty members have been required to submit national plans for job creation, but they have been defined in the neoliberal terms of the British memo, that is, supply-side measures of training and business incentives that respect the stability criteria of Maastricht, and had no impact on divergent national policies (*Analyses & Documents economiques*, CGT, no. 81, Dec. 1999, pp. 4–8).

Links of the social to the democratic deficit

The social deficit of the EC is connected to the democratic deficit. Social policy requires democratic pressure and legitimation. But this process is thwarted by the institutional basis of the EC, the reliance on Commission initiative, inter-governmental assent, and a subaltern parliament. The complexity and elitist bias of decision-making makes it difficult to activate popular movements and opinion over European issues. Europe is regarded as a rich man's club for a self-appointed elite; it has always been regarded with suspicion by working people in most countries (Lindberg and Scheinberg, 1970, pp. 264–75). Decision-making tends to be technical, consensual and depoliticized. The public lacks the familiar signposts of Right and Left, government and opposition, that structures politics in their own country. Maastricht in an attempt to reduce the deficit has aggravated it by making the legislative system even more complex and opaque, providing no less than six legislative procedures from consultation to assent, with Council, whose decisions are largely unaccountable before public opinion, having the final say (Neunreither, 1994).

The European Parliament is not about to replace national parliaments as a source of legitimacy and power. European elections have been called 'second-order' with a low turnout, an incentive to punish national incumbents and preoccupation with domestic issues. Abstention in European elections has continued to grow since 1979 reaching over half of the electorate in 1999. Elections are demotivating because they do not lead to a change of government or tangible legislation. The lack of transnational media and a common language renders the work of the parliament obscure. There is no party discipline in voting, with cross-cutting national, regional and sectoral interests deciding the result. Legislation controlled by rapporteurs is often passed without discussion (Jacobs *et al.*, 1995, pp. 7, 90–3).

The complex procedure seems to demand a consensual mode. The working majority was for a long time a centrist alliance between Socialists, who ran the gamut between the neoliberalism of Tony Blair to the interventionism of Jospin, with Christian Democrats, who were more openly business-friendly. It resembled the crosscutting class and regional consensual politics of postwar Belgium (De Winter, 1993) rather than the clearer left–right split of France and Germany. The only strong interventionists were on the extreme Left, which was divided and little committed to Europe. The centrist consensus avoiding political cleavage gave resolutions an idealistic deracinated character, fostering the illusion that integration was ideologically neutral (Ladrech, 1996, pp. 292–6).

In the byzantine corridors of EC power business lobbyists have a distinct advantage over labour or other popular organizations. They have the know-how and resources to master all the stops in the complex decision-making process through the Commission, Council and Parliament. The Commission depends heavily on interest groups for the content of legislation. UNICE is the best financed lobby in Brussels. Associations of business vastly outnumber those of labour with 20 unions facing 332 associations of industry (Streeck and Schmitter, 1991, pp. 136–8). The consultative Economic and Social Committee on which labour is well represented has accomplished little. While labour is divided on national and political grounds employers are united in opposition to European industrial regulation. Their power was seen in the defeat of the 1980 Vredeling proposal on European works councils when they were able to coordinate pressure simultaneously on Christian Democrats in parliament and governments in Council (Devos, 1989, pp. 175–9).

Though its power is diminished, labour is still much better organized for political action on the national rather than on the European level. Unions depend on social norms, ideology and legislation that are not available on the European level where they are divided by linguistic, cultural and political barriers (Lemke and Marks, 1992, p. 16). Whatever unions may have gained from the EC – training schemes, works councils, health and safety legislation – they have lost in spades through EC-sponsored deflation and deregulation. Deregulation may have occurred to some degree without the EC – it was part of a profound reversal – but the EC provided an alibi and justification for governments, particularly social-democratic ones, disinclined to act alone. Rather than accept responsibility for economic and social policy, they chose to tie their hands with EMU.

Many social democrats hope that the discontents created by EMU will induce popular demands for European government such as the French have made, but the idea is anathema to the Germans and other members. There was only limited enthusiasm for extending codecisional powers of Parliament at Amsterdam. Further transfers of state sovereignty to the EU are highly unlikely for many reasons.

First, as we have shown, the EC lacks the constitutional and institutional foundations for an interventionist government. Second, it lacks democratic legitimacy, the primary support and loyalty of a European people or demos. Third, policy disagreements among the major partners, especially Germany, France and Britain, make agreement on new tax or social legislation or macroeconomic policy extremely problematic. Employers will always be able to find a state willing to veto such new proposals. Interventionist measures might also clash with the fundamental competitive law of the EC. Fourth, the prospect of enlargement to the much poorer states of Eastern Europe threatens existing constructive measures such as structural and agricultural funds, not to speak of any attempted extension of them. Finally, states may have reached the limit of their transfer of sovereignty without losing their coherence as constituting bodies for society. They are especially unlikely to yield more control of social and economic policy, which is a main source of their legitimacy.

Conclusion

In view of the failure of constructive integration and the social dimension in the EC, Europeans, but especially the working class, must look primarily to the nation state for their physical security and economic and social welfare. Primary loyalty is everywhere to the member state and only secondarily to the EU, which at best is viewed as an adjunct. Globalization, which can ruin firms, industries and regions, makes the nation state even more important as an instrument of regulation (cf. Garrett, 1995) because it is the strongest bastion of class and democratic solidarity. It is still the principle framework for both the organization and contestation of capitalist hegemony.

To say this is not to deny the pressure of international market forces, but to recognize the power of national governments based on popular coalitions to channel and tame them. The state remains the most powerful institution to regulate markets for the purpose of employment, education, research, health, financial integrity, job training, labour relations, infrastructure and justice. Even with globalization the state has the capacity to secure markets and industry and attract long-term investment. It has no peer as a source of public power for economic governance (Boyer and Drache, 1996). International cooperation in regulating financial flows, launching new technologies or controlling pollution is more necessary than ever, but it can usually be more easily achieved through inter-state cooperation outside the market-oriented framework of the EC.

These basic facts about the EC and nation state have been obscured by a 'lib–lab' Europhilia reigning in academic discussion that views the history, law and institutions of the Community through rose-coloured glasses. Nations have lost some capacity to regulate markets on their own but not as much as many believe. Currency speculation may have made the cost of borrowing for budgetary deficits greater, but reflationary public spending and devaluation can still be effective in reviving growth and employment (Baker *et al.*, 1998). To the extent such policies are subverted by speculators and the forces of capital, socialist governments will have to return to the alternative strategies of nationalization, worker control and redistribution propounded by left socialists and Communists in the 1970s, perhaps more emphatically in the future as a transition to socialism.

Notes

1 The EC created by the Treaty of Rome in 1957 remains the main pillar of the wider European Union (EU) established in 1992 under the Treaty of Maastricht.
2 A quasi-academic critique was Holland (1980). See political critiques by Rocard *et al.* (1973) and in Haack (1983). Trotsky argued against Lenin for the advancement of a United States of Europe. In that vein Ernest Mandel of the Fourth International asserted that the EC was the expression of the multinationals' need for a superstate.
3 This self-doubt was expressed in Haas (1975) and in the proliferation of studies in the 1990s on the directionless complexity of multilevel governance.
4 Eric Olin Wright (Walker, 1979) locates intellectuals in a contradictory class position, but that definition tells us little about the situation of particular academics (cf. Frindjonsdottir, 1987).

Bibliography

Alter, K. and Meunier-Aitsahalia, S. (1994) 'Judicial Politics in the European Community: European Integration and the Pathbreaking *Cassis de Dijon* Decision', *Comparative Political Studies*, 26.
Bairoch, P. (1996) *Mythes et paradoxes de l'histoire économique* (Paris: La Découverte).
Baker, D., Epstein, G. and Pollin, R. (eds) (1998) *Globalization and Progressive Economic Policy* (Cambridge: Cambridge University Press).
Belassa, B. (1975) 'Trade Creation and Trade Diversion in the European Common Market: An Appraisal of the Evidence', in Belassa, B. (ed), *European Economic Integration* (Amsterdam: American Elsevier).
Bossuat, G. (1996) *L'Europe des Français, 1943–1959* (Paris: Publications Sorbonne).
Bourgeois, J. and Demeret, P. (1995) 'The Working of EC Policies in Competition, Industry and Trade', in Buiges, P. *et al.* (eds), *European Policies on Competition, Trade and Industry* (Aldershot: Edgar Elgar).
Bourry, C. (1993) 'Existe-t-il une industrie européenne?', *Etudes et recherches*, ISERES, CGT, no. 131.

Boyer, R. and Drache, D. (eds) (1996) *States against Markets: The Limits of Globalization* (London: Routledge).

Brittan, L. (1994) *The Europe We Need* (London: Hamish Hamilton).

Cartelier, L. (1996) 'Services publics européens entre la théorie économique et droit communautaire' in Cartelier, L. *et al. Critique de la raison communautaire: utilité publique et concurrence dans l'Union européenne* (Paris: Economica).

Cecchini, P. (1988) *The European Challenge, 1992: The Benefits of a Single Market* (Aldershot: Gower).

Coates, K. and Santer, J. (1996) *Dear Commissioner, Will Unemployment Break Europe?* (Nottingham: Spokesman).

Cockfield, Lord (1994) *The European Union: Creating the Single Market* (London: Wiley Chancery).

Cohen, E. (1995) 'National Champions in Search of Mission', in Hayward, J. *Industrial Enterprise and European Integration: From National to International Champions* (Oxford: Oxford University Press).

Cutler, T., Haslam, C., Williams, J. and Williams, K. (1989) *1992: The Struggle for Europe: A Critical Evaluation of the EC* (Oxford: Berg).

Debène, M. and Raymundie, O. (1996) 'Sur le service universel: renouveau du service public ou nouvelle mystification?' in Cartelier, L.

Denton, G. (1969) 'Planning and Integration: Medium-Term Policy as an Instrument of Integration', in Denton, G. *Economic Integration in Europe* (London: Weidenfeld and Nicolson).

Devos, T. (1989) *Multinational Corporations in Democratic Host Countries: US Multinationals and the Vredeling Proposal* (Aldershot: Dartmouth).

De Winter, L. (1993) 'Socialistes belges entre région et Europe', in Telo, M. *De la nation à l'Europe: paradoxes et dilemmes de la social-démocratie* (Brussels: Bruyand).

Dinan, D. (1994) *Ever Closer Union? An Introduction to the European Community* (London: Macmillan).

Eichengreen, B. and Frieden, J. (1994) 'The Political Economy of European Monetary Unification: An Analytical Introduction', in Eichengreen, B. and Frieden, J. (eds), *The Political Economy of European Monetary Unification* (Boulder: Westview Press).

Evans, A. and Martin, S. (1991) 'Socially Acceptable Distortion of Competition: Community Policy on State Aid', *European Law Review,* 16.

Featherstone, K. (1988) *Socialist Parties and European Integration: A Comparative History* (Manchester: Manchester University Press).

Feldstein, M. (1997) 'The Political Economy of the European Economic and Monetary Union: Political Sources of an Economic Liability', *The Journal of Economic Perspectives,* 11.

Fligstein, N. and Brantley, P. (1995) 'The 1992 Single Market Program and the Interests of Business', in Eichengreen, B. *et al.* (eds), *Politics and Institutions in an Integrated Europe* (New York: Springer).

Fontagné, L. *et al.* (1997) 'Trade Patterns Inside the Common Market', *CEPII*, Doc. 97.

Fridjonsdottir, K. (1987) 'The Modern Intellectual: In Power or Disarmed?', in Eyerman, R. *et al.* (eds), *Intellectuals, Universities and the State in Western Modern Societies* (Berkeley: University of California Press).

Friedman, G. (Forthcoming) 'Has European Economic Integration Failed?', in Moss, B. (ed.), *The Triumph of Monetarism in the European Union: Economies, Ideas, Politics* (London: Macmillan).

Garrett, G. (1995) 'Capital Mobility, Trade and the Domestic Politics of Economic Policy', *International Organization*, 49.

Gillingham, J. (1991) *Coal, Steel and the Rebirth of Europe: The Germans and French from Ruhr Conflict to the Economic Community* (Cambridge: Cambridge University Press).

Goyder, D. (1988) *EEC Competition Law* (Oxford: Clarendon).

Haack, W. (1983) 'The Selectivity of Economic Integration Theories: A Comparison of Some Traditional and Marxist Approaches', *Journal of Common Market Studies*, 21.

Haas, E. (1959) *The Uniting of Europe: Political, Economic and Social Forces, 1950–57* (London: Stevens & Sons).

Haas, E. (1975) *The Obsolescence of Regional Integration Theory* (Berkeley: Institute of International Studies).

Hall, M. (1992) 'Behind the European Work Council Directive: The European Commission's Legislative Strategy', *British Journal of Industrial Relations*, 30.

Hall. M. and Gold, M. (1994) 'Statutory European Works Councils: The Final Countdown?', *Industrial Relations Journal*, 25.

Hallstein, W. (1972) *Europe in the Making* (London: George Allen & Unwin).

Hartley, T. (1994) *The Foundations of European Law* (Oxford: Clarendon).

Hayward, J. (1995) 'Europe's Industrial Champions', in Hayward, J. *Industrial Enterprise and European Integration* (Oxford: Oxford University Press).

Hine, C. (1985) *The Political Economy of European Trade: An Introduction to the Trade Policies of the EEC* (London: Harvester).

Hobsbawm, E. (1977) *Revolutionaries: Contemporary Essays* (New York: Quartet).

Holland, S. (1980) *The Uncommon Market* (London: Macmillan).

Holland, S. (1996) *The European Imperative: Social and Economic Cohesion in the 1990s* (Nottingham: Spokesman).

Jacobs, F., Corbett, R. and Shackleton, M. (1995) *The European Parliament* 3rd edn (London: Catermill).

Kapteyn, P., Gormley, L. and Verloren van Thematt, P. (1989) *Introduction to the Law of the European Communities after the Coming into Force of the Single European Act* (Boston: Kluwer).

Ladrech, R. (1996) 'Political Parties in the European Parliament', in Gaffney, J. (ed), *Political Parties and the European Union* (London: Routledge).

Lafay, G. (1997) *L'Euro contre l'Europe* (Paris: Arléa).

Lemke, C. and Marks, G. (1992) 'From Decline to Demise? The Future of Socialism in Europe', in Lemke, C. and Marks, G. (eds), *The Crisis of Socialism in Europe* (London: Duke University Press).

Lindberg, L. and Scheinberg, S. (1970) *Europe's Would-Be Polity* (Englewood Cliffs, NJ: Prentice Hall).

Maier, C. (ed) (1991) *The Cold War: Era of a Divided Continent* (New York: Marcus Wiener).

Martin, A. (1995) *European Institutions and the Europeanization of Trade Unions: Support or Seduction*? (Brussels: ETUI).

Martin, J. (1996) *EC Public Procurement Rules: A Critical Analysis* (Oxford: Clarendon).

Martin, J. and Stehmann, O. (1991) 'Product Market Integration versus Regional Cohesion', *European Law Review*, 16.
Mertens de Wilmar, J. (1993) 'The Case Law of the Court of Justice in Relation to the Review of the Legality of Economic Policy in Mixed Economy Systems', in Snyder, F. (ed), *European Community Law* 2 vols. (Aldershot: Dartmouth).
Milward, A. (1992) *The European Rescue of the Nation State* (London: Routledge).
Monnier, L. (1996) 'Politique économique et raison communautaire', in Cartelier, L.
Moravcsik, A. (1991) 'Negotiating the Single European Act', *International Organization*, 45.
Moravcsik, A. (1998) *The Choice for Europe: Social Purpose and State Power from Messina to Maastricht* (Ithaca: Cornell University Press).
Moss, B. (ed) (forthcoming) *The Triumph of Monetarism in the European Union: Economies, Ideas, Politics* (London: Macmillan)
Moss, B. and Michie, J. (eds) (1998) *The Single European Currency in National Perspective: A Community in Crisis*? (London: Macmillan).
Neunreither, K. (1994) 'The Democratic Deficit of the European Union: Toward Closer Cooperation Between the European Parliament and National Parliaments', *Government and Opposition*, 29.
Oliver, P. and Baché, J.-P. (1989) 'Free Movement of Capital Between the Member States: Recent Developements', *Common Market Law Review*, 26.
Olson, M. (1965) *The Logic of Collective Action: Public Goods and the Theory of Groups* (Cambridge, MA.: Harvard University Press).
Padoa-Schioppa, T. (1987) *Efficiency, Stability and Equity: A Strategy for the Evolution of the Economic System of the European Community* (Oxford: Oxford University Press).
Pernin, A. (1996) 'Des Dysfonctionnements de la raison communautaire: une analyse à partir du contrôle des transfers Etats-entreprises', in Cartelier, L.
Philip, A. (1957) 'Social Aspects of European Economic Cooperation', *International Labour Review*, no. 76.
Pinder, J. (1969) 'Problems of European Integration', in Denton, G.
Pivetti, M. (1998) 'Monetary versus Political Unification in Europe', *Review of Political Economy*, 10.
Rocard, M. *et al.* (1973) *Le Marché commun contre l'Europe* (Paris: Seuil).
Ross, G. (1993) 'Social Policy in the New Europe', *Studies in Political Economy*, 40.
Saint-Martin, O. (1996) 'L' Anti-Politique industrielle de l 'U.E', in Cartelier, L.
Salesse, Y. (1996) 'Institutions européennes, déficit démocratique et intérêral général', in Cartelier, L.
Salesse, Y. (1997) *Propositions pour une autre Europe: construire Babel* (Paris: Arléa).
Sharp, M. (1993) 'The Community and New Technologies', in Lodge, J. (ed), *European Community and Challenge of the Future* (London: Pinter).
Shaw, J. (1994) 'Twin-Track Social Europe – The Inside Track?', in O'Keefe, D. and Twomey, P. (eds), *Legal Issues of Maastricht* (London: Wiley).
Silvia, S. (1991) 'The Social Charter of the European Community: Defeat for European Labour', *Industrial and Labour Relations Review*, 44.
Snyder, F. (ed) (1996) *Constitutional Dimensions of European Economic Integration* (The Hague: Kluwer).
Streeck, W. (1995) 'From Market Making to State Building? Reflections on the Political Economy of European Social Policy', in Liebfried, S. and Pierson, P.

(eds), *European Social Policy: Between Fragmentation and Integration* (Washington, DC: The Brookings Institution).

Streeck, W. and Schmitter, P. (1991) 'From National Corporatism to Transnational Pluralism: Organized Interests in the Single European Market', *Politics and Society*, 19.

Szyszczak, E. (1994) 'Happy Tale or Remaking the Fairy Tale?', in O'Keefe, D. and Twomey, P. (eds), *Legal Issues of Maastricht* (London: Wiley).

Taylor, P. (1983) *The Limits of Integration* (London: Croom Helm).

Tinbergen, J. (1965) *International Economic Integration* (Amsterdam: Elsevier).

Van Paridon, C. (1996) 'European Economic Integration: Did It Matter in the Past, Will It Matter in the Future?', in Tilly, R. and Wolfens, P. *European Economic Integration as a Challenge to Industry and Government* (New York: Springer).

Verdun, A. (1996) 'An "Asymmetrical" Economic and Monetary Union in the EU: Perceptions of Monetary Authorities and Social Partners', *Journal of European Integration*, 20.

Verloren van Thematt, P. (1996) 'Propositions on the Legal Analysis of Economic and Monetary Union', in Snyder, F.

Walker, P. (ed) (1979) *Between Labour and Capital* (Boston: South End).

Weiler, J. (1991) 'The Transformation of Europe', *Yale Law Journal*, 100.

Weiler, J. (1993) 'The Community System: The Dual Character of Supranationalism', in Snyder, F.

6
The European Union and its Periphery: Inclusion and Exclusion*

Mike Haynes

Conventional economic theory suggests that a cluster of strong states such as those that make up the European Union should create powerful equilibrating forces which will help even out the level of economic development. But the pattern of actual development in the European Union, both internally and in the states along its borders, appears to be marked by inequalities between rich and poor states and rich and poor regions. This chapter discusses the evidence for developmental convergence within the European Union and between it and its immediate geographical periphery. It then argues that the ideology of 'Europeanness' which underpins the 'European' project serves in part to justify the European Union as a relatively exclusive 'rich man's club', keeping its distance from its poorer neighbours. New boundaries are being developed along the borders of the European Union which emphasize protecting this rich man's club by the control of 'soft security' issues concerned with limiting access to the European Union for migrant labour, drugs and crime and what is loosely seen as the threat of fundamentalists and terrorism.

Rich and poor Europe

The 15 states of the European Union (EU) make up one of the most powerful cores of the world economy. The population of the EU is over 370 million, equivalent to that of the US and Japan combined and, at the turn of the twenty first century, it produced over 20 per cent of world GDP, a similar amount to the US and far exceeding the 7.8 per cent produced by Japan. The economies of the European Union are responsible for more than one-fifth of world trade, some 60 per cent of which is internal to the union (with an even higher share for internal trade in manufactures). Overall the high trade share makes the EU the world's biggest import market. The EU countries also form a magnet for foreign direct investment which is reckoned to amount to over US$500 billion and in turn FDI by Europe in third countries makes up one quarter of world-wide FDI.[1]

But, of course the EU, has not achieved the same level of integration characteristic of the American and Japanese economies. Within it there remain considerable national inequalities of development, power and influence. Table 6.1 sets out the main economic characteristics of the 15 member states. In terms of economic output Germany remains preponderant with 23 per cent of the GDP of the EU15. Four economies – Germany, France, Italy and the UK, account for 68 per cent of the output of the EU. This reflects their weighting in terms of population and level of development. If we compare the EU countries on the basis of crude exchange rates we find very wide differences in output per head, with a spread of 1:4 when comparing Portugal, the poorest state to Luxembourg, the wealthiest in 1995. A more realistic comparison of output per head can be based on what economists call purchasing power standards – PPS. These are artificial exchange rates which are designed to minimize the uncertainties of comparisons based on actual rates by reflecting a truer picture of relative purchasing powers. In the case of the EU these

Table 6.1 Characteristics of the economies of the European Union[2]

	Population 1999 (1000)	**GDP per capita 1998 (ecu)**	**GDP per capita 1998 (PPS)**	**PPS GDP per capita EU-15 =100**
EUR-15	373 460	21 100	21 100	100
Luxembourg	429	38 200	36 400	173
Denmark	5 314	28 200	24 000	114
Belgium	10 14	21 900	22 600	108
Austria	8 083	23 300	22 200	106
Netherlands	15 760	22 300	21 900	104
Germany	82 057	23 400	21 800	104
Ireland	3 745	18 400	21 200	100
France	58 967	21 500	20 400	97
Italy	57 613	18 400	20 400	97
Sweden	8 854	23 700	20 100	96
United Kingdom	59 390	21 100	20 200	96
Finland	5 160	22 300	20 200	96
Spain	39 394	13 200	16 400	78
Portugal	9 979	9 800	14 600	69
Greece	10 522	13 200	13 700	65

PPS calculations are made regularly by the European Union's Eurostat organization. As can be seen in Table 6.1 on this basis the spread reduces to 1:2.6 between Greece and Luxembourg. But to take Luxembourg as the standard makes little sense as it is a small country and perhaps more akin to a wealthy capital city region, boosting its wealth by its concentration of services and commuting. The more realistic comparison is with a more significant economy and, as Table 6.1 shows, the next economy in terms of wealth is Denmark whose output per head is 114 per cent the EU average. This reduces the spread in output per head to 1:1.7 between Greece and Denmark.

Within the EU there are also significant regional differences in GDP per head. In the past decades there has been a significant growth of 'regional' consciousness in Europe which has, in part, reflected dissatisfaction with the role of the nation state. Led initially by people in disadvantaged regions this regional focus now extends to demands for a politics that is also built around what Harvie calls 'bourgeois regions' – the competitive demands of more dynamic and privileged areas of Europe for a degree of autonomy (Harvie, 1994; see also Applegate, 1999). But defining regions is much harder than defining states whose boundaries are more or less clear. And measuring regions is often more difficult still as the statistics we have are produced as a result of the existence of administrative units whose borders may not coincide with either the consciousness of region or the spatial processes of economic differentiation. The EU has developed its regional statistics based around a Nomenclature Territorial Units for Statistics (abbreviated to NUTS). NUTS regions are essentially administratively defined areas which can then be subdivided into different levels for more detailed comparison. There are 77 NUTS1 regions (the highest level of aggregation) similar in size to the German Länder. At a lower level of aggregation there are some 208 NUTS2 regions (similar to French regions). Slight changes of administrative definition can produce significant changes in results. Thus in measuring the European regional hierarchy in the early 1990s EU statisticians put Hamburg at the head but the reclassification of inner London put it in the first place in the calculations for the second half of the 1990s. But such definitional problems do not affect the fundamental character of the hierarchy, which is what we wish to focus on.

GDP spread at this level is around 5 comparing inner London, the wealthiest region, with the poorest, Ipeiros in Greece or 4.4 if we take Hamburg as the rich base. But if we add in the overseas territories that some states hold on to as a remnant of Empire and which are treated by

Table 6.2 Range of values of regional per capita GDP in PPS for NUTS 2 regions in the EU member states in 1996[4]

Member	Minimum value % EU average	NUTS 2 region with minimum value	Maximum value as % EU average	NUTS 2 region with maximum value	Spread factor richest to poorest
Belgium	81	Hainaut, Namur	173	Brussels	2.14
Germany	61	Thuringia	192	Hamburg	3.15
Greece	44	Ipeiros	77	Attiki	1.75
Spain	55	Extremadura	101	Madrid	1.84
France	78	Languedoc-Rousillon	160	Ile de France	2.05
Italy	59	Calabria	132	Lombardy	2.24
Netherlands	75	Flevoland	134	Groningen	1.79
Austria	71	Burgenland	167	Vienna	2.35
Portugal	50	Açores	89	Lisbon e Vale do Tejo	1.78
Finland	74	Itä-Suomi	130	Uusimaa	1.76
Sweden	92	Oestra Mellansverige	123	Stockholm	1.34
United Kingdom	73	Merseyside	140	Greater London	1.91

the EU as 'Europe' then the spread widens.[3] Table 6.2 shows the variation within countries at the NUTS 2 level (no regional breakdown is made at this level for Denmark, Ireland and Luxembourg). What is of interest here is not only the variation within countries but also that between countries if we compare the national regional leaders with the most advanced EU region – Hamburg. Thus while the gap between Spain and Germany is 1: 1.3 on the basis of PPS per capita output the gap between Spain's richest region and Hamburg is 1: 1.9 (Eurostat News Release, 1999a; for earlier data see Eurostat, 1998).

The richest regions tend to be capital or large city regions, concentrating high value added industry and services. The list is headed by inner London in the United Kingdom and Hamburg in Germany and another four of the top regions are in that country. In addition we find regions like Brussels and the Paris centered Île de France. At the very bottom are those regions that have a long history of disadvantage and populations that have been struggling against a legacy of backwardness and underdevelopment. None of these are in the North. They form a broad southern European band which includes all the Portuguese regions with the exception of Lisbon, rural Spain, southern Italy and all of Greece. A second problem group consists of regions that were once cores of the European economy but which came to be characterized by outdated industrial and commercial structures which were slow to change (including the 5 Länder of the former East Germany.) Difficult though the situation is in these declining regions (the per capita income of the old mining area of Hainault in Belgium, for example, is less than 50 per cent that of neighbouring Brussels), if we exclude the regions of the former East Germany as a special case, none of these regions fall below the EU problem threshold of having a per capita income of less than 75 per cent of the average EU level save two, both in Britain – Merseyside (73 per cent) and South Yorkshire (74 per cent).

These kind of national and regional inequalities within the EU, combined with differing levels of political commitment to the Union, have led to arguments for a multispeed Europe. This has to some extent already come about with the creation of a partial Eurozone. Supporters of the broader idea of a Union built upon a more dynamic, developed and integrated core argue that it would allow policy deadlocks to be broken and assist flexibility. For its pro-European opponents, however, a multispeed Europe would be a major retreat from the ideal of a united Europe, while for Euro-sceptics such a strategy is made unattractive by the fear that states will lose their blocking veto and end up being marginalized. The result is that progress for the foreseeable future is likely to be based on an extension of the existing approach and therefore profoundly affected by the inequalities that exist with the European Union.

What then of the development gap between the EU and its external periphery? There are currently 12 candidate applicants for EU membership comprising the three Baltic states – Estonia, Latvia and Lithuania; Poland; the Czech and Slovak Republics; Hungary, Romania, Bulgaria, Slovenia from the Former Republic of Yugoslavia and the two island economies of Malta and Cyprus. If we leave aside the latter two minor economies then what we have is a swathe of economies all of which are significantly less developed than even the weaker southern European EU members. As part of the long accession process the statistical basis of these economies is being revised and their data, still subject to some quality and comparability doubts, integrated into the EU's Eurostat system. The latest data reported in Table 6.3 shows that GDP per head in PPS in 1998 for these economies as a whole was around a third of the EU average and still under half of the GDP per head figure for Greece, the least wealthy EU member. Taken together the total output of these economies is under 4 per cent of EU output measured at current

Table 6.3 Characteristics of selected economies on the border of the European Union[5]

	Population 1996–1997 mill	Area 000 sq. km	$ GDP per head 1997	GDP per head in 1998 as % EU average PPS	% Urban 1994	Life Expectancy 1996	Adult Literacy % 1996
Ex Soviet Bloc							
Baltic							
Estonia	1.5	45	3 330	37	73	70	n.a.
Latvia	2.5	65	2 430	27	73	70	n.a.
Lithuania	3.7	65	2 230	31	71	71	n.a.
Central Europe							
Poland	38.6	313	3 590	36	64	73	n.a.
Czech Republic	10.3	79	5 200	60	72	74	n.a.
Slovak Republic	5.4	49	3 700	46	58	73	n.a.
Hungary	10.2	93	4 430	48	64	70	n.a.
Romania	22.7	238	1 420	27	55	69	n.a.
Balkans							
Ex-Yugoslavia (1994)	23.9	256	n.a.	n.a.	n.a.	73	93
Slovenia	2	20	9 680	68	63	75	n.a.
Bulgaria	8.3	111	1 140	23	70	71	n.a.
Albania	3.5	29	750	n.a.	n.a.	72	n.a.
Turkey	63.5	779	3 130	37	67	69	82
Israel	5.5	21	15 810	n.a.	90	77	n.a.
Mashreq							
Syria	16.1	185	1 150	n.a.	51	69	71
Lebanon	3.45	10.4	3 350	n.a.	n.a.	70	85
Jordan	4.3	89	1 570	n.a.	71	71	86
Egypt	61.4	1 001	1 180	n.a.	45	66	51
Maghreb							
Libya	5.6	1759	n.a.	n.a.	n.a.	n.a.	n.a.
Tunisia	9.1	164	2 090	n.a.	57	70	67
Algeria	28.6	2 382	1 490	n.a.	55	70	62
Morocco	28.3	447	1 250	n.a.	48	66	44

exchange rates and 9 per cent measured in PPS. Table 6.3 also shows the variation between these countries. In terms of size the economies range from Poland with a population of some 39 million and 35 per cent of the output of the group as a whole to Estonia with a population of 1.5 million and 1 per cent of the output of the group. The most developed candidate is Slovenia with a PPS per capita output of 68 per cent of the EU level (and 105 per cent of the Greek level) while, at the other extreme is Bulgaria with a PPS per capita output of 23 per cent of the EU average (and 35 per cent of the Greek level).

As we move further around the periphery of the EU we come to even less developed economies. Turkey remains one of the most problematic neighbours for the EU having been a long time applicant for membership but continually held at arms length. The refusal to incorporate Turkey into the current accession negotiations consequently precipitated angry exchanges which in the aftermath of Nato's war in Kosovo led to what might be described as a 'positive fudge' in which Turkey was encouraged without being included in the accession process. In order to create a basis for developing relations with these economies on the southern edge of the Mediterranean the 1995 Barcelona Euro – Mediterranean conference created the basis for EU – Mediterranean cooperation by drawing these economies into what is expected to be a new and long term systematic relationship (Hakura, 1997; Nsouli *et al.*, 1996). Turkey, Syria, Lebanon, Israel, Gaza-Jericho (the Palestinian state), Jordan, Egypt, Libya, Algeria, Morocco and Tunisia, and the two island economies of Cyprus and Malta (which also appear in the candidate group) are now treated as a group by the EU. Table 6.3 also reports the latest available data for these economies from which the development gap is apparent compared to the EU as a whole, its southern members and the candidate members in the east. Nominal output per head is estimated to be around 10 per cent of the EU average for the southern Mediterranean countries (excluding Israel) and around 20 per cent if relative purchasing power is considered (Rhein, 1996, p. 81).

The less developed character of these economies is also reflected in their trade structure. In 1995 9.3 per cent of EU exports went to the non-EU Mediterranean and 7.2 per cent of imports came from there with EU trade shares falling rather than rising reflecting the comparative problems of these economies. The EU has a large trade surplus with this area on the basis of its export of manufactures in return for imports 60 per cent of which consist of fruits and vegetables, textile yarns and fabrics, clothing and petroleum products. The unevenness within the region is reflected in the fact that three economies are responsible for over 50 per cent of EU–Mediterranean trade – Turkey (26 per cent), Israel (16 per cent) and Algeria (12 per cent) (Eurostat Memo, 1997).

Economic convergence and divergence

From the sixteenth century it is possible to see a qualitative change taking place in the development of Europe and especially Western Europe associated with the 'rise of capitalism'. But it was only with the onset of industrialization in the late-eighteenth century that this qualitative differentiation came also to be reflected in large quantitative differences in output per head. As the first successful industrialization occurred in countries and regions so the gap in output per head began to open up. In a now classic discussion Simon Kuznets (1966) suggested that this pattern of growing inequality was a temporary phenomenon which would disappear over the long run as follower areas and countries began to develop and experience what is now called 'catch-up'. The mobility of capital, labour and technology would help to even out development and even if factor mobility where hindered then trade could also play the same role. Economic integration, whether it occurred on a world scale through globalizing economic processes or on a regional scale through integration structures, should reinforce this process by allowing greater factor mobility and greater trade.

Not everyone, of course, was so confident and especially on the left various theories were developed that suggested that development gaps might well be self-perpetuating not, as neo-classical discussion suggested, because of market imperfections but because of deficiencies in the capacity of market mechanism itself to generalize the benefits of development. But it has only been in the past two decades that a real debate has emerged about the evidence for divergence and convergence. This has partly been due to the creation and continual updating of long-run comparable data sets for a large sample of countries and regions which allow for the statistical testing of basic hypotheses about convergence. But it has also been due to a concern that the decline in world-wide growth rates from those of the golden age after World War II might have significant implications for the possibilities of 'catch-up'. It is not that growth is not taking place as some very pessimistic theories once suggested. Rather the question is whether more backward areas are sustaining higher rates of growth over long enough periods to allow convergence to occur.

The evidence here does not admit of a simple answer. Two things appear crucial. First, a number of studies have suggested forces assisting convergence will be more apparent when the world economy grows strongly than when its performance is weak. The strength of the convergence effect after World War II when the world economy was uniquely prosperous may not therefore be easily repeatable. Second, it can also be argued that there are 'convergence clubs' – smaller groups of economies and regions which do exhibit convergence but whose experience may not be typical of larger groups. Both of these issues are crucial when we turn to the experience of the European Union and its periphery.

Table 6.4 presents the evidence for the EU and its periphery taken from the dataset constructed by Angus Maddison.[7] It seems clear that the OECD countries and the EU group do form related 'convergence

Table 6.4 Long run GDP per capita in 1990 international dollars in European Union members and periphery countries, 1820–1992[6]

	1820	**1900**	**1913**	**1950**	**1973**	**1992**
Current EU members						
Austria	1 295	2 901	3 488	3 731	11 308	17 160
Belgium	1 291	3 652	4 130	5 346	11 905	17 165
Denmark	1 225	2 902	3 764	6 683	13 416	18 293
Finland	759	1 620	2 050	4 131	10 768	14 646
France	1 218	2 849	3 452	5 221	12 940	17 959
Germany	1 112	3 134	3 833	4 281	13 152	19 351
Italy	1 092	1 746	2 507	3 425	10 409	16 229
Netherlands	1 561	3 533	3 950	5 850	12 763	16 898
Sweden	1 198	2 561	3 096	6 738	13 494	16 927
United Kingdom	1 756	4 593	5 032	6 847	11 992	15 738
Greece			1 621	1 951	7 779	10 314
Ireland	954	2 495	2 733	3 518	7 023	11 711
Portugal		1 408	1 354	2 132	7 568	11 130
Spain	1 063	2 040	2 255	2 397	8 739	12 498
Arithmetic average EU 14	1 210	2 531	3 090	4 447	10 947	15 430
First wave						
Czech Republic	849	1 729	2 096	3 501	7 036	6 845
Hungary		1 682	2 098	2 480	5 596	5 638
Poland				2 447	5 334	4 726
Second wave						
Bulgaria			1 498	1 651	5 284	4 054
Slovak Republic						
Romania				1 182	3 477	2 565
Excluded						
Turkey			979	1 299	2 739	4 422
ex Yugoslavia			1 029	1 546	4 237	3 887
USSR	751	1 218	1 488	2 834	6 058	4 671
North Africa						
Egypt		509	508	517	947	1 927
Morocco				1 611	1 651	2 327

clubs', especially for the period since 1950. The greatest period of convergence appears however to have been during the 'golden age' of postwar growth.[8] Before then the evidence of convergence is less persuasive and since then although a continuing narrowing of gap in GDP per head has occurred this has been at a slower rate.

How this should be interpreted is another matter. Baumol in his original investigation implied that a successful 'convergence club' might be capable of emulation and this has been echoed in a quite unqualified way by some commentators. (Abramovitz, 1986; Baumol, 1986; Williamson, 1996) However De Long (1988) pointed out that this argument rests on a tautology in as much as if the club selected is already wealthy then convergence is assured *ex post* by sample selection. What has to be demonstrated is the convergence potential of a group of economies selected *ex ante* on the basis of similar characteristics and potential. Unfortunately this is harder to operationalize historically or statistically though De Long's interpretation is less favourable to the convergence case than its supporters.[9]

Another problem is that convergence can occur within a convergence club for two reasons. One is that the weaker economies grow significantly faster (what is sometimes termed upwards convergence) and some of the catch-up is accounted for in the EU in this way. But convergence can also arise because of the poor performance of some of the leaders (downward convergence) and here any analysis of the situation in Europe must have regard to the two problems. The first is the difficulties of British capitalism and the long fall of the British economy not only from a position of absolute dominance (a fall that was unavoidable) but from its position of relative dominance reflected in its overtaking in terms of output per head so that today it is what Hutton (1996) has called 'a fading middle aged economy protesting its great power ambitions'. By the end of the nineteenth century Britain had already given way to the United States in terms of output per head but it was not until the 1960s and 1970s that its main European competitors overtook it. But the gap had been closing before, albeit unevently. Indeed some economic historians locate the origins of relative decline in the late nineteenth century. William Kennedy, for example, has suggested that had British businessmen at this time proved as adept at exploiting technological change as their ancestors during the industrial revolution then output per head in 1913 could have been as much as 50 per cent higher (Hutton, 1996, p. 123). Others argue that this type of retrospective critique would have required decisions that could not be justified by the available knowledge of opportunity costs. How this problem is resolved is of some importance for the convergence debate.

One school of thought, popular in Britain, has seen relative decline as an expression of organizational deficiencies within British capitalism itself. Here the 'British problem' appears as part of the debate over models of capitalism. According to this view there are a variety of capitalist models – the Anglo-Saxon, the European social or Rhine-Alpine model, the Asian model and so on. Hutton argues that British capitalism stands in a category of its own, failing to achieve the flexibility of the American model or the high wage, high productivity base of the European model. How exactly this argument is formulated is not important here. The key point is that if it is correct then the problem is 'the peculiarities of the British' and there is no necessary reason to expect more 'successful' models of capitalism to come under pressure to give up their lead. The hierarchical ordering of the most developed economies can be expected to be maintained into the foreseeable future.

Against this it has been argued that the problems of the British economy reflect pressures immanent in all advanced economies. In an initial discussion of the issue that continues to provoke interest Kaldor argued that the problem arose from Britain's very early industrialization which meant it was less able to capture productivity gains from the reallocation of resources than economies developing latter (Kaldor, 1966). Thus sooner or later as follower countries industrialized they would experience similar slowdowns. A different approach, which points to similar conclusions, has stressed the competing demands created by the past history of world leadership. The burden of formal and informal empire, the Pax Britannica and then military expenditure in the Cold War and the reluctant recognition of reduced status all acted to divert resources and attention in ways that created problems for the future. The precise argument differs but the central point is that world leadership imposes costs on the leader which makes it difficult to sustain its position in the long run – what Paul Kennedy has called 'imperial over-reach' drags great powers back towards the pack of follower countries (Kennedy, 1988). If any of these accounts are correct then the implication is that it will be more difficult to retain a stable long-run hierarchy at the top of the world economy than might initially be imagined.

Whereas the relative problems of the British economy have been of long standing a second element of downward convergence through problems 'at the top' has arisen because of the unification of the West and East German economies. Although this increased the absolute size of the German economy, the per capita output level of the new

Germany was less than that of the former West Germany partly because the level of development in the former GDR was significantly lower and partly because subsequent economic growth was probably restricted by the costs of subsidizing the transition. Nearly a decade of intra-German transfers from West to East (which dwarf the total transfer of resources and aid between the West and the former Soviet bloc at large) has resulted in some movement upwards of the GDR component of the new Germany. But the average per capita output of the 5 ex-GDR Länder in 1994 to 1996 was still 62 per cent of the EU level, 57 per cent of the German average and 52 per cent of the West German average. German GDP per head in 1994 to 1996 was 110 per cent of the EU average. Crudely removing the ex-GDR states (without taking into account the negative growth effects of unification) would raise the relative per capita GDP of the former West Germany to 119 per cent of the EU level thus restoring the leading role of West Germany.[10]

So far we have approached this issue in national terms but we can extend this discussion of convergence–divergence to incorporate regional differentials within the European Union. Long-run regional GDP per head data is less easily available than data at the national level but attempts can be made to piece the history of pre-1945 regional divergence and convergence using both the descriptive and quantitative work of economic historians (Molle and Boeckout, 1995). Some more recent trends can be established using NUTS data but this is restricted to a small number of countries before the late 1970s. Nevertheless broadly similar trends again emerge from these studies. The regional gap has been reduced from the 1950s (on one account from 1:4 to 1:3). This reduction is significant but as we have seen it still leaves a considerable gap. Moreover as with national data the evidence is that the strongest regional catch took place before the 1970s and, if the data set is widened to include the more peripheral regions now within the EU, then regional catch up in the south was less marked than regional catch up in the north. In the 1970s the overall rate of catch up declined and during the 1980s it was low, and on some estimates, barely existent.[11]

Regional performance is affected by state and EU transfers. Within countries resource transfers through unemployment pay and social security systems tend to go more to poor regions. Similarly states use national programmes of regional aid to stimulate development. At the EU level resource transfers (on a smaller scale than most state regional aid programmes) occur through the deployment of EU structural funds. The dominant fund here is the Common Agricultural Policy which, despite reforms, still channels most EU aid and which acts as an indirect form of regional support. Beyond this EU regions are divided for the purposes of direct assistance into 'Objective 1' – regions which are marked by historically lagging development and which receive 70 per cent of EU structural funds and 'Objective 2' regions which are more developed but now characterized by industrial decline and which receive some 11 per cent of EU structural funds.

If we leave aside the extreme free market argument which disputes the value of all such aid there would appear to be four problems with seeing these transfers as a cause of and possible route to further *strong* regional convergence. First, social security programmes are in themselves mainly palliative, aimed more at poverty reduction than growth. Second, pressures towards convergence and divergence are often a product of global trends which are not easily susceptible to state or EU control. Third, regional aid often appears to involve the leaders of poorer regions trying to compete among one another to 'play' these global forces to their own advantage but in a way that can be self-defeating overall. Finally, the idea that broader corrective aid programmes can be developed not only neglects the difficulties of generating the political will to do this but also the constraints on both states and the EU to direct resources in other more 'profitable' directions so that from the point of view of lagging regions the state can appear as one of the problems rather than the solution. The contradictions that these tensions produce in European Union regional policy can be seen in the response to the creation of the Eurozone. On the one hand policy makers have apparently responded positively to the need for a stronger regional policy by extending the scope of regional policy with a greater concentration on the regions most in need of assistance. But they have then planned a level of assistance for the period after 2000 which is lower in real terms than that at the end of the 1990s. As Thirwall (2000) bluntly puts it, 'on regional policy, the structural funds are simply inadequate'. Moreover if this is true of the current situation in the 15 it hardly augurs well for the capacity of the EU to respond to the even more massive regional problems of potential new members.

What then of the periphery of the EU? Analysis of experience of the former Soviet bloc is complicated by the debate over output measurement but the most widely accepted data shows clear evidence of a significant degree of catch-up in the 1950s and 1960s that was impressive for the time. However growth then slowed and in the latter stages of these regimes fallback occurred especially when their performance was compared to that of some of the weaker southwest European economies. The transition crisis everywhere resulted in a general slump in output, which led to an even more dramatic fallback compared to the situation in the EU. Again the precise scale of this is disputed but some measure of it can be seen in Maddison's data for 1992 in Table 6.4. It had been hoped that the transition crisis would be short lived and that these economies would then soon recover lost ground. But the subsequent recovery has been very uneven. In order to maintain the momentum of the transition and to encourage laggards there is a tendency among many commentators to put the best possible gloss on the evidence of recovery arguing that the scale of the crisis was exaggerated by data problems and the scale of the recovery underestimated for similar reasons. But a contrary case can equally be made. To put the recovery data in the best possible light many statistical series are now presented starting from 1991–92 rather than 1989 (or before) when the transition crisis began. Beyond this presentational sleight of hand an argument can also be made that output data, even in a supposed success story like that of Poland, exaggerates recovery more than overstates it.[12]

But even if we accept the most optimistic data for the economies at the forefront of the transition in this part of the EU's periphery we must not forget that recovery does not in itself mean convergence since these economies are chasing a moving target. When the transition economies recover their 1989 levels of output they therefore still remain relatively farther behind than they were at that date. In the years 1989 to 1998, for example, while the transition crisis was being experienced in Eastern Europe, in the European Union as a whole output per head rose by 19 per cent while in a successfully backward economy like Ireland it grew by much more (UN Commission for Europe, 1999). Convergence requires them to sustain higher rates of growth over a sufficiently long period to recover the initial relative gap and then to begin to close it. A large question mark must remain as to whether they have the capacity to do this and it seems likely that in the foreseeable future these economies will remain the moderately poor neighbours of the rich man's club – with the greatest poverty in South Eastern Europe (apart from Slovenia).

In 1999 Eurostat published the first results of an analysis of regional differentiation in the Central and Eastern European (CEC) applicant countries based on an informal extension of its NUTS classification system (at level 2 and, in some cases, level 3). Eighty-nine sub regions were identified (some of which were the whole of the very smallest countries) and 77 were found to have a PPS per capita income that was less than 50 per cent of the EU average with 34 having a per capita income less than 30 per cent of the EU average. These very poorest regions were to be found in Bulgaria and Romania and in the eastern areas of Poland and Latvia and Lithuania. Within the Central and East European countries the spread of regional incomes was roughly 1 to 5 – more or less the same as in the European Union. But the EU–CEC spread was found to be nearer 1 to 10. Whereas Ipeiros, the poorest EU region, had a per capita income of 44 per cent of the EU average, that of the regions of Eastern Poland was as low as 23 per cent of the average. The scale of the regional problem in this area is reflected in a Eurostat calculation of eligibility for Objective 1 regional funds which automatically go to regions whose income per head is less than 75 per cent of the EU average. Even though this average would fall sharply if the 10 CEC countries joined the EU (a possibility we will later question) it would still be the case, according to Eurostat, that 85 out of the 89 regions identified would be eligible for such assistance.

Under communism regional differentiation was partially suppressed without being fundamentally eliminated. The Eurostat data confirms that while some of the more backward countries like Bulgaria and Romania have regional income spreads similar to EU the spread is increasing and in a number of cases is now much greater than the national spread in the different EU members. This can be clearly seen in Hungary, which has a better record than most in attracting foreign investment. What is revealing, however, is its internal distribution, 'of the $15 billion foreign investment which Hungary has received since 1990, about 75 per cent has gone to Budapest and the western counties, according to ministry of trade statistics. Only an estimated one per cent of this capital went to each of the four western counties of eastern Hungary.' This is an extreme case but it reflects a wider problem and it suggests that regional divergence is likely to be more marked in the future than in the more recent past (Kaplar, 1997; Nizamova, 1997).

For the Mediterranean area too the evidence of convergence remains unimpressive. Israel stands out with a quite atypical level of output per head for the region, a performance that can only be explained by the peculiar circumstances of that state. In contrast much of the rest of the region is mired in difficulties though there is less concern with the development potential of Turkey which is thought by some EU insiders to be good than for the EU's Arab neighbours in the Maghreb and Mashrak which, it is argued, pose 'a formidable challenge that exceeds by far the one the EU has been shouldering in Eastern Europe since 1990' (Blunden, 1994; Rhein, 1996, pp. 80–1).

The Mediterranean countries generally have a larger population than the EU's central and eastern European neighbours, a lower level of per capita output and, especially worrying to EU policy makers, a longer tradition of migration to the EU. In 1992 there were 4.6 million Mediterranean migrants in the EU compared to 0.7 million from eastern Europe. The 1995 Mediterranean agreement was provoked in part by the laudable desire to overcome past uneasy relationships but beneath this lay the less pleasant concern to deal with the Mediterranean as a zone of potential instability. Policy makers in the EU states and the Commission itself have tended to argue that the root of this instability lies in economic weakness. In the run up to the new agreement the Commission apocalyptically warned of huge pressures towards divergence arguing that unless there was a change the 'wealth gap which presently stands at a level of "one to ten" would be on its way to reach the level of "one to twenty" [by 2025]' (Rhein, 1996, pp. 80–1). Even allowing for the scare mongering designed to enlist support for a policy the point remains that the indicators are pointing strongly away from convergence – even on an optimistic evaluation of the capacity of this area for change. The EU objective is to encourage the formation of a huge free trade zone by 2010 based on free trade in manufactures with the EU, free trade among the Mediterranean countries themselves and preferential access to the EU market for agricultural products. If successful this will create the biggest free trade area in the world uniting some 600 to 800 million people in 30 to 40 countries in the EU, eastern Europe and the Mediterranean. One OECD commentator describes this as 'a venture worth the risk' for the Mediterranean countries themselves but acknowledges that the problems are considerable. Studies predict that in the first instance there will be an increase in traditional areas of specialization in the Mediterranean; heavier trade deficits; lower government revenue and therefore pressure on government expenditure or higher taxes and inflation. 'Unemployment and poverty will not diminish'. Longer-term success is supposed to come from 'a major shift in flows of foreign investment'; enhanced labour skills through education which will allow for economic diversification and the general productivity gains from trade and market liberalization (Garson, 1997–98).

But the past record of the region in attracting foreign investment is not impressive, only 1 per cent of global private European investment has gone to the Southern Mediterranean countries. Similarly although the EU is anxious to limit migration from the area it is likely to continue disproportionately to want cheap skilled labour. A realistic evaluation of the prospects of creating a prosperous and converging non-EU Mediterranean points therefore towards a pessimistic conclusion. The development gap and level of poverty on the Southern flank of the EU will remain much greater than that on the Eastern flank but in both areas the problem of the relationship of the EU's external periphery will remain serious.[13]

In the heady days of the collapse of the Soviet bloc Chancellor Kohl of Germany said, 'there must be no borders which perpetuate the prosperity divide' (quoted Burgess, 1997, p. 163). But these borders clearly exist both in the perceptual world of politicians and policy makers and in the real world of controls on movement. They also infect the very language of discussion. So far as internal EU development is concerned we find 'the language of cohesion, integration, unity, community and security'. The rhetoric of discussion for Eastern Europe is also positive but implies a greater distance focusing on 'aid' and 'assistance' to meet 'conditions'. For the Mediterranean the distance is greater with language oscillating between a rhetoric of inclusion which dominates the grand strategy and a rhetoric of exclusion which dominates the detail. The two rhetorics are not as opposed as might at first sight appear for it is easy to find policy makers slipping from one to the another in the same breath. 'The Mediterranean is to be progressively turned into a zone of peace, stability and prosperity. Who would dare not to subscribe to such a slogan . . . ?', asks one EU official. Who indeed? But he then goes on immediately to write 'expressed in less solemn terms, Europe wishes to see at its southern rim a group of countries that will not: be at war with one another; be destabilized by socio-political conflicts; export terrorism or drugs to Europe; threaten Europe's social stability by continued or even sharply increased flows of illegal immigration' (Rhein, 1996, p. 81).[14]

This suggests that what we are looking at externally is a poor Europe which will act as a buffer zone. There are clear parallels here with the southern flank of the United States and some commentators have spoken of the Mexicanization of eastern Europe and the Mediterranean area. According to this view these regions are becoming 'a source of controlled immigration, cheap energy and agricultural imports, and demand for European products, accommodation for mass tourism and the location of industries (the equivalent of Maquilladoras) . . . ' (Hadjimichalis, 1997, p. 25).[15] A cynic might reply that even this Mexicanization might be an improvement and advantageous for these regions especially if the alternative is complete exclusion. But this is hardly an adequate response if the possibility exists to do more and to eliminate 'the borders which perpetuate the prosperity divide'. Judged against this standard the policy of the EU looks niggardly and perhaps self-defeating.

First, policy appears to be driven by narrowly conceived self-interest which the Commission may occasionally declare to be 'enlightened' but which in reality is much focused on a calculus of immediate costs and benefits. The contrast between the generosity of the internal assistance programme between the former West and East Germany and the much less impressive external programme is striking. Moreover when priorities multiply this tends to result in a redirection of existing funds rather than a commitment to new funding. Thus a case can be made that assistance to Eastern Europe has led to a redirection of funding away from other causes and the same claims are also made by critics of the EU–Mediterranean policy.[16] Second, the particular agenda of the EU in respect of its periphery is driven by the fear of crisis and instability on the rim. These lead to a concern with development which would be positive were it not for the fact that the actual formulation of policy is subordinate to this 'crisis' ethos rather than a generous, structured programme based on real cooperation.

This creates a third difficulty in as much as it traps the peripheral governments in a vicious circle where they are required to meet implicit or explicit EU targets without necessarily being able to guarantee their populations early improvements in their situation. This is evident in EU negotiations with Eastern Europe. The potential new EU applicants from the former Soviet bloc have little bargaining power. Russia is no longer an alternative pole of attraction either economically or politically and EU membership is seen, in the words of Petre Roman the Romanian Foreign Minister in early 2000, as a movement 'from the bad side of history... [to] ... the right side' (*Guardian*, 16 February 2000). EU policy has, however, treated these countries more as supplicants than applicants. Its responsiveness to their needs often seems to reflect the balance of 'strain' and 'gain'. Within the EU countries themselves considerable doubts exist about the capacity to tolerate the strain of accession, doubts played on by politicians like Jörg Haider in Austria and to a degree given wider legitimization by the acceptance of his Freedom Party as a 'normal' governing party. 'Gains' on the other hand are more variable. Prior to the Spring of 1999 enormous doubts existed as to whether the balance would lead to speedy progress towards accession. Then NATO's war over Kosovo transformed the situation, at least temporarily, by consolidating the further integration of the former Soviet satellites into the western bloc. A flurry of promises was made about the need for zones of prosperity and at the turn of 2000 the EU respond by formalizing the stages of the accession negotiations. On this basis Poland, Hungary, the Czech Republic, Slovenia and Cyprus are seen as potential fast track candidates with the possibility of staggered membership from 2003. Bulgaria, Latvia, Lithuania, Malta, Romania and Slovakia are now also formally identified as part of a second wave. But the commitment here is to negotiations – not membership. Membership will be the outcome of these negotiations in which the formal aim is to 'strike the right balance between two potentially conflicting objectives in the enlargement process: speed and quality. Speed is of the essence because there is a window of opportunity for enhanced momentum in the preparations for enlargement, in accordance with the expectations of the candidate countries. Quality is vital because the EU does not want partial membership, but members exercising full rights and responsibilities.' These are the words of Günter Verheugen, the Commissioner for Enlargement (European Commission, 1999). But less decorously as the potential gain factor reduces again, post Kosovo, then the balance may well swing back towards heavier weighting for the 'strain' element. Moreover, even if the EU honours its paper commitments, the staggering process invites a further differentiation between favoured and unfavoured applicant and builds up more complications and divisions to become incorporated into EU policy making.[17]

The formal problem for the candidate members is to adopt the *acquis* (the community body of law) which will require continuing reforms as well as other costs. Negotiation involves agreement about how this can be achieved as well as agreements on transition periods and derogations. But because these economies are weak they have little leverage over the EU to secure better terms:

> At the end of the day . . . the Union holds all of the cards. Although it clearly has a lot to gain from new members in the east, the Commission stresses it is the applicants, not the EU, that are doing the demanding. If they do not convince the Union that they can, within a reasonable periods of time, fulfil the entry conditions, they will not join. That simple fact will probably ensure that the talks last for a long time.

This argument was put more bluntly by François Lamoureux, the European Commission official in charge of partnership agreements, 'Opt-outs are for us. Not for them' (*Guardian* 28 March 1998). But it can also be seen in EU–Mediterranean relations. Ironically therefore EU policy looks to be a factor that might provoke further instability as governments are caught between the competing demands of the EU and their own domestic constituencies. Peripheral governments are forced to make choices based on the imperatives of the EU where their area of manoeuvre is restricted to offering concessions in one area in order to win better deals in another.[18]

Finally, the justification for this stance has involved the attempted development of an ideology of inclusion/exclusion from the EU club. But the impact of this ideology cannot be restricted to the external periphery. The idea that people can be divided into those who are more or less European also has an internal impact within the EU. As a result of past immigration control and different citizenship laws, the EU now has a significant minority population with uneven access to basic rights. Indeed some even talk of there being a 'sixteenth state' of EU inhabitants with less than full citizenship rights. The development of ideas which underpin the concept of external distance and exclusion inevitably affects the position of this 'sixteenth state' by creating legitimacy for their further exclusion from full citizenship of the EU.[19]

Europe and its other

The European Union today is built on the idea of the single market defined as 'an area without frontiers in which the free movement of goods, persons, services and capital is ensured' (European Union, 1986). But the EU is only a limited attempt to achieve this and EU leaders and policy makers must therefore also define themselves against the rest of the world even as they welcome the bringing down of internal barriers. The ideological tangle this creates was well illustrated by Mrs Thatcher's infamous declaration that 'we have joined Europe to have the free movement of goods . . . I did not join Europe to have the free movement of terrorists, criminals, drugs, plant and animal diseases and illegal immigrants' (quoted in Baimbridge *et al.*, 1994, p. 422). In her xenophobic vision this threat came from outside the EU but also, to an extent, from inside too. But even on the more avowedly European right this rhetoric is common place. The French politican Eduard Balladur summed this up in 1991 when he warned that 'there is always a danger in the East and there is always a danger in the South' (quoted in Manfrass, 1992, p. 395). We have seen how this discourse affects the language of EU officials and mainstream politics as in the discussion of the EU's Mediterranean policy but what is it that makes Europe 'European' and therefore justifies exclusion?

We must immediately reject the idea that there is some self-evident European geographical identity. Only in the west does geography provide a clear marker. To the south the Mediterranean has always been a sea easily crossed and for much of known history it has been a unifying force for the communities around its shores; the Bosphorous, which is conventionally said to divide Turkey 'in Europe' from

'Turkey in Asia', can be swum and there is no obvious physical dividing line to the East. In fact the definition of Europe is a political act based on conceptual boundaries which include some and exclude others (Haynes, 1999).

Despite attempts to backdate this idea of 'Europe' into the distant past a strong argument can be made that this 'geography of difference' is essentially a product of the rise of capitalism and especially the development of industrialization, paralleling the economic divergences we have noted. This involved a twofold separation. The first was between an idea of 'Europe' and the rest of the world. The second was an internal differentiation within Europe where the degree of 'Europeanness' reflected the peripheralisation of the South and the East. 'Africa begins at the Pyrennes' Napoleon is reported to have said while Metternich claimed that he could see Asia when he looked East from his windows in Vienna. The idea of Europe thus came to be dominated by the ideas and interests of those in north-western Europe. But despite this growing elaboration of an idea of 'Europe' other divisions continued to be as, if not, more important. The idea of nation and empire created powerful practical and ideological ties that cut across continental boundaries and which were in some respects strengthened in the imperial 'high noon' of the inter-war years. When the EU was formed in the 1950s its supporters had only a vague concept of a Europe as it exists today and it must be remembered that some of the founder states were still clinging determinedly to their old imperial possessions.[20] But the loss of empire and the development of a more internally focused European Union has involved a redefinition of the perceptual geography of Europe which has meant a cutting of these ties and made outsiders of former 'insiders'. This shift has been further encouraged by three more recent factors, the increased integration of the world economy and especially its rich heartlands; the catching-up process of the south of the EU which has meant that although these regions retain a peripheral status within the EU they are now more of a magnet to their non EU neighbours; and the ending of the Cold War which has unfrozen the borders of the former Soviet bloc and created the possibility of the establishment of a denser network of relationships.

The modern rhetoric of 'Europe' is being constructed in part through the debate over the limits of EU expansion and the need to protect Europe's borders. Article 237 of the Treaty of Rome, reiterated in article 49 of the consolidated Treaty on European Union, says that 'any European state may apply to become a member of the community' but it does not define what a European state is and a glance at other international organizations which include the title European shows that the concept is capable of enormous expansion.[21] EU insiders recognize this ambiguity, one Commission publication described it this way, 'the term "European" has not been officially defined. It combines geographical, historical and cultural elements which all contribute to European identity. The shared experience of proximity, ideas, values and historical interaction cannot be condensed into a simple formula and is subject to review by each succeeding generation...' It then went on to talk of prospective members meeting 'the three basic conditions of European identity, democratic status, and respect of human rights.' (European Commission, 1992)

The first potential applicant to stumble here was Morocco in 1987, which applied to join with Turkey. Morocco was firmly rejected because it 'clearly did not meet EEC criteria' (Bahaijoub, 1993; *Times*, 14 September 1987). Turkey by contrast continued to be held at arms length with doubts about its 'European identity, democratic status and respect of human rights'. Without in any sense wishing to endorse the policies of the Turkish state, it is difficult not to feel the smell of hypocrisy here in EU policy. As a *Times* journalist put it, 'since the EU's doors have been held ajar for undemocratic Slovakia and bankrupt Bulgaria, the Turks are understandably furious at being shut out' (*Times*, 14 March 1998). Similarly poor though Turkey's human rights record might be it has opened its borders in the recent past to large numbers expelled from Bulgaria and large numbers of Kurds. Indeed the schizophrenia of many European commentators and governments is reflected in their condemnation of Turkish repression of the Kurds and their refusal to grant many of these same Kurds refugee status, with some European politicians demanding that Turkey further control their right of exit.

Behind this dialectic of inclusion–exclusion it is 'culture' that often substitutes for the role that race has played in the past. It is obvious in the debate on the southern limits of Europe where Islam is seen as a cultural divider from Christian Europe but in the East too Burgess has shown how this cultural rhetoric can take other forms. The argument then becomes a self-perpetuating one. 'Cultural difference' becomes a convenient alibi for failure of policies on the periphery and a recipe for more of the same. What 'Europe' did was correct, it was simply 'they' who failed to respond appropriately and we must therefore do more of the same to help them to respond more appropriately in the future (see Burgess 1997). The effect of this has been well put by Hadjimichalas (1997, p. 14),

> Eastern Europeans, Oriental people, and neighbours across the sea demand their rights of entry into the Single European Space. In earlier centuries, as Braudel teaches us, they were part of it; they have contributed to its wealth and culture; they were 'inside', and they cannot accept some of the current European notions which portray Europe's lines of inclusion / exclusion as outcomes of new global relations.[22]

Soft security borders and identity

What is of interest to us here is the way in which this has also come to underpin so-called soft security policies, which involve the policing of the EU border regions. More detailed border control policies began to develop in the EU in *ad hoc* way in the 1970s, often at a tangent to the formal EU structure.

Under the 1992 Maastricht Treaty an attempt was made to give the EU itself a wider role in directing and consolidating these concerns. These were set out in article K1 of the treaty which identifies nine areas of common interest – (1) asylum policy; (2) movement across borders; (3) immigration policy; (4) drug addiction; (5) international fraud; (6) judicial cooperation on civil issues; (7) judicial cooperation on criminal issues; (8) customs cooperation; (9) police cooperation on terrorism, drugs, and other forms of international crime.

This has led to a more determined attempt to develop coherent structures but it must be recognized that this has yet to be completely successful. This is partly because of clashing national visions, partly because of imprecision over objectives and partly because of the difficulties of rationalizing such policies. By looking only at the aspirations of these policies it is possible to derive a vision of a self-enclosed 'fortress Europe'. By looking only at the messy application on the other hand it is possible to see a still porous 'Europe' with much less precise boundaries than its leaders want. The truth is somewhere in between and it is important to complement any critique of the high level exclusionary rhetoric of 'Europe' with an appreciation of the irrational and frequently contradictory application of the detailed policies that flow from this.[23]

The most fundamental issue here is that of migration. Both national and EU policies are permised on the idea that migration to the EU area is a 'problem'. The argument is that countries of immigration must be safeguarded from this external threat. Unless controlled, migration will occur on an enormous scale because driving it is social and political instability underpinned by poverty and demographic crises. The vast majority of migrants will be 'economic' migrants and therefore it is important to create deterrent asylum procedures to help sift the very few who have legitimate asylum claims from the very many who will try to use such claims as a disguise for their economic motives.

These arguments have become so deeply grounded that it is often forgotten that the effective control and criminalization of the movement of the poor across international boundaries is a creation of the twentieth century. As late as 1889 the International Immigration Conference could 'affirm the right of the individual to the fundamental liberty accorded to him by every civilized state to come and go and dispose of his person and his destinies as he pleases.' Today no such human right of 'coming and going' is recognized, especially by the EU and its members (Harris, 1996, p. 6).

We can identify three different elements in EU policy. The first is the debate on the role of labour migration in the accession process for any new members.[24] Part of the hostility to Turkey's application is motivated by the fact that there are well-established migration links between Turkey and especially Germany. But there is also a clear suspicion that an integration of Turkey into the EU would increase the possibility of migrant flows which, given the dominant framework of analysis, is then pictured as a potential destabilizing factor in Western Europe. The same problem exists in the East though here it is less compounded by ideas of 'cultural' difference. In the aftermath of 1989 there was wild talk of the huge potential scale of migration from the former Soviet bloc. This has not materialized but the rhetoric of immigration control has made politicians and the media sensitive to even very small movements (Fassmann, 1994; Manfrass, 1992). In the accession negotiations therefore this issue is likely to loom large or at least to loom large in the subtext of discussion. For the applicant countries any qualification of the rights of their citizens to move in an expanded EU would be an institutionalization of their second class status. But EU policy makers are caught in a dilemma both by their crude approach to the dynamics of migration and the panics that ensue about 'migrant tides'. Thus Rolf Timans, one of the European Commission's ambassadors, has warned Poland that demands for free movement of labour would only 'raise the temperature in EU countries' (*Guardian*, 24 March 1998).

Beyond the issue of accession is that of solidifying EU external borders against third country migrants. Here the countries of northern Europe are partly protected by their geographical position and partly by the tightness of their established control structures. In the south, however, the picture is different. There until the mid-1980s immigration was limited and barely controlled.[25] Since then a complex of restrictive laws have been passed dealing with immigration, asylum and naturalization. Baldwin-Edwards has argued that initially these laws may have simply been part of the modernization process in Southern Europe but that in the 1990s they have reflected the interaction of panics about refugee movements (especially from Albania) and a wider emulation, with encouragement, of EU practice. However 'geography, economy and [inefficient] bureaucracy' in the southern EU members mean that these controls are likely to be much more inconsistently and inefficiently applied than in the rest of the EU – a prospect which may reinforce doubts about the centrality of these economies to the core integration process (Baldwin-Edwards, 1997; Hamilton, 1997).

A third strand of EU policy has been to push migration control, into the hands of external border countries. Under the Dublin convention, agreed by EU leaders, responsibility for asylum falls on the first country of entry and this has been re-inforced by carrier liability legislation which forces carriers to undertake the role of immigration controllers. To enable this to operate, the EU countries put pressure on the external periphery and give resources to encourage their governments to create systems, which mean that potential 'illegal' immigrations do not even reach EU border controls.

The issue of migration is seen by many as one part of a wider criminal threat to Europe's borders which can only be met by the development of Europe-wide policing measures. The fear of transnational crime is an issue, which has become a staple of international discussion, some would say a staple myth, since the end of the Cold War. Traditionally international police cooperation has relied on bilateral agreements and international conventions which have primarily involved the exchange of information since police powers themselves have been seen as close to the core of state sovereignty. But the process of 'globalization' and the creation of 'borderless' economies and, in the case of the EU the commitment to free movement of goods, services, capital and persons and especially the partial achievement of the latter through Schengen, eliminates the border monitoring that was a cornerstone of past controls. Then the transition crisis in Eastern Europe and Russia has boosted the level of criminal activity there and led to much concern with 'criminal mafias' as different groups have sought to capitalize on the transition in a way which the authorities fear will spill over into 'Europe'.[26] Frameworks of regulation of all kinds are notoriously lax in the region and compromised even more by corruption.[27] This leads to the fear of 'the infiltration of Eastern European crime syndicates into

Western Europe, North America and other regions. Illicit trafficking in drugs, human beings, nuclear materials, weapons and property is increasingly routed through the European continent' (Council of Europe, 1997a).[28]

Unfortunately much of the discussion of crime is based on anecdote and panic in a way that is similar to the moral panics about crime within European countries. The effect of this is to re-inforce fears about 'identity' in a way that diverts attention from more serious issues and not least the considerable abuse of state and corporate power that exists as well as those policies in the East that contribute towards establishing a climate of uncertainty in which criminality of all kinds can flourish.[29] The horrific example of Albania's descent into chaos as this process spiralled out of control, even as Western advisors were lauding the Albanian leadership, for their commitment to change is only the most extreme case of this pattern.

The policies that result hardly match up to the problems discussed. For example, the consequences of the conventional argument about 'protecting Europe' from the criminal threat on its borders underpin the development of policing structures that even the European Parliament has worried are beyond public control and which serve as much to perpetuate problems as solved them. One example of how this happens is the concern to resist the 'invasion' of 'Europe' by prostitutes from the east, a concern which has united much of the political spectrum including feminists, ostensibly as an act of protection for the women themselves. This has allowed lurid pictures to be painted. Thus in the Council of Europe it was suggested that 'during 1995, at least 500 000 women were thought to have been victims of trafficking towards members states of the EU.' To prevent this various measures were discussed,

> these could include strengthening police co-operation – particularly by setting up specifically trained police units... involving the immigration services, consulates and embassies which gave out visas and work permits; providing legal, medical, and psychological aid, along with physical protection, to victims of trafficking, especially if they were willing to give evidence to a court (granting temporary residence permits, for example), and closing establishments where sexual exploitation took place (Council of Europe, 1997b)

The agenda is clear and repressive. It fails to address the extent to which it is poverty that puts women in this position and causes them to look for a solution through migration to the west as potential prostitutes.[30] It fails to address the fact that since these women cannot freely migrate they therefore become the object of a vicious cycle of criminalization as illegals with no rights. Then, as the extract makes clear, within this structure of analysis there is no solution to the problem because its roots in poverty and immigration restriction are not addressed. Instead we are offered a solution based upon further controls and regulation in which the women are promised at best 'temporary residence permits' if they cooperate with the possible implication that once they have served their purpose for the authorities they will be sent back to their countries of origin. Thus is the vicious circle of fear underpinned not only by their immediate exploiters but also the wider system of building barriers between insiders and outsiders.

Similar sensitivities in terms of border controls are reflected in the 'drug fear' as an outside threat. It was only in the late 1980s that concerted action against drugs began to be taken on an EU scale. Since then the drugs trade has become a major policy issue not only internally but as an issue of border security. EU policy is concerned with drug production in its more loosely regulated border states including the chemical production of drugs or their 'precursor substances' which is thought to be a problem in Eastern Europe.[31] There is also concern about cannabis production in Egypt, Morocco and the Lebanon. But the border states, especially in southeastern Europe, are also seen as a significant route for incoming opium-based drugs.

This concern with drug trafficking finds its reflection in the rising EU expenditure on the fight against drugs as well as expenditure through the individual states. In 1987 the EU made its first financial commitment of ecu 5.5 million which rose to 14.8 million in 1991, 27.9 million in 1995 and ecu54 million in 1996. In 1995, 47 per cent of this expenditure was undertaken within the EU mainly on health, information and the coordination of anti-drugs policies. Of the 53 per cent that was spent outside the European Union 34 per cent went to the PHARE countries of Eastern Europe and 23 per cent to the countries of the Mediterranean. But alongside this there has been a succession of organizational initiatives. In 1989 the European Committee to Combat Drugs (ECCD) was set up, in 1991 action was taken to try to limit money laundering. The Lisbon summit of June 1992 agreed to make drug trafficking one of the priorities of the Common Foreign and Security Policy. Then the Maastricht Treaty came into force in November 1993 making the drug fight a matter of common concern. The same year also saw the creation of the Lisbon based European Monitoring Centre for Drugs and Drug addiction (EMCDDA). The 'fight against drugs' has become a high profile issue in the Heads of State meetings, incorporated into the common foreign and security policy and a current issue in the enlargement process since 1992. Clauses about drugs and money laundering are written into the Europe agreements and active operational cooperation has been part of the PHARE framework since 1992. The issue also figures importantly in the development of the European Union's Mediterranean policy in the south (European Union, nd).

But critics of the 'war on drugs' argue that it is driven both by moral panics internally and, insofar as it comes to influence the wider relations of the EU to its periphery, broader goals that can be conveniently achieved under the flag of drug control. Drug control also has the wider function of allowing the demonizing of some social groups and legitimizing pressure on the poorer periphery of Europe. In this latter case the association of these areas with lax laws in respect of production or trafficking allows the image to be re-enforced that here is a zone of instability which threatens the peace and prosperity of 'Europe'. Supplicant governments are forced to accede to an EU opposed agenda of drug control as part of the price of their continuing relationships even though domestically this might not be a priority and indeed might involve a considerable diversion of resources.[32]

But it is in the south that many of these elements come together through the development of controls based on the idea of the threat of Islam, Islamic fundamentalism and Islamic terror. There is now an extensive literature disparaging the idea that there is a coordinated threat from Islamic fundamentalism and setting what has been called 'Islamophobia' in the context of longer term 'orientalist ideas' (Runnymeade Trust, 1997). It is not clear how seriously this threat is taken at the level of foreign policy. One British defence expert, Jonathan Eyal, has termed the idea of Islamic threats and clashes between civilization blocks, 'a puerile search for the certainties of the Cold War, with their unity of purpose and single enemy; it makes gripping reading, but is useless for strategic thinking' (*Observer*, 1 June 1997).

However, at the level of political rhetoric and debate the idea continues to fascinate many and, especially in the absence of networks of subversive communist spies, networks of subversive Islamicists can play a useful role in legitimating police and border controls. Here the argument turns full circle because the terrorist threat comes not only from without but from within and this contributes to police and state pressure on migrant communities and their descendants who continue to be discriminated against and denied full rights. In the run up to the World Cup in France in 1998, for example, there was coordinated police action across Europe to arrest suspected 'Islamic terrorists' intent on disrupting the tournament through bombings. Police and governments boasted of the European cooperation that this involved and the way that it reflected the success of international policing of the suspect groups, and by implication the communities in which they lived. But despite the propaganda of the authorities nothing of substance was found to identify those who were arrested as potential bombers. A flavour of the mentality of the action that the authorities lauded can be seen in the code names given to the police operations which ranged from 'Vendetta' in Britain to the even more astonishing 'Operation Crusades' in Italy. With this officially blessed insensitivity it is not difficult to see that such actions risk further alienating local communities, which might even provoke the very actions it was ostensibly designed to forestall.[33]

In each of these ways we have seen how this rhetoric of the insider–outsider, the European and the non-European reflects and contributes to the practical controls that are built into the walls of the prosperity divide around Europe. This is bound to be a source of continuing instability and frustration. But the paradox of the collapse of the Soviet model has been the creation of a situation where there is a lack of a powerful alternative ideology to challenge this structure. Only in the Islamic world does an alternative political ideology exist and even here Fukuyama's judgement that this lacks an alternative focus to liberal market ideology retains a considerable element of truth.

Yet the evidence is that the liberal market also cannot fulfil its promise and within its failure we see nurtured a whole series of far less pleasant arguments and polices. Changing the direction of development here will involve unravelling the hidden assumptions of these arguments, attacking the substance of the practical policies of exclusionary control and going beyond this to the root of the problem in terms of the failure to offer a feasible solution to the problems of uneven development and divergence in the foreseeable future.

Notes

*This is a revised and updated version of an earlier publication which appeared in *Economic and Political Weekly*, 29 August 1998.

1 Current general EU data can be accessed through the EU's Eurostat webpage at http://europa.eu.int/comm/eurostat/

2 Taken from Eurostat (2000).

3 As a percentage of the EU average per capita output, measured in purchasing power standards, for these 'external' EU areas in 1996 was as follows: Canaries

74 (Spain); Madeira 54, Açores 50 (Portugal); Martinique 40, Guyana 54, Reunion 48, Gouadeloupe 47 (France).

4 Data taken from Eurostat News Release (1999a). On regions see European Commission (1996).

5 Data taken from Eurostat Memo (1999) plus various World Bank data and other sources for countries not reported by Eurostat.

6 Calculated from Maddison, A. (1995) passim.

7 Calculated from Maddison, A. (1995) passim.

8 See Crafts (1995); Toniolo (1998); Tortella (1994).

9 For a good recent summary of the issues see Ben-David (1997).

10 Author's calculations based on data in Eurostat News Release (1999a).

11 See Abraham and Van Rompuy, (1995); Armstrong (1995); Barro and Sala-i-Martin (1991); Fagerberg and Verspagen (1996); Neven and Gouyette (1995).

12 For a critique of the transition, including a questioning of the extent of real recovery see Summers and Andor (1998).

13 If we assume a stable population in the EU and a long-run per capita growth rate of 2 per cent then with 2 per cent population growth in the Maghreb–Mashrak these countries would need a sustained 4 per cent rate of GDP growth to hold their position and a much higher one to make an impression on the development gap.

14 Note that the author seems to think that existing illegal immigration levels are a serious problem.

15 Ellingstad (1997) elaborates the maquiladora model in respect of Eastern Europe but Martin (1998) argues that even this is too optimistic a prognosis for the short-to medium-term future of these economies.

16 EU aid runs at 0.37 per cent of GNP making it the second largest source of multi-lateral aid after the World Bank. Disbursements (rather than pledges) have swung heavily to Eastern Europe at the expense of both the Mediterranean and the rest of the world. The character of aid has also changed, now including a higher consultancy element which goes straight back to Western Europe. See Overseas Development Institute (1997).

17 For a strong social democratic critique of the narrow-minded response of the EU to the Eastern European problem see Eatwell *et al.* (1997).

18 Collinson (1996, p. 60), for example, argues that governments in North Africa are trading restrictions on immigration in return for better deals elsewhere.

19 *De jure* this 'sixteenth state' is made up of those with less than full citizenship rights, *de facto* it is also based on colour and religion. Sometimes in some countries the three come together. At the moment much attention is being paid to Muslim minorities. For an estimate of their numbers and composition see Peach and Glebe (1995).

20 France, for example, considered Algeria – now a pariah state across the Mediterranean, as a département.

21 (European Union, 1997). The elastic definitions of Europe can be seen in the differing membership of such organizations as the EU, the Western European Union, the Council of Europe, Conference on Security and Cooperation in Europe. It is worth noting as well that the key article does not say that non 'European' states cannot apply though this is implicitly what it has come to mean.

22 The reference to Braudel is to the famous French historian whose classic work was on the unity of the Mediterranean in the sixteenth century.
23 For an outsider view see Butt–Philip (1994). For an insider view of EU Calloui (1992). For a valuable summary of the actual barriers to movement see Convey and Kupiszewski (1995).
24 See Dale and Cole (1999) for discussions of policy towards external migration within the current EU.
25 Until the 1980s southern Europe was an area of out-migration. Since then it has become an area of in migration. See, for example, Blanco Fdez de Valderramam (1993).
26 For a typical discussion of this problem see Shelly (1995).
27 Reuvid (1995) – a work produced with the support of the British government.
28 The slipshod analysis is illustrated in the following passage from the same source, 'From 1991–1995, the number of criminal groups in Russia increased from 952 to 8222 and the number of identified members from 15,000 to 32,000. At the end of 1996, there were an estimated 400 organised crime groups in Poland, with Russian, former Yugoslav, Vietnamese, Italian and Colombian contacts'. The spurious accuracy of the estimate of the number of criminal groups appears designed to mislead and the author does not appear to have noticed that if true then the average size of a Russian criminal group has declined from 15 to 4!
29 See Box (1983) for a discussion of how the idea of crime has been constructed in Europe and Pearce and Woodiwiss (eds) (1993) for critiques of the conventional idea of what constitutes international crime.
30 The same also applies with the much vaunted return flow of 'western sex tourists' to the periphery of Europe and beyond which is increasingly the subject of international police cooperation without the roots of the problem being seriously addressed. As Petr Zelasko, the Czech coordinator of youth crime investigation, put it of the problem in that country, 'the day the [Czech] koruna has the same value as [Deutsch] mark will be the day the last paedophile comes over here'. A Czech child prostitute described his relationship with his client, 'Mum and Dad were giving me between 100 and 200 crowns a month ($3–5) which was too little. Chris…would give me 1,000 every time. I bought myself Adidas shoes, a Nike jacket and I have a golden ring for my mum for Christmas. I spent all my money' (Campbell and Connolly 1997).
31 See, for example, the articles collected as Various (1996).
32 Fighting drugs is not the central Europeans' number one priority' said one commentator in 1996. (Thomson, 1996).
33 *Le Figaro*, 27 May 1998, *Libération*, 27 May 1998, *Times*, 27 May 1998.

Bibliography

Abraham, F. and Van Rompuy, P. (1995) 'Regional Convergence in the European Monetary Union', *Papers in Regional Science*, 74, 2.

Abramovitz, M. (1986) 'Catching Up, Forging Ahead and Falling Behind', *Journal of Economic History*, 46, June.

Applegate, C. (1999) 'A Europe of Regions: Reflections on the Historiography of Sub-national Places in Modern Times', *American Historical Review*, 104, 4.

Armstrong, H. W. (1995) 'Convergence Among Regions of the EU, 1950–1990', *Papers in Regional Science*, 74 2.

Bahaijoub, A. (1993) 'Morocco's Argument to Join the EEC', in Joffé G. (ed.), *North Africa: Nation, State and Region* (London: Routledge).

Baimbridge, M. *et al.* (1994) 'The Maastricht Treaty: Exacerbating Racism in Europe?', *Ethnic and Racial Studies*, 17, 3, July.

Baldwin-Edwards, M. (1997) 'The Merging European Immigration Regime: Some Reflections on Implications for Southern Europe', *Journal of Common Market Studies*, 35, 4, December.

Barro R. J. and Sala-i-Martin, X. (1991) 'Convergence Among States and Regions', *Brookings Papers*, no. 1.

Baumol, W. (1986) 'Productivity Growth, Convergence and Welfare', *American Economic Review*, 76, December.

Ben-David, D. (1997) 'Convergence Clubs and Diverging Economies', *Working Paper Tel Aviv University*, October.

Blanco Fdez de Valderramam, C. (1993) 'The New Hosts: The Case of Spain', *International Migration Review*, xxvii, 1.

Blunden, M. (1994) 'Insecurity on Europe's Southern Flank', *Survival*, 36, 2, Summer.

Box, S. (1983) *Power, Crime, and Mystification* (London, Routledge).

Burgess, A. (1997) *Divided Europe. The New Domination of the East* (London: Pluto Press).

Butt-Philip, A. (1994) 'European Union Immigration Policy: Phantom, Fantasy or Fact', *West European Politics*, 17, 2, April.

Calloui, G. (1992) 'Regulation of Immigration in 1993: Pieces of the European Community Jigsaw Puzzle', *International Migration Review*, xxvi, 2.

Campbell, D. and Connolly, K. (1997) 'Inside Europe's sex supermarket', *Guardian*, 17 December.

Collinson, S. (1996) *Shore to Shore: The Politics of Migration in Euro–Maghreb Relations* (London: Royal Institute of International Affairs).

Convey, A. and Kupiszewski, M. (1995) 'Keeping up with Schengen: Migration and Policy in the EU', *International Migration Review*, xxix, 4.

Council of Europe (1997a) Second Summit of the Council of Europe 10–11 September. *Special Document. The Fight Against Organised Crime in Europe* (http://www.coe.fr/summit/ecorruption.html.).

Council of Europe (1997b) 'Assembly Calls for Measures to Combat Traffic in Women and Forced Prostitution', *Council of Europe Press Release*, Ref. 246 (97).

Crafts, N. (1995) 'The Golden Age of Economic Growth in Western Europe, 1950–1973', *Economic History Review*, xlviii, 3.

Dale, G. and Cole, M. (eds) (1999) *The European Union and Migrant Labour* (Oxford: Berg).

De Long, J. Bradford (1988) 'Productivity Growth, Convergence and Welfare: Comment', *American Economic Review*, 78, 5.

Eatwell, J., Ellman, M., Karlsson, M., Mario Nuti, D., and Shapiro, J. (1997) *Not 'Just Another Accession': The Political Economy of European Union Enlargement to the East* (London: Institute of Public Policy Research).

Ellingstad, M. (1997) 'The Maquiladora Syndrome: Central European Prospects', *Europe-Asia Studies*, 49, 1, January.

European Commission (1992) 'Europe and the Challenge of Enlargement', *Bulletin of the European Commission Supplement*, no. 3.

European Commission (1996) *First Report on Economic and Social Cohesion*, Luxembourg.

European Commission (1999) 'Regular Report from the Commission on Progress towards Accession by Each of the Candidate Countries', October 13.

European Union (1986) *Single European Act*, Luxembourg.

Eurostat (1998) 'Facts through figures' (Luxembourg: Office for Official Publications of the European Communities).

European Union (n.d.) *The European Union and the Fight Against Drugs* (Luxembourg: Office for Official Publications of the EU).

European Union (1997) *Consolidated Treaties*. (Luxembourg: Office for Official Publications of the European Communities).

Eurostat (2000) 'GDP in 1998', *Statistics in Focus: Economy and Finance Series*, no. 2.

Eurostat Memo (1997) 'Step forward in Euro–Mediterranean Statistical Co-operation', 3/97 15 April 1997.

Eurostat Memo (1999) 'EU Enlargement. Key data on candidate countries', Memo 10/99, 7 December 1999.

Eurostat News Release (1999a) 'European Regions with Highest and Lowest GDP Per Person', 11/99, 9 February.

Fagerberg, J. and Verspagen, B. (1996) 'Heading for Divergence? Regional Growth in Europe Reconsidered', *Journal of Common Market Studies*, 34, 3, September.

Fassmann, H. (1994) 'European East-West Migration, 1945–1992', *International Migration Review*, xxviii, 3.

Garson, J. P. (1997–98) 'Opening Mediterranean Trade and Migration', *OECD Observer*, no. 209, December–January.

Hadjimichalis, C. (1997) 'What kind of Europe?', *Soundings*, no. 6, Summer.

Hakura, F. S. (1997) 'The Euro-Mediterranean Policy: The Implications of the Barcelona Declaration', *Common Market Law Review*, 34.

Hamilton, K. A. (1997) 'Europe, Africa and International Migration: An Uncomfortable Triangle of Interests', *New Community*, 23, 4, October.

Harris, N. (1996) *The New Untouchables. Immigration and the New World Order* (Harmondsworth: Penguin).

Harvie, C. (1994) *The Rise of Regional Europe* (London: Routledge).

Haynes, M. (1999) 'Setting the limits to Europe as an imagined community', in Dale G. and Cole M. (eds), *The European Union and Migrant Labour*.

Hutton, W. (1996) *The State We're In* (London: Vintage).

Kaldor, N. (1966) *The Causes of the Slow Rate of Growth of the United Kingdom* (Cambridge: Cambridge University Press).

Kaplar, Z. (1997) 'Hungary Tries to Bridge the Gap', *The European*, 12–18 June.

Kennedy, P. (1988) *The Rise and Fall of the Great Powers. Economic Change and Military Conflict from 1500 to 2000* (London: Fontana).

Kuznets, S. (1966) *Modern Economic Growth: Rates, Structure and Spread* (New Haven: Yale University Press).

Maddison, A. (1995) *Monitoring the World Economy 1820–1992*, Paris: OECD.

Manfrass, K. (1992) 'Europe: South–North or East-West Migration?', *International Migration Review*, xxvi, 2.

Martin, R. (1998) 'Central and Eastern Europe and the International Economy: The Limits to Globalisation', *Europe-Asia Studies*, 50, 1.

Molle, M. and Boeckout, S. (1995) 'Economic Disparity under Conditions of Integration – A Long-Term view of the European Case', *Papers in Regional Science*, 74, 2.

Neven, D. and Gouyette, C. (1995) 'Regional convergence in the European Community', *Journal of Common Market Studies*, 33.

Nizamova, A. (1997) 'The Regional Differentiation of Poverty in East-European Countries', *Luxembourg Income Study Working Papers*, no. 161, May.

Nsouli, S. M. Bisat, A. and Kanaan, O. (1996) 'The European Union's new Mediterranean Strategy', *Finance and Development*, 33, 3, September.

Overseas Development Institute (1997) *Insights for Policy Makers*, no. 24, December.

Peach, C. and Glebe G. (1995) 'Muslim Minorities in Western Europe', *Ethnic and Racial Studies*, 18, 1, January.

Pearce, F. and Woodiwiss M. eds. (1993) *Global Crime Connections. Dynamics and Control* (Basingstoke: Macmillan).

Rhein, E. (1996) 'Europe and the Mediterranean: A Newly Emerging Geopolitical Area', *European Foreign Affairs Review*, 1, 1.

Reuvid, J. (1995) *The Regulation and Prevention of Economic Crime Internationally* (London: Kogan Page).

Runnymeade Trust (1997) *Islamophobia. A Challenge to Us All*, (London: Runnymeade Trust).

Shelly, L. (1995) 'Transnational Organised Crime', *Journal of International Affairs*, 48, 2, winter.

Summers, M. and Andor, L. (1998) *Market Failure: A Guide to Eastern Europe's Economic Miracle* (London: Pluto Press).

Thirwall, T. (2000) '*European Unity Could Flounder on Regional Neglect*', *Guardian*, 31 January.

Thomson, T. (1996) 'EU unsure of policies on fighting drug consumption,' *European Dialogue*, no. 4, July–August.

Toniolo, G. (1998) 'Europe's Golden Age, 1950–1973: Speculations From a Long-run Perspective', *Economic History Review*, 2, May.

Tortella, G. (1994) 'Patterns of Economic Retardation and Recovery in South-western Europe in the Nineteenth and Twentieth Centuries', *Economic History Review*, xlviii, 1, February.

Williamson, J. (1996) 'Globalisation, Convergence and History', *Journal of Economic History*, 56, 2, June.

UN Commission for Europe (1999) *Economic Survey of Europe*, no. 2, United Nations, Geneva.

Various (1996) 'Drugs – A CIS Growth Industry', *Transition*, 2, 19, 20 September.

7
Britain and the Question of Europe[1]

Werner Bonefeld

The contention that the relationship of Britain to European integration is peculiar summons common wisdom. Britain has time and time again been characterized as an 'awkward' (George, 1994) or 'semi-detached' (Bulmer, 1992) partner. However, despite its 'awkwardness', Britain has in fact signed and ratified the Maastricht Treaty.[2]

The fact that the UK negotiated an opt-out from the European single currency is widely assumed to mean that the monetary union obligations set out in the Maastricht Treaty are of little importance unless the UK opts to join the single currency (*Financial Times*, 30.11.98). As a result, there is a belief that monetary policy, including exchange rate policy, will remain a matter of political 'choice' for the UK. However, and importantly, Britain's opt-out clauses relate only to Stage 3 of monetary union.[3] However, the Protocol to the Treaty which embodies Britain's opt-out, obliges the UK to take part in Stages 1 and 2 of monetary union (Howe, 1996, pp. 287–88). The UK need not take part in Stage 3 unless it opts to do so. However, under Stage 3, the UK is treated as a member state with a derogation (ibid, pp. 287–88). The Treaty confers, as Howe explains, obligations on the conduct of Britain's monetary and exchange rate policies. Stage 2 of monetary union requires member states, amongst other things, 'to endeavour to avoid excessive budget deficits' and 'restrict lending by central banks to governments and public sector bodies' (ibid., p. 286). It also envisages that member states avoid devaluation, and that independence wil be granted to the central banks of member states. The 'Treaty envisages', then, that those member countries that have a derogation from full monetary union will continue to strive to 'achieve the convergence criteria' (ibid, 288). The vacillations over Europe could not be better expressed than by Britain's forceful campaign to retain its 'sovereignty' over monetary policy and its – two-third – membership in EMU.

The chapter assesses the *raison d'être* of Britain's position. The argument contends that the question of Europe, especially monetary union, poses an impasse for the British ruling class. Britain's vacillations over Europe will be explained by the miserable experience of monetarism in Britain and the particular character of British economic structures in relation to its main rivals on the world market. Britain, so the argument goes, is the most internationalized economy, probably in the world. The conclusion sums up the argument and assesses Labour's employment policies. The key to the understanding of Britain in relation to Europe is inter-imperialist rivalry over competitive rates of growth in labour productivity.

EMU and disarray

The construction of 'Europe' over the past two decades seems to indicate that Britain was able to Europeanize its neo-liberal domestic policy agenda.[4] The Single European Act dovetailed with the politics of the Thatcher administrations of the 1980s. Thatcher, as Anderson (1997, p. 171) argues, collaborated 'in the interest of deregulating financial markets, in which British banks and insurance companies saw prospects of large gains'. Of course, monetary union was and remains a deeply contentious issue. Yet, EMU endorses, and puts on to a legal basis, the neo-liberal politics of tight money, labour market deregulation, and the liberalization of capital and financial markets. EMU supports the scaling down of the welfare state. It imposes deregulatory pressure on existing protectionist and regulative functions of member states, leaving a politics of sound money as the sole 'regulator' that imposes adjustment to tight monetary conditions as if it were an automatic pilot. In short, as Gill (1992) reports, EMU was designed to lead to the obliteration of what was left of the Keynesian legacy. Grahl (1997, p. 129) makes a similar point when he argues that the 'Maastricht Treaty... inscribed the monetarist project into the EU's agenda for the rest of the century and beyond'. What, then, do we make of Britain's two-third membership in EMU?

There is no need here to review the history of Britain's relations to the development of the European enterprise. The question of whether to join the Common Market has split both major parties since the 1950s. In the first decade after Britain's accession to the EC in 1973, European integration was characterized by 'Eurosclerosis'. This allowed the British state to reconcile two conflicting agendas. On the one hand, it was able to seek the modernization of its domestic economy within the framework of the Cold War and, on the other, it could claim to have contained the European question. However, the revitalization of European integration during the 1980s shattered this 'settlement' and sceptical assessments of Britain's role in an integrating Europe put at risk the cohesion of the then Thatcher government. The debate over Europe became even more bitter against the background of the unification of Germany and especially after the pound's expulsion from the ERM in September 1992. The crisis of 1992 paralysed not only the Major government. It also affected Labour's economic policy stance. Under the leadership of Kinnock and Smith, Labour adopted a pro-European stance. Labour endorsed the view that ERM membership would 'depress inflationary expectations by denying employers the option of a competitive devaluation if they succumbed to pay claims too easily' (Shaw, 1994, p. 98). Were employers not able to depress the growth of wages and achieve lower unit labour costs, they would 'price themselves out of markets with the result – as [the later Labour Leader John] Smith pointed out [in 1990] – that "there would be unemployment, wouldn't there?"' (ibid). This endorsement assessed the virtues of ERM membership in similar terms to those of the then Conservative government.

The new Labour government under Tony Blair has sought more amicable relations with other European states. During the Amsterdam IGC of 1997, Blair claimed the role of a European leader for himself because, as he saw it, of his successful reconciliation between the German and the French governments over the issue of 'employment' within EMU (Robinson, 1998). However, behind the rhetoric of a New Britain at the heart of a New Europe lurks the familiar uncertainty and reluctance towards Europe. The Labour government soon ran into difficulties over the proposals by the new SPD-led government in Germany to introduce, as the French government under Jospin had demanded for some time, a European employment pact to run in parallel with monetary union. Furthermore, the new German government's call for the harmonization of business tax rates across Europe did not receive an enthusiastic endorsement in Britain. The tax proposals projected Germany's regulative model on to a European plane, seeking to avoid competitive tax pressures that might entice tax bases to migrate to low tax countries. The German view was anathema to the British Labour government. It seeks, on the basis of comparatively lower tax-levels, to attract foreign direct investment. Britain, in the conception of both the Conservative party and the Labour party, is to participate in the single market as a competitive offshore island for global capital guaranteeing access to the European market and offering a low tax regime and a deregulated labour market as a competitive advantage. Proposals for tax regulation, and indeed an active European employment policy are viewed as taking away at least some of these advantages and imposing a regulative regime that the British economy might find very difficult to absorb without further exposure of its relative weakness in relation to its 'partners', especially Germany. In sum, the honeymoon between New Labour and Europe, if indeed it ever existed, has fallen on hard times.

Of course, one of the first acts of the Labour government was to sign up to the European Social Charter that sets out minimal rights for European labour, and to announce that Britain would defer decision on entry into monetary union to early 2002 at the earliest. Labour's acceptance of the Social Charter, however, has not in any way softened its emphasis on labour market deregulation as a means of maintaining its competitive position on the world market. Blair's endorsement of a politics of 'employability' signals that much. As the conclusion will show, the Labour government's endorsement of workers' rights is not what it seems. It interprets and seeks to implement these rights within a framework of neo-liberal labour market reforms. Labour espouses deregulated and flexible labour markets and stresses the 'democratic virtues' of choice and individual responsibility.[5] In short, under Blair, Britain is governed 'in the spirit of Thatcher' (cf. Ali, 1999). For Labour, as Ali reports, 'there is only one successful model in Europe and that is the British model. Death to tax and spend. Long live flexible labour markets'.

The Labour government, in sum, views Britain's low wage economy and its deregulated labour market as a competitive asset in relation to the so-called 'overregulated' European economies, most of whose economic performance is superior to Britain's (Young, 2000, p. 24). However, Blair's endorsement of labour market flexibility and deregulation is not only concerned with the defense of these assets *vis-à-vis* its more productive European 'partners'. His espousal of deregulated labour relations reflects also the miserable experience of monetarism in Britain.

Monetarism and the search for an anchor

In the European context, Thatcher's Britain of the 1980s stands out both for the severity of its monetarist experiment and the failure of monetarism. In contrast to Britain, France under Mitterand in the early 1980s pursued what for reasons of brevity might be termed a programme of 'Keynesianism in one country'. Against the background of the recession of the early 1980s, this programme was soon abandoned and economic policy in France shifted decisively towards austerity that was anchored by the German Mark in the ERM. In short, France adopted an 'external' anchor for its domestic programme of tight money (*franc fort* – strong franc).[6] In Britain, the programme of monetarism in one country, that is the Medium Term Financial Strategy, was also discontinued in the early 1980s. In contrast to France, Britain did not commit the pound to the ERM. The making of monetarist policy was left without a firm anchor, leaving the British state without a basis for its continued quest to effect disinflation. Furthermore, during the 1980s, the so-called relative economic decline of the British economy was not reversed[7] and, instead, the 'parasitic' character of the British economy became more accentuated. Making money out of money became more important and emphasized, than the productive accumulation of capital.

After the disaster and subsequent abandonment of the Medium Term Financial Strategy in the early 1980s (see Bonefeld, 1993), the Thatcher government was deeply divided over the conduct of monetary policy. The divide centred on whether Britain should lock the pound into the ERM or whether the pound should be allowed to find its own level.[8] The then British Chancellor, Nigel Lawson, endorsed membership in the ERM as a means of putting the economy on auto-pilot.[9] By fixing the exchange rate to that of a stronger and more stable economy, the British economy would be forced to adjust in order to remain competitive and government would be shielded from the consequences of such adjustment because it would be imposed on Britain ostensibly from the outside, from Europe. This would help to depoliticize the making of economic policy and thereby insulate the government from the consequences of ERM-enforced economic and social adjustment and the likely electoral backlash such adjustment might cause.

Lawson lost the argument to Thatcher who argued that the exchange rate should be determined by market forces and that it was the task of government to create the conditions, particularly labour market conditions, that would support employers in their attempt to reassert their right to manage, i.e. to increase labour productivity.[10] Yet Thatcher agreed, against the background of a severe economic downturn, to link the pound to the ERM in 1990.[11] During the 1980s, Lawson's search for a stable exchange rate regime reflected his despair at the failure of monetarism in one country (see Lawson, 1992). When the boom of the

1980s came to an end, first signalled by the crash of 1987, and then by growing inflationary pressure and an increase in deficits by the late 1980s, Thatcher was adamant that the serious economic downturn was the result of Lawson's apparently 'clandestine' shadowing of the German mark from 1987 to 1988. For the Eurosceptics, monetarism had not failed but, rather, it was Lawson's misguided exchange rate policy that was at fault (see for example, Redwood, 1997). Growing differences over the conduct of economic policy focused on the increasingly bitter debate over whether or not Britain should join the ERM. This debate, ostensibly over the issue of national sovereignty, was about the failure of the British economy during the Thatcher period to catch up with its main competitors. During the pound's membership in the ERM, the fault lines of the British economy were clearly exposed and commentators assessed the impact of ERM-membership in terms similar to those suffered by the former GDR after monetary and economic union with the FRG in July 1990 (*Financial Times*, 12.3.91).

Britain entered the ERM at the start of the deep recession of the early 1990s. The then Chancellor, Norman Lamont, was quite clear on the 'benefits' of the deflationary discipline exerted by ERM-membership: 'Rising unemployment and business failures "were a price worth paying" for the defeat of inflation' (Smith, 1993, p. 188). ERM-membership was heralded a success and Lamont took the opportunity of emphasizing the 'sea-change in attitudes to inflation' that had occurred in Britain since joining. The Chancellor stressed that a regime change in monetary policy had occurred inasmuch as industry and labour would be taught once and for all that high pay awards 'translate directly into a loss of competitiveness and hence of market share, profits and jobs' (*Financial Times*, 20.5.92). The centre of gravity was the Deutschmark, with the pound kept within limits set by the German mark. This enabled the government to argue that Britain had to adapt to an environment in which inflation performance must match or even undercut that of Germany.

Lamont's assessment of ERM-membership was widely shared. The *Financial Times* proclaimed that 'sterling's years of living dangerously are over' (*Financial Times*, 29.4.91) and that the UK was 'about to enter a period when making things is more important than moving paper' (*Financial Times*, 8.2.91). However, these early assessments missed an important point. During the 1980s there had been a large scale shake out of labour (Crafts, 1994) and the Keynesian nexus between wages and public expenditure had been attacked (Rowthorn, 1992). There had not been, however, a decisive breakthrough in labour productivity, productive investment or a reduction in average wages relative to other European states (Deakin, 1992). The depth of the recession of the 1990s was to a great extent a response to the ballooning of debt on a global scale. The boom of the 1980s rested on the continued accumulation of credit. The longer this was sustained without increased investment and thus a corresponding exploitation of social labour power, the deeper the attendant recession, 'the greater the accumulation of fictitious capital on which [the boom] rests, the greater the dangers of a catastrophic crisis and a devastating depression' (Clarke, 1992, p. 147).

The *sine qua non* of the pound's stability within the ERM was a reduction in unit labour costs and increased productivity. Failure to achieve these ends made it unlikely, as indeed was the case, that the pound would survive inside the ERM without provoking serious political and social conflict. Unless unit labour costs in Britain improved to match the levels in Germany, pressure on the pound would increase because the pound's exchange rate would not be backed by productivity performance and the creation of assets against which to balance the money supply. Between 1985 and 1992, GDP in Germany grew uninterrupted, with unemployment reaching only 4.6 per cent in 1992 and net output per worker running 25 per cent higher than in Britain (see Bonefeld and Burnham, 1996). The underlying strength of the German industrial economy underpinned the Deutschmark. Britain had to accommodate to German unit labour costs and rates of inflation or lose jobs to German competition. The ERM operated like an automatic pilot of national and international reconstruction putting, in the absence of a real breakthrough in labour productivity, growing pressure on high inflation and low productivity memberstates. As Peter Jay (1994, p. 183) summarizes: 'Since interest rates cannot be substantially different in two economies linked by supposedly immutable exchange rates and capital movements, the EC economies outside the natural greater German economy (Germany, Austria, Holland, Belgium and Luxembourg) faced a choice between devaluing (or floating down) against the German mark and raising their interest rates to compete with German rates, thereby subjecting their already cyclically weak economies to further deflationary pressures.' As the costs of German unification rocketed, the Bundesbank tightened monetary policy, driving German interest rates up. The Deutschmark appreciated pushing its partner currencies to the lower end of the fluctuation margin. Pressure on the pound increased rendering a reduction in the rate of interest in Britain impossible at a time of deepening recession.

Towards the end of August 1992 the Deutschmark appreciated sharply against the dollar and the Bank of England lost $1bn in an attempt to prevent sterling falling below its ERM floor (see Bonefeld and Burnham, 1996). As exchange rate volatility increased and dollar exports weakened, it became apparent that the pound's continued membership of the ERM depended on further interest rate rises, consigning the UK's manufacturing and construction industries to further decline and job loss and reinforcing financial pressures on personal debtors. Lamont's last throw of the dice occurred on the 3rd of September when he announced a foreign currency borrowing plan designed to strengthen sterling within the ERM – and finally scotch suggestions of devaluation. In a move dubbed by the *Financial Times* (4.9.92) as more 'often associated with the lax finances of banana republics', Lamont borrowed ecu 10bn (£ 7.27bn), over half in Deutschmarks, as insurance in the event of a French 'No' vote in the September 20th referendum on Maastricht. Lamont's hopes were pinned on a significant German cut in interest rates. But on 14 September the Bundesbank announced a reduction of only 0.25 per cent and the then Bundesbank President, Helmut Schlesinger, indicated that in his view a wider realignment was still required. This could only mean one thing to the dealers on the floors of the world's financial markets – that sterling's position within the ERM was under threat. Wednesday 16 September saw the Bank of England intervene in foreign currency markets on an unprecedented scale, losing £16bn in an attempt to maintain sterling at its ERM floor of DM2.77. As sterling continued to collapse – 'it was sold like water running out of a tap' (*Financial Times*, 19.9.92) – the financial markets knew the game was up – as indeed it was.

After the pound's dramatic and humiliating exit from the ERM in 1992, a further attempt to achieve the aims of monetarism focused on the institutional reform for the conduct of monetary policy, especially central bank independence. Central bank independence is claimed to increase the credibility of commitments to price stability, assure a high priority on fighting inflation, reduce changes in monetary policy resulting from general elections, reduce pre-electoral manipulation of monetary policy and inflationary tendencies resulting from political manipulation of monetary policy, and put up barriers to the monetization of government expenditure (Posen, 1993, p. 42). Regardless of the validity of these claims, independence is seen to enhance the credibility of the conduct of monetary policy, satisfying financial markets.

There is, of course, no institutional 'fix' to the problem of 'inflation' (Fine, 1979; Posen, 1993), and Britain's competitive asset of a low-wage economy is precarious in that any upturn in the economy might reactivate class conflict and lead to higher wage settlements. Operational independence is important in that it replaces discretionary policy making by a rule-based system, which allows the government to claim that its 'macroeconomic hands' are tied. Furthermore, the granting of central bank operational independence extends the politics of depoliticization. Although the Chancellor and the Governor of the Bank of Endland might have public disputes over interest rates, there is no reason why these should jeopardize the political benefits of independence. On the contrary, publicized disputes support the Chancellor's political role at the same time as the Bank of England emphasizes its responsibility in monetary matters. Thus disputes put distance between the Chancellor and the Bank exploiting the depoliticizing potential that controversies between different state-apparatuses can produce when one appears to argue against the other in the pursuance of the 'national interest'. The political conflict between government and the working class becomes thus transformed into a friendly, consensus-creating dispute between different aspects of the state.

The government's search for a 'new framework', for another way of depoliticizing economy policy began immediately following expulsion from the ERM.[12] On 8 October 1992, in a memorandum to the House of Commons Treasury and Civil Service Committee, the then Chancellor, Norman Lamont, set out the policy framework which would replace the ERM (Jay, 1994, p. 187; Lamont, 1992). Counter inflationary credibility would now be sought by restructuring the institutional relationship between the Treasury and the Bank of England in order, apparently, 'to make the formation of policy more transparent and our decisions more accountable' (Lamont, 1992). In an effort to bear down on inflation, the government would produce: a) publicly announced long-term inflation targets of 1 to 4 per cent; b) a unified budget which examined spending and revenue together; and c) monthly monetary reports published by the Treasury. Furthermore, a team of independent forecasters would advise the Chancellor while the Bank of England would be responsible for publishing quarterly Inflation Reports and, importantly, would acquire progressively more independence from the Treasury in the execution of monetary policy. Under Kenneth Clarke, as Chancellor, in 1993, the Bank was given the right of deciding the timing of interest rates and, in February 1994, Clarke outlined a new framework for monetary policy decision making: decisions concerning interest rates would be taken at meetings between the Chancellor and the Governor and minutes would subsequently be published (on this: Thompson,

1995). In sum, since September 1992, the Bank of England's role and influence in monetary policy has increased significantly (Treasury, 1993–94, p. 10). The Bank's quarterly Inflation Reports, which examine the government's progress towards meeting the newly announced inflation targets, were initially commented on by the Treasury prior to release. However since the Fourth Report, the Bank has been wholly responsible for its publication and the Bank's directors have admitted that this move represents 'a significant departure from the pattern of the past 35 or 40 years' (Treasury, 1994; Treasury, 1993–94, p. 9).

Nevertheless, these measures stopped well short of giving full political independence to the Bank of England. Indeed, John Major, when announcing the appointment of Eddie George as the new Governor of the Bank of England in 1993, reaffirmed that the British government remained opposed to the idea of full central bank independence (*The Times*, 23.1.93). However, Major's opposition to operational independence was more rhetorical than real. Indeed, it did not reflect the government's actual stance on the topic. Under Major, recommendations were reviewed to enshrine price stability in statute as the primary objective of monetary policy and to follow the Bank of France by creating an independent Monetary Policy Committee within the Bank to oversee the making of policy (Treasury, 1993–94, pp. 19–21). The potential of this development was well assessed by the Governor of the Bank of England: 'The embodiment of the stability objective in statute... is actually important because I think the credibility of arrangements which would simply be with Government would be a good deal less' (ibid, p. 16). In short, while the issue of central bank independence remained politically divisive, there were powerful forces within the Major government that sought to enhance counter inflationary credibility by moving, at least in principle, in the direction of French and German versions of bank independence.

The incoming Labour government, elected on 1 May 1997, under Tony Blair as Prime Minister and Gordon Brown as Chancellor, lost no time in securing operational independence for the setting of interest rates to the Bank of England. The new Labour Chancellor defended his decision on 'grounds of domestic policy and increased credibility with financial markets' (*Financial Times*, 7.5.97, p. 10). His defence echoed an earlier assessment of the former Chancellor Nigel Lawson: 'An independent Bank was to some extent an alternative way of entrenching the commitment to stable prices... An independent Bank would not, of course, have had the merit of ERM membership of replacing discretion by rules. But it would at least... be seen to be locking a permanent anti-inflationary force into the system, as a counter-weight to the strong inflationary pressures which are always lurking' (Lawson, 1992, p. 868; see also Thompson, 1995). Labour's speedy proposal for greater operational independence could not have happened, as David Smith (1997, p. 11) points out, without the reforms of Norman Lamont and Kenneth Clarke who formalized the Bank's explicit role in monitoring and forecasting inflation and offering advice on the setting of interest rates, made public after six weeks.

Independence for the Bank of England is of course a requirement of Stage 2 of EMU. However, the Labour Chancellor, Gordon Brown, did not advocate central bank independence as a European commitment. Instead, it was endorsed as a prudent step to remove the making of monetary policy from the electoral battlefield, and to place it, instead, into the hands of those with 'impartial' understanding of monetary requirements. Brown thus seems to have taken to heart the neo-liberal prescription to resolve the so-called crisis of 'ungovernability'.[13] During the 1970s, neo-liberal commentators had argued for institutional reforms to remove economic policy from electoral pressures. The aim was to reduce the apparent economic costs of democracy. As Brittan (1976) saw it, 'excessive expectations are generated by the democratic aspects of the system' (p. 97). and 'the temptation to encourage false expectations among the electorate becomes overwhelming to politicians' (p. 105). The granting of operational independence to the Bank of England under Gordon Brown recognizes and reflects this concern.

Globalization and European integration

The most fashionable term used to describe contemporary developments is globalization.[14] There is no need here to rehash the at times opaque nature of the debate on globalization. Without doubt, we are witnessing the creation of what Marx called the world market society (on this: Agnoli, 2000). This society, in contrast to the proponents of 'globalization', is neither characterized by the creation of 'homogeneous' economic conditions nor does it amount to an escape of the 'economic' from the 'political'. As Murray (1997, p. 28) puts it, 'far from representing a "globalising" trend in economic affairs, one smoothing out contradictions between nation states, developments in trade are actually signalling a fiercer struggle between them'. There is, then, a re-ordering of political space through the regionalization of the world economy around the sphere of influence of the USA, Japan and Germany (Negri, 1996). The world market society is founded on the creation of regional power blocs and, as such, is characterized by inter-imperialist rivalry between and withing these blocs. And the UK?

The difficulties of the British political class to commit itself to Europe, and the full-scale integration of its political economy into a regionalized economic power-bloc dominated by Germany,[15] has much to do with the structure of the British economy. Britain, as Callinicos (1997, p. 43) puts it, 'is probably the most internationalized of the major capitalisms'. There is no doubt, as Rowthorn (1975) argued in the 1970s, that the global strength of British big capital has compounded the debility of 'British capitalism'. The global reach and operation of big 'British capital' helps, as Gamble (1986, p. 109) suggested in the 1980s, to 'account for one of the great paradoxes of British decline – why an economy performing so poorly should nevertheless have produced more multinational companies than any other country apart from the United States'. There is no reason to suggest that the global orientation of 'British capital' has changed (see Radice, 1999) and that it has become more European in outlook.

The long debate and divisions over Europe reflect and address the specific character of Britain's integration into the world market. This character concerns not only the global role of the City and the importance of financial institutions within the structure of the British economy. Nor does it merely concern the potential threat to the City by an integrated euro-bloc. It concerns also the high degree of capital concentration in British industry and the global role played by British transnational corporations (Radice, 1999). Britain has an exceptionally high rate of capital export and 'British capital', from its inception, was much more 'globally' oriented than its European competitors. For 'British capital', Britain is the basis from which its global operations divorced from domestic market constraints are conducted. From this perspective it seems that Britain has less interest in the 'regionalization' of the world economy and, instead, much to gain from a stable world-wide system for profit-making, a system in which, as its proponents see it, the powers act in concert to order the affairs of the world (cf. Jamieson, 1996). 'Globalization', in short, appears to be 'Britain's natural and logical style' (Murray, 1997, p. 77). Germany in contrast has been and remains in its political perspective, and economic orientation (Hufschmidt, 1994; 1998), a much more regionally focused power – better: it seeks to 'cover' its global aspiration through European institutions and to spread the costs of its world economic power position to its

'European partners' (Connolly, 1995). Germany cultivates Europeaness (see Kirchner, 1996) and does so in order to have a secure basis and cover for its international aspirations and operations (see Halevi, 1999).[16] Britain, in contrast, directly addresses its domestic concerns as global concerns and *vice versa*.

The 'global' perspective of British capital also helps to account for Britain's strong and persistent endorsement of a European free trade area and its lack of enthusiasm for incorporation into a Europe that is circumscribed by German economic power and political aspirations. Britain is a 'moderately poor EC member'; it fails to 'meet German productivity rates' (Moravcsik, 1999, pp. 425, 427); and its exposure to German interest rates during the membership of the pound in the ERM had shown for many the dangers that membership in monetary union might entail. The view that Britain would have serious problems of competitiveness in a fixed exchange regime is emphasized by Burkitt and Baimbridge (1996, p. 177) who argue that in order, 'to ensure its survival as a prosperous and self-governing nation, Britain must disengage from damaging integration trends, so that it can seize the tremendous opportunities open to it as an inherently cooperative, yet independent, country'. In other words, locking Britain into EMU is seen to impose upon it a deflationary force that would further weaken its economic status. This position holds that within an integrating Europe, Britain's so-called relative economic decline is not expected to be reversed but, rather, to become more emphasized. The disengagement from Europe appears thus to be endorsed as a means of returning Britain to the status of a global trading nation, permitting Britain as Jamieson (1996) sees it, to pursue free market policies as an offshore island for global capital. Yet, as a territorialized landing strip for global capital, Britain's national economy might well develop even further in the direction of a 'parasitic economy'. It might, however, not be 'a comfortable fate for sterling' to remain an independent currency that wobbles 'between the dollar and the euro as a speculator's toy currency' (Riley, *Financial Times*, 5/6.12.98). In the meantime, with a much weaker than expected euro, Britain suffered its worst trade deficit for a decade in 1999 'as imports surged and the strong pound started to hurt exporters' (*Guardian*, 24 February 2000).

In sum, Heseltine's warning is well founded: 'the coming of the single currency will unleash a wave of competitive pressure, which will sweep through this huge common market' (Heseltine, in *Guardian*, 15.10.99). He urges Britain to prepare for membership to withstand the pressure. Heseltine, like Lawson in the 1980s, views 'Europe' as a means of anchoring a domestic policy of tight money. This policy which is ostensibly about the maintenance of price stability and the control of inflation, involves the redistribution of wealth from labour to capital with the aim of strengthening the link between working class consumption and labour producitivity.[17] Against this backgrond, the ideological function of the debate on globalization seems clear. Globalization is said to demand the transformation of the state into a 'competition state', replacing discretionary policy-making by a rule based system in order to reduce the economic costs of democracy (cl. Hirsch, 1997 with Bonefeld, 1999b). 'Globalization', then, allows governments to legitimate tight monetary policies and, importantly, to adopt depoliticizing strategies that are ostensibly demanded by globalization.

There is no doubt that the deregulation of financial markets provides the strongest possible public justification governments can muster for maintaining downward pressure on wages to combat inflation and thereby achieve price stability (see, for example, van Dormael, 1997).[18] The capacity of the national state(s) to impose austerity upon the working class is 'policed' through speculative capital movements (see Bonefeld and Holloway, 1995). In many ways, therefore, the deregulation of the financial markets enhances the 'power' of the state *vis-à-vis* the working class since it can be argued forcefully that price stability really is the crucial determinant in the global economy and lack of 'competitiveness' translates directly into a loss of jobs and profits. Globalization in this sense is far from being a 'mere' ideology.[19]

There is of course the danger that anti-inflationary policies might heighten class conflict with the ultimate risk that such conflict spills over into a political crisis. To prevent the realization of this scenario, governments seek to insulate themselves from such 'spill over'. In this they are served by an 'automatic pilot' (cf. Goldthorpe, 1978) which takes responsibility for imposing financial discipline upon social relations.[20] As Clarke (1990, p. 27) argues in a different context, the driving force behind the state's endeavour to restructure social relations is not so much the attempt to provide a resolution of 'economic crisis', as the attempt to resolve the 'political crisis' of the state by trying to separate the state from the economy, disengaging the government politically from the economic sphere and seeking to depoliticize the making of economic policy by rendering it 'non-political'. This is attempted, for example, by removing monetary policy from the electoral battlefield or by shielding government through institutional reforms towards a more 'rule-based' decision-making system which attempts to build 'automaticity' into the system by formally limiting government's room for manoeuvre.[21] Concerning the issue of depoliticization, membership in the ERM was, initially, successful for the Major government. Since the expulsion of the pound from the ERM, British governments have sought to anchor their tight monetary policies through central bank independence and indeed through secrete membership in EMU.

Conclusion: EMU and employability

The precise scope of Britain's obligation within EMU is open to interpretation. Yet, there is little doubt that the UK is obliged to ensure economic and monetary convergence.[22] Of course, the UK would not be operating in defiance of the Treaty if its attempt of achieving convergence would fail. What matters is that the 'Treaty obligations are framed in terms of *policy intentions*' (Howe, 1996, p. 292). Under Stage 3, Britain's derogation from full membership in EMU entails that it has to be seen to be trying to achieve the common objectives of monetary union.

There is no reason to doubt the new Labour government's tight monetary policy stance. It has adopted the budgetary constraints of its predecessor in office and is staunchly opposed to a politics of 'socialist re-distribution'. Its emphasis falls on 'low inflation' and the inflation target is set at 2.5 per cent. For Labour, the basis of 'economic reform' is a sound monetary and fiscal policy. Independence was granted to the Bank of England precisely for that reason. The UK has pursued and continues to pursue the same neo-liberal policies of tight money that monetary union institutionalizes on a European plane. Artis (1998) has commented that Britain's membership in the ERM in the early 1990s, did not amount to a restriction of the policy-making autonomy of the British government. This was so, he argues, because the policy-stance in the UK and that of the ERM converged. In other words, the domestic policy agenda of the then Major government was reflected in the deflationary discipline of the ERM. Under Blair the European politics of tight money, disinflation and deregulation continue to characterize Britain's domestic policy agenda. When the decision was taken in Spring of 1998 about which member states qualified for Stage 3, the UK was one of the few countries that qualified without fudging its accounts for membership in Stage 3. The UK opted to 'stay out'.

The trouble, then, for Britain is not that monetary union institutionalizes a neo-liberal regime of tight money and deregulation. Rather, the trouble is that full membership in EMU would commit Britain whole-heartedly to Europe exposing its competitive weakness *vis-à-vis* the German-dominated euro-bloc. For the British political economy, the most disappointing feature of the past two decades has been the inability to achieve a decisive breakthrough in labour productivity. In the face of Britain's relatively high unit labour costs and apprehensions over the ability of those workers in the skilled labour market to achieve wage increases, Britain's 'secrete' membership in EMU amounts, then, to an attempt to establish the sort of counter-inflationary credibility that Lawson advocated during the 1980s. Membership in Stage 2 provides an institutional anchor for Britain's tight monetary policy. At the same time, Britain has retained a degree of monetary flexibility and exchange rate 'independence' within the supranational rule-based system of EMU – its two-third membership provides 'discretionary' room for manoeuvre in a rule-based system. In other words, Britain has anchored its macroeconomic policy in Europe. At the same time, the British state has retained – in part – the ability to accommodate relatively low labour productivity to internationally competitive standards through, for example, exchange rate devaluations within the limits set by the euro-bloc. Britain, then, has opted to be a secrete member of EMU, keeping up the appearance of independence and seeking to exploit any margin of competitive advantage that non-membership in Stage 3 confers on Britain. Appearances are, of course, all important, particularly in a world where anti-inflationary credibility is not only an advantage but where, also, the anti-inflationary stance is policed by the movement of speculative capital (cf. Marazzi, 1995).

For sceptics and Blairite Europhiles alike, the UK's future does not lie in an economic alliance with a Europe that it weighted down by allegedly sclerotic and over-regulated labour markets. Indeed, Europe's unemployment problem is seen by many to be at the heart of scepticism about monetary union (see, for example, Eltis, 2000). Commentators, such as Eltis, argue that the European economies have not created any jobs since the 1970s, even in periods of economic expansion; that Europe lags far behind US American job creation, and that European labour market policies mask the underlying problems by promoting early retirement or work sharing. Thus, open unemployment appears to be reduced: a consequence not of an increased demand for labour but of a reduction in the supply of labour. According to the IMF, such measures 'tend to improve the bargaining position of insiders and raise their real wages, with little benefit to outsiders who are likely to remain unemployed' (IMF, *Economic Outlook* October 1997, cited in Eltis, 2000, p. 155). In short, 'Europe' undermines the functioning of the labour market! In Eltis' (2000, pp. 155–6) view, Europe is following a path advocated by Marx! Full membership in an integrating Europe is thus seen as economically dangerous and disadvantageous. In comparison with its more productive European 'partners', Britain's asset is its comparatively low wage economy and deregulated labour market. These 'assets' have to be defended!

The politics of labour market deregulation was, of course, one of the major aims of the previous Conservative governments. The new Labour government has confirmed that it is no less dedicated to the deregulation and flexibilization of labour markets. It has done so, however, under the cover of a semantic innovation: its labour market policy is neither called 'deregulation' nor employment policy. Instead, the Labour government endorses its labour market policy in terms of 'employability'.[23]

'Employability' appears to set out to improve the employment prospects of the working class. The term has a positive connotation, at first sight at least, in that it raises the issues of training, skill and education. There is, of course, nothing wrong with a skilled, educated and well trained labour force. However, the term 'employability' does not lack its sinister side and it is this sinister side that provides substance to the term 'employability'.

During the 1980s, the rate of unemployment not only in Britain, but on a global scale, remained high and this despite the long boom. The boom of the 1980s did not re-integrate the unemployed into the production relation.[24] Furthermore, and importantly, the unemployed did not seem to work in the classic conception of the reserve army of labour. There was, in particular, no recognizable wage-pressure exerted by the reserve army of labour on those workers whose skills were not only in demand but also in short supply. In Britain, during the 1980s, average wage levels increased. This increase disguised the dramatic fall in the income of the unskilled, the unemployed and of those whose skills were no longer required. There developed, then, a 'dual' labour market between highly paid and lowly paid workers. The Thatcherite labour market reforms, especially its anti-trade union policies, were designed to deregulate and flexibilize the labour market. However, the demarcation between 'labour market insiders' and 'labour market outsiders' meant that those with skills were able to take 'advantage' of their position on the labour market leading to the regulation of the labour market on the basis of skill shortages.

The endorsement of 'employability' can thus be seen as an attempt to 'deregulate' the skilled-based demarcation of the labour market that protected skilled workers, on the one hand, and created a vast amount of marginalized labour, on the other. The current British Chancellor,

Mr Brown, has argued that macroeconomic stability and coordination are not the only essential conditions for employment growth. The other is flexible labour markets (see Robinson, 1998). Further deregulation of labour markets, then, is seen to hold the key for the success of Britain plc. As Robinson (1998, p. 193) puts it, 'in the new labour market, governments could not guarantee employment growth, never mind full employment, but instead could only create the conditions in which labour would adapt continously to the changing needs of business'. The new adaptability of the working class would mean that the privileged insiders in the labour market are no longer in a protected position *vis-à-vis* the 'unskilled' outsiders, reducing job security, exerting wage-pressure, and making employment more flexible for all.[25] Whether labour market deregulation and the withdrawal of employment protection would cut unemployment is, of course, a different question. Capital, as the last three decades have shown, is unable to treat the unemployed as an exploitable resource. In other words, 'employability' will not reduce unemployment but increase the risk of unemployment and render work conditions more precarious. Employability makes unemployment invisible.

In sum, the viability of Britain's second-tier membership depends on the achievement of competitive unit labour costs to support the pound as a national currency whose international role is squeezed by the euro, the yen, and the dollar. Keeping Britain outside Stage 3 might transform the British pound into a toy-currency for speculators (cf. Riley, *Financial Times*, 5/6.12.98). The politics of making Britain a 'mega-Singapore' (cf. Callinicos, 1997) would run into serious difficulties with its European partners. EMU entails a politics of deregulation. It does, however, not entail a domestic policy of competitive free riding where member states seek competitive advantage through 'social dumping' or, for those with a derogation, competitive deflation. On the other hand, full scale membership in EMU might well mean a further decline in the competitive position of Britain's political economy. For Labour, deregulated labour markets and a relatively low tax regime are espoused as offering a solution. Whatever the future development of the relationship between Britain and the EU, the achievement of relatively more competitive labour productivity holds the key.

Notes

1 I am most grateful to Peter Burnham for his very useful comments and advice. The usual disclaimers apply.

2 This chapter draws in part on Bonefeld (1999a); and Bonefeld and Burnham (1996, 1998).
3 This part draws on Howe (1996).
4 This part draws on Bonefeld (1999a).
5 See Holloway (1987) for an instructive assessment of labour market deregulation within the framework of workers rights.
6 See Moss (1998) for an account of France's political economy in relation to Europe. See also the contribution by Moss to this volume.
7 This is acknowledged, for example, by Martin Wolf of the *Financial Times* (8.4.97): 'To have halted, or even slowed, the pace of relative decline is comforting. But delight must be tempered by awareness of the reason for this sucess. This is the deterioriation in performance elsewhere, above all on the European continent'. In other words, the relative decline was not reversed, but was merely halted or slowed; and this not because of a stronger economic development in Britain but because of a slower economic development in the rest of Europe. On Britain's relative decline see Coates (1994).
8 This part draws on Bonefeld and Burnham (1996).
9 On this see Goldthorpe (1978, pp. 186–214) and below.
10 On Thatcher's position see Wooley (1992).
11 On this and subsequent developments: Bonefeld *et al.* (1995, ch. 4).
12 This part draws on Bonefeld and Burnham (1998).
13 On this see King (ed) (1976) and Crozier *et al.* (1975). See also Bonefeld (chapter 4) in this volume.
14 For an assessment of conventional accounts on globalization see Burnham (1997).
15 On EMU as a means of forcing the adjustment of European labour productivity to German levels, see Carchedi's contribution to this volume.
16 See also the contribution of Callinicos to this volume.
17 On this see Bonefeld *et al.* (1995).
18 This section draws on Burnham (1997, p. 154).
19 On this see Agnoli (2000) and Burnham (2000).
20 One of the most important lessons of the 1920s was that by switching from 'discretion' to 'rules' in economic policy, governments could 'externalize' the imposition of financial discipline. The stronger the set of 'rules', the greater manoeuvrability the state would achieve, increasing the likelihood of attaining objectives. This was the logic behind Britain's return to gold in Spring 1925 at a pre-war parity of £1 = $4.86. The move was subjected to a devastating critique by John Maynard Keynes who argued that the pre-war parity was too high and would impose painful and useless deflation on the British economy (Block, 1977, p. 17). Leading supporters of the return to gold, in particular John Bradbury and Otto Niemeyer in the Treasury, were adamant that the gold standard would make the British economy 'knave-proof', free of manipulation for 'political or even more unworthy reasons' (Rukstad, 1989, p. 440). For its supporters, the gold standard was seen as an 'automatic corrective mechanism' and thus the best guarantee against inflation. The parallel between Britain's return to gold in the 1920s and Major's determination to depoliticize 'economic' adjustment by joining the ERM in 1990 is striking. Both 'regimes' seemed to offer an automatic corrective to inflation and both, in the short-term, were successful in imposing austerity upon the working

class. On this see also Bonefeld and Burnham (1996, 1998); Burnham (2000). See also Ludlam (1992) on Labour's 'use' of the IMF in the 1970s.

21 For an overview of the literature on rule based systems, see: Keech (1992, pp. 259–78) and Kydland and Prescott (1977, pp. 473–91). See also the useful discussion of 'new constitutionalism' in Gill (1995, pp. 399–423; 1998, pp. 5–26).

22 On this see Howe (1996).

23 For a useful discussion see Levitas (1998, esp. pp. 118–21).

24 This part draws on Bonefeld (1993).

25 Labour's labour market philosophy draws in terms of its ideological justification from, for example, Reich (1992) who argued that globalization requires maximum flexibility and work-force adaptability to reduce labour market rigidities and to allow governments to preside over prosperous economies. In Britain, the ideological underpinning of Labour's third way philosophy is provided by, for example, Giddens (1998, 1999).

Bibliography

Agnoli, J. (2000) 'State, Market, and the End of History', in Bonefeld, W. and Psychopedis, K. (eds).

Ali, T. (1999) 'All quiet on the EU front...', *Observer*, 17th January.

Anderson, P. (1997) 'The Europe to Come', in Gowan, P. and Anderson, P. (eds), *The Question of Europe* (London: Verso).

Artis, M. J. (1998) 'The United Kingdom', in Forder, J. and Menon, A. (eds), *The European Union and National Macroeconomic Policy* (London: Routledge).

Bellofiore, R. (ed) (1999) *Global Money, Capital Restructuring and the Changing Patterns of Labour* (Cheltenham: Edward Elgar).

Block, F. (1977) *The Origins of International Economic Disorder* (London: University of California Press).

Bonefeld, W. (1993) *The Recomposition of the British State During the 1980s* (Aldershot: Dartmouth).

Bonefeld, W. (1999a) 'British Experience: Hiding Behind Europe', *Journal of European Area Studies*, 7, 1.

Bonefeld, W. (1999b) 'Globalization and the State', *Studies in Political Economy*, 58.

Bonefeld, W. and Burnham, P. (1996) 'Britain and the Politics of the European Exchange Rate Mechanism', *Capital & Class*, 60.

Bonefeld, W. and Burnham, P. (1998) 'The Politics of Counterinflationary Credibility in Britain, 1990–94', *Review of Radical Political Economics*, 30, 1.

Bonefeld, W. and Holloway, J. (eds) (1995) *Global Capital, National State and the Politics of Money* (London: Macmillan).

Bonefeld, W. and Psychopedis, K. (eds) (2000) *The Politics of Change* (London: Macmillan).

Bonefeld, W., Brown, A. and Burnham, P. (1995) *A Major Crisis* (Aldershot: Dartmouth).

Brittan, S. (1976) 'The Economic Contradictions of Democracy', in King, A. (ed).

Bulmer, S. (1992) 'Britain and European Integration: of Sovereignty, Slow Adaption, and Semi-Detachment', in George, S. *Britain and the European Community* (Oxford: Oxford University Press).

Burkitt, B. and Baimbridge, M. (1996) 'Britain and the European Community', in Holmes, M. (ed).
Burnham, P. (1997) 'Globalisation: States, Markets and Class Relation', *Historical Materialism*, 1.
Burnham, P. (2000) 'Globalisation, Depoliticisation and "modern" economic Management', in Bonefeld, W. and Psychopedis, K. (eds).
Callinicos, A. (1997) 'Europe: The Mounting Crisis', *International Socialism*, 75.
Clarke, S. (1990) 'Crisis of Socialism or Crisis of the State?', *Capital & Class*, 42.
Clarke, S. (1992) 'The Global Accumulation of Capital and the Periodisation of the Capitalist State Form', in Bonefeld, W. *et al.* (eds). *Open Marxism*, vol. I (London: Pluto).
Coates, D. (1994) *The Question of UK Decline* (London: Harvester Wheatsheaf).
Connolly, B. (1995) *The Rotten Heart of Europe* (London: Faber).
Crafts, N. (1994) 'Industry', in Kavanagh, D. and Seldon, A. (eds).
Crozier, M. *et al.* (1975) *The Crisis of Democracy* (New York: New York University Press).
Deakin, S. (1992) 'Labour Law and Industrial Relations', in Michie, J. (ed).
Eltis, W. (2000) 'British EMU Membership Would Create Instability and Destroy Employment', in Baimbridge, M., Burkitt, B. and Whyman, P. (eds), *The Impact of the Euro* (London: Macmillan).
Fine, B. (1979) 'World Economic Crisis and Inflation', in Green, F. and Nore, P. (eds), *Issues in Political Economy: A Critical Approach* (London: Macmillan).
Gamble, A. (1986) *Britain in Decline* (London: Macmillan).
George, S. (1994) *An Awkward Partner*, 2nd edn (Oxford: Oxford University Press).
Giddens, A. (1998) *The Third Way* (Cambridge: Polity).
Giddens, A. (1999) *Runnaway World* (London: Profile).
Gill, S. (1992) 'The Emerging World Order and European Change', *Socialist Register 1992* (London: Merlin).
Gill, S. (1995) 'Globalisation, Market Civilisation and Disciplinary Neoliberalism', *Millennium*, 24, 3.
Gill, S. (1998) 'European Governance and New Constitutionalism: Economic and Monetary Union and Alternatives to Discplinary Neoliberalism in Europe', *New Political Economy* 3, 1.
Grahl, J. (1997) *After Maastricht* (London: Lawrence & Wishart).
Goldthorpe, J. (1978) 'The Current Inflation', in Hirsch, F. and Goldthorpe, J. (eds), *The Political Economy of Inflation* (London: Martin Robertson).
Halevi, J. (1999) 'The Accumulation Process in Japan and East Asia as Compared with the Role of Germany in European Post-war Growth', in Bellofiore, R. (ed).
Hirsch, J. (1997) 'Globalization of Capital, Nation-States and Democracy', *Studies in Political Economy*, 54.
Holloway, J. (1987) 'The Red Rose of Nissan', *Capital & Class*, 32.
Holmes, M. (ed.) (1996) *The Eurosceptical Reader* (London: Macmillan).
Howe, M. (1996) 'Monetary Policy after Maastricht', in Holmes, M. (ed).
Hufschmid, J. (1994) *Wem gehört Europa?*, 2 vols., (Heilbronn: Distel Verlag).
Hufschmid, J. (1998) 'Hoist with its own Petard', in Moss, B. and Michie, J. (eds).
Jamieson, B. (1996) 'Worlds Apart?', in Holmes, M. (ed).
Jay, P. (1994) 'The Economy 1990–94', in Kavanagh, D. and Seldon, A. (eds).
Kavanagh, D. and Seldon, A. (eds) (1994) *The Major Effect* (London: Macmillan).

Keech, W. (1992) 'Rules, Discretion, and Accountability in Macroeconomic Policymaking', *Governance*, 5, 3.
King, A. (ed) (1976) *Why is Britain Becoming Harder to Govern?* (London: BBC Books).
Kirchner, E. (1996) 'Germany and the European Union', in Smith, P., Paterson, W. E. and Padgett, S. (eds), *Developments in German Politics 2* (London: Macmillan).
Kydland, F. and Prescott, E. (1977) 'Rules Rather than Discretion', *Journal of Political Economy*, 85, 3.
Lamont, N. (1992) *Mansion House Speech*, 29 October.
Lawson, N. (1992) *A View from Number 11* (London: Bantam Press).
Levitas, R. (1998) *The Inclusive Society?, Social Exclusion and New Labour* (London: Macmillan).
Ludlam, S. (1992) 'The Gnoms of Washington: Four Myths of the 1976 IMF Crisis', *Political Studies*, 30, 4.
Marazzi, C. (1995) 'Money in the World Crisis: The New Basis of Capitalist Power', in Bonefeld, W. and Holloway, J. (eds).
Michie, J. (ed) (1992) *The Economic Legacy 1979–1992* (London: Academic Press).
Moravcsik, A. (1999) *The Choice for Europe* (London: UCL Press).
Moss, B. (1998) 'France: Economic and Monetary Union and the Social Divide', in Moss, B. and Michie, J. (eds).
Moss, B. and Michie, J. (eds) (1998) *The Single European Act in National Perspective* (London: Macmillan).
Murray, A. (1997) *Flashpoint* (London: Pluto).
Negri, A. (1996) 'The Crisis of Political Space', *Common Sense*, 19.
Posen, A. (1993) 'Why Central Bank Independence does not Cause Law Inflation', in O'Brien, R. (ed) *Finance and the International Economy* (Oxford: Oxford University Press).
Radice, H. (1999) 'Britain under New Labour: A Module for European Restructuring?', in Bellofiore, R. (ed).
Redwood, J. (1997) *Our Currency, Our Country* (Harmondsworth: Penguin).
Reich, R. (1992) *The Work of Nations* (New York: Vintage).
Robinson, A. (1998) 'Why "Employability" Won't Make EMU Work', in Moss, B. and Michie, J. (eds).
Rowthorn, B. (1975) 'Imperialism in the 1970s – Unity or Rivalry?', in Radice, H. (ed), *International Firms and Modern Imperialism* (Harmondsworth: Penguin).
Rowthorn, B. (1992) 'Government Spending and Taxation in the Thatcher Era', in Michie, J. (ed).
Rukstad, M. (1989) *Macroeconomic Decision Making in the World Economy* (London: Dryen).
Shaw, E. (1994) *The Labour Party since 1979* (London: Routledge).
Smith, D. (1993) *From Boom to Bust* (Harmondsworth: Penguin).
Smith, D. (1997) 'The Bank's First Task is to Get the Rate Right', *The Sunday Times*, 11 May.
Thompson, H. (1995) 'Globalisation, Monetary Autonomy and Central Bank Independence' in Lovenduski, J. and Stanyer, J. (eds), *Contemporary Political Studies 3* (Exeter: PSA).
Treasury (1993–94) Treasury and Civil Service Committee. *The Role of the Central Bank of England 1 (First Report)* (London: HMSO).

Treasury (1994) *Chancellor Publishes Minutes of Monetary Meetings,* March, (London: HM Treasury).
van Dormael, A. (1997) *The Power of Money* (London: Macmillan).
Wooley, J. (1992) 'Policy Credibility and European Monetary Institutions', in Sbragia, A. M. (ed), *Euro-Politics* (Washington, DC: Brookings Institute).
Young, H. (2000) 'Blair Can No Longer Afford to be Vague About the Euro', *Guardian*, 24 February.

Index

Abraham, F. and P. van Rompuy, 165
Abramovitz, M., 145
abstract equality, 3, 82
accumulation of capital and capitalist crisis, 3, 4, 5, 7, 13, 28, 31–2, 37, 39–46, 52–4, 65, 67, 74–9, 96–7, 176
Achcar, G., 35
Adenauer, K., 12
adjustment, 42–4, 51, 52, 64, 66–7, 73, 77–8, 88–9, 174–6
  and currency devaluation, 18, 40–6, 64, 76, 89, 131, 172
  and labour, 3, 18, 19, 50–1, 57, 64, 73, 76–8, 88–9, 94, 95–7, 98, 100, 174, 175–7
  and fiscal policy, 18, 19, 47, 64–5, 87–8, 91–5, 100
  see also Economic and Monetary Union (EMU) and Stability Pact
Adorno, T., 9
Agnoli, J., 102, 180, 188
Albert, M., 11, 34
Ali, T., 173
Alter, J. and S. Meunier-Aitsahalia, 117
Altvater, E., Blanke, E., and Chr. Neusüss, 59
Anderson, P., 2, 5, 8, 34, 73, 88–9, 89, 99, 171
Andor, L., *see* Summers, M. and L. Andor
Andreotti, G., 16
Applegate, C., 138
Armstrong, P., Glyn, A., and J. Harrison, 102
Armstrong, H.W., 165
Artis, M. J., 184
Ash, T. G., 15
Atkinson, D., *see* Elliot, L. and D. Atkinson
Auschwitz, 5, 15

Baché, J.-P., *see* Oliver, P. and J.-P. Baché
Backhaus, H.-G., 102
Bahaijoub, A., 157
Baimbridge, M., 155
  see also Burkitt, B. and M. Baimbridge
Bairoch, P., 109
Baker, D. Epstein, G. and R. Pollin, 131
Baldwin-Edwards, M., 160
Balladur, E., 155
barbarism, 5–7, 34
Barber, L., 25
Barro, R. J., and X. Sala-i-Martin, 165
Baruch, B., 83, 86
Baumol, W., 145
Beetham, D. and C. Lord, 8
Belassa, B., 109
Bell, P. and H. Cleaver, 102
Ben-David, D., 165
Benson, G., 103
Bentham, J., 82
Bernholz, P., 103
Bisat, A., *see* Nsouli, S. M., Bisat, A. and O. Kanaan
Bladen-Hovell, R., 61
Blair, T., 21, 24, 26, 29, 31, 33, 128, 172–3, 179, 184
Blanco Fdez de Valderramam, C., 166
Blanke, B., *see* Altvater, E., Blanke, B., and Chr. Neusüss
Block, F., 188
Blunden, M., 150
Boeckout, S., *see* Molle, M. and S. Boeckout
Bonefeld, W., 4, 5, 7, 8, 102–3, 174, 183, 188, 189
Bonefeld, W. and P. Burnham, 61, 102, 176–7, 188–9
Bonefeld, W., Brown, A. and P. Burnham, 188
Bonefeld, W. and J. Holloway, 102, 183
Bossuat, G., 108
Bourgeois, J. and P. Demeret, 123
Bourry, C., 109, 118

Box, S., 166
Boyer, R. and D. Drache, 130
Bradbury, J., 188
Brantley, P., *see* Fligstein, N. and P. Brantley
Braudel, F., 158, 166
Brenner, R., 35
Bretton Woods, 45–6, 68, 72, 74
Brittan, L., 117
Brittan, S., 80–1, 189
Brown, G., 21, 179–80, 187
Brown, A., *see* Bonefeld, W., Brown A. and P. Burnham
Brzezinski, Z., 21, 35
Bundesbank, 14, 15, 17, 23–5, 57, 72, 82, 110, 176–7
Burgess, A., 152, 157
Burkitt, B. and M. Baimbridge, 182
Burnham, P., 187, 188, 189
  see also Bonefeld, W. and P. Burnham; and Bonefeld, W., Brown, A. and P. Burnham
Busch, K., 79
Busch, K., Schöller, W., and W. Seelow, 59
Bush, G., 27
Butt-Phillip, A., 166

Callaghan, J., 70
Callinicos, A., 4–7, 29, 34–5, 181, 187–8
Calloui, G., 166
Campbell, D. and K. Connolly, K., 166
Carchedi, G., 4, 5, 7, 37, 38, 39, 58, 59, 61, 65, 73–4, 88–9, 188
  see also Freeman, A. and G. Carchedi
Carchedi, G. and W. de Haan, 58
Cartelier, L., 119
Carter, J., 70
Cecchini, P., 114, 115
Central Bank independence, 16–17, 17, 82, 90, 98–9, 170, 184
  Bank of England, 17, 177–80, 184
  Bank of Japan, 17
  see also European Central Bank (ECB)
Chévènement, J., 22
Chirac, J., 22, 24, 33
Clarke, K., 178, 180
Clarke, S., 69, 102, 176, 183
Cleaver, H., 76
  see also Bell, P. and H. Cleaver
Clinton, B., 26, 27, 28
Coakley, J., 61
Coates, K. and J. Santer, 123, 127
Coates, D., 188
Cockfield, Lord, 114
Cohen, E., 121, 122
Cole, M., *see* Dale, G. and M. Cole
Collinson, S., 165
Commission, 12, 23, 24, 64, 113–14, 116–17, 119–29, 152, 154, 157
Common Agricultural Policy, 27, 117–18, 147–48
Connolly, B., 12, 14, 34, 102, 182
Connolly, K., *see* Campbell, D. and K. Connolly
convergence and divergence, 143–7
  and regional differences, 137–40
  and enlargement and/or accession, 8, 130, 140–2, 148–54, 156–7
Convey, A. and M. Kupiszewski, 166
Corbett, R., *see* Jacobs, F., Corbett, R. and M. Shackleton
Council of Ministers, 12, 20, 116–17, 122–3, 127–29
Crafts, N., 165, 175
Crozier, M., 79, 188
Currie, D., 95
Cutler, T., Haslam, C., Williams, J. and K. Williams, 109

d'Estaing, V. G., 13
Dale, G. and M. Cole, 166
de Gaulle, C., 12, 27, 109, 118
de Brunhoff, S., 102
de Long, J., 145
de Haan, W., *see* Carchedi, G. and W. de. Haan
Deakin, S., 176
Debène, M. and O. Raymundie, 119
Delors, J., 2, 8, 11, 13, 111, 114, 121, 123–27
Demeret, P., *see* Bourgeois, J. and P. Demeret
democratic deficit, 5–6, 65, 82, 85–6, 90–1, 99, 128–30
Denton, G., 122

depoliticization, 17, 49–51, 67, 78–9, 81–2, 84, 87–8, 90, 92, 99, 128, 174, 178, 184, 188
Deubner, Chr., Rehfeld, U., Schlupp, F. and G. Ziebura, 59
Devos, T., 126, 129
Dinan, D., 118
Drache, D., *see* Boyer, R. and D. Drache
Duisenberg, W., 24, 25

Eastern Europe, *see* convergence and divergence, and enlargement; and labour and migration, moral panics and policing
Eatwell, J., Ellman, M., Karlsson, M., Mario Nuti, D., and J. Shapiro, 165
Economic and Monetary Union (EMU), 2–3, 5, 7, 10, 11, 13–14, 20, 21, 23, 25, 31, 34, 46, 49, 50–1, 64–7, 82, 86–7, 89–90, 92, 94–100, 107, 127, 129, 171–2, 182, 184–5, 187
  and convergence criteria, 19–20, 22, 23, 33, 37, 50, 61, 64, 72, 95, 97, 110, 115, 170
  see also Stability Pact
Ecu, 46–7, 48
Eichengreen, B., 92, 94
Eichengreen, B. and J. Frieden, 110
Ellingstad, M., 165
Elliot, L. and D. Atkinson, D., 23
Ellman, M., *see* Eatwell, J., Ellman, M., Karlsson, M., Mario Nuti, D., and J. Shapiro
Eltis, W., 101, 185
Emerson, M., 2, 8, 82, 86, 91–5
employment and employability, 8, 19, 38, 49, 52, 61, 93, 94, 100, 110, 113, 115, 119, 121, 127, 151, 171–73, 175–6, 185–7
  see also adjustment and labour; and labour
Enlightenment, 1, 6
Epstein, G., *see* Baker, D., Epstein, G. and R. Pollin
Erhard, L., 12
Euro, 2, 10, 16, 18–21, 30, 37, 50–1, 58, 73, 92, 100–1, 148, 182, 185, 187
Europe versus America, 7, 11, 25–30, 72, 124
European Council, 12, 23, 127
European Parliament, 12, 125–9, 161
European law and negative integration, 115–117, 118–22
European Central Bank (ECB), 16, 17, 22, 23, 24, 25, 51, 64, 65, 67, 72, 73, 82, 87, 89–91, 92, 96
European Monetary System (EMS) 13, 46, 69, 78, 87
European Exchange Rate Mechanism (ERM), 12, 14, 18, 21, 46, 48–52, 60–1, 69, 71, 87, 103, 110, 124, 175–6, 179, 184, 188
  and crisis of 1992/93, 17, 15, 18, 22, 49, 71–2, 172, 176–7
  and DM-zone, 14–15, 18, 23, 48, 49, 71, 174, 182
European Payments Union (EPU), 68
European Coal and Steel Community (ECSC), 108, 112
European Court of Justice (ECJ), 113–117, 119, 121, 123
Europeaness
  ideology of, 8, 136, 155–8
  see also Labour and moral panics
Evans, T., 61
Evans, A. and S. Martin, 120
exchange rate and appropriation of value, 39–46, 177
Eyal, J., 163

Fagerberg, J. and B. Verspagen, 165
Fassmann, H., 159
Feathersone, K., 107
Feldstein, M., 9, 30, 109
Fine, B., 177
fiscal federalism, 86, 92–4, 100–1
  see also adjustment, Hayek, Keynesianism, and Stability Pact
Fligstein, N. and P. Brantley, 108
Fontagné, L., 109
France forte, 14, 17, 71, 174
Franco–German relations, 5, 7, 12, 14, 16, 22, 24–5, 69, 72–3, 86–7, 92, 102, 107–8, 112, 124
Freeman, A., 61
Freeman, A. and G. Carchedi, 60

Frieden, J., *see* Eichengreen, B. and J. Frieden
Friedman, G., 110
Friedman, M., 70, 84, 102
Frindjonsdottir, K., 131
Fukuyama, F., 11, 164

Galbraith, J., 34
Gambino, F., 3
Gamble, A., 181
Garret, G., 91–2, 130
Garson, J.P., 151
Geir, J., 35
Geir, J. and A. Shawki, 35
Georg, E., 179
George, S., 170
German, L., 35
Germany
  dominant position in Europe, 13–15, 48–50, 69–73, 88, 124, 137, 147, 176, 181–2, 185
  see also Franco–German relations
Giddens, A., 8, 93, 189
Gill, S., 61, 98, 99, 171, 189
Gillingham, J., 108
Glebe, G., *see* Peach, C. and G. Glebe
Glyn, A., 61, 102
  see also Armstrong, P., Glyn, A., and J. Harrison
Godley, W., 88
gold standard, 188
Gold, M., *see* Hall, H. and M. Gold
Goldthorpe, J., 183, 188
Gouyette, C., *see* Neven, D. and C. Gouyette
Gowan, P., 99
Goyder, D., 120
Grahl, J., 12, 16, 34, 61, 66, 73, 90, 171
Gramsci, A., 111
Greenspan, A., 28
Gromley, L., *see* Kapteyn, P., Gromley, L. and P. Verloren van Thematt
Gros, D. and N. Thygessen, 86–7

Haack, W., 131
Hass, E., 111, 131
Hadjimichalis, C., 152, 157–58
Haider, J., 153
  and Freedom Party, 25, 153
Hakura, F.S., 142
Halevi, J., 72, 182
Hall, M., 126
Hall, M. and M. Gold, 126
Hallstein, W., 119, 122
Hamilton, K.A., 160
Harley, T., 116
Harman, C., 34, 35
Harris, N., 159
Harrison, J., *see* Armstrong, P., Glyn, A., and J. Harrison
Harvie, C., 138
Haslam C., *see* Williams, J., Williams, K., and C. Haslam; *see also* Cutler, T., Haslam, C., Williams, J. and K. Williams
Hayek, F., 1, 2, 8, 70, 79, 84–6, 93, 96, 98–103
  see also inter-state federalism
Haynes, M., 3, 4, 8, 103, 156
Hayward, J., 122
Helleiner, E., 79
Henning, C.R., 73, 96
Hennis, W., 102
Heseltine, M., 182
Hine, C., 124
Hirsch, J., 183
Hirst, P. and G. Thompson, 35
Hix, S., 3
Hobsbawm, E., 111
Holland, S., 8, 119–20, 122–23, 131
Holloway, J., 8, 79, 102, 188
  see also Bonefeld, W. and J. Holloway
Holloway, J., and E. Peláez, 102
Holloway, J. and S. Picciotto, 8
Howe, M., 170, 184, 188, 189
Hufschmid, J., 181
Hutton, W., 34, 145, 146
immigration, 25, 56, 152, 155, 159, 160, 165
  as human right, 159
  see also labour and migration, fortress Europe
inter-imperialist rivalry, 4–5, 7–8, 12, 31, 58, 65, 72, 102, 171, 180
  see also convergence and divergence, and Enlargement

inter-state federalism, 2, 84–5, 95
  see also F. Hayek

Jacobs, F., Corbett, R., and M. Shackleton, 128
Jamieson, B., 181, 182
Jay, P., 176, 178
Jospin, L., 22, 24, 29, 30, 128, 172
Juppé, A., 24, 33

Kaldor, N., 146
Kanaan, O., *see* Nsouli, S.M., Bisat, A. and O. Kanaan.
Kant, I., 2, 5, 6
Kaplar, Z., 150
Kapteyn, P., Gromley, L. and P. Verloren van Thematt, 107, 113, 116, 119
Karlsson, M., *see* Eatwell, J., Ellman, M., Karlsson, M., Mario Nuti, D., and J. Shapiro
Keech, W., 189
Kemp, T., 102
Kennedy, P., 146
Keynes, M. J., 188
Keynesianism, 38, 66, 70–1, 79, 80, 85–6, 92, 99, 102, 171, 174–5
King, A., 80–1, 188
Kinnock, N., 172
Kirchner, E., 182
Kohl, H., 8, 11, 14–16, 22–5, 27, 152
Krugman, P., 35
Kupiszewski, M., *see* Convey, A. and M. Kupiszewski
Kuznets, S., 143
Kydland, F. and E. Prescott, 189

Labour theory of value, 37–9, 58, 67, 75
  see also Adjustment and labour
Labour, 2–5, 7–8, 33, 44, 49, 50–2, 57–8, 62, 65–7, 70–1, 73–9, 81–6, 88, 91–2, 95–7, 99, 101–2, 129–30, 171–73, 178, 183, 185, 187
  and migration, 3, 8, 95, 100, 118, 151, 158
  and 'fortress Europe', 8, 158–164
  and asylum, 3, 158–60
  and moral panics and policing, 159–164, 166
Ladrech, R., 128
Lafay, G., 110
Lafontaine, O., 25, 34
Lambert, R., 30
Lamont, N., 175, 177, 180
Lamoureux, F., 154
Lawson, N., 70, 85–6, 87, 174, 175, 179–80, 183, 185
Lemke, C. and G. Marks, 129
Lenin, I., 131
Levitas, R., 189
Lindberg, L. and S. Scheinberg, 119, 128
Lindsey, L., 18
Lord, C., *see* Beetham, D. and C. Lord
Ludlam, S., 189
Luttwak, E., 16
Luxemburg, R., 5, 6, 8, 34

Maddison, A., 144, 149, 165
Maier, C., 108
Major, J., 21, 179, 184, 188
Mandel, E., 8, 35, 102, 131
Manfrass, K., 155, 159
Marazzi, Chr., 76, 185
Mario Nuti, D., *see* Eatwell, J., Ellman, M., Karlsson, M., Mario Nuti, D., and J. Shapiro
Marjolin, R., 124
Marks, G., *see* Lemke, C. and G. Marks
Marsh, D., 15, 34
Marshall Plan, 26
Martin, P., 20
Martin, R., 165
Martin, S., 121, 127
Martin, S. and O. Stehmann, 121
  see Evans, A. and S. Martin
Marx, K., 2, 3–4, 4, 6, 58, 82, 102, 180, 186
Matthews, R., 102
Mattick, P., 76
Mertens de Wilmar, J., 115
Metternich, Klemens Lothar-Wenzel Fürst von, 156
Meunier-Aitsahalia, S., *see* Alter, K. and S. Meunier-Aitsahalia

Mexicanization
Eastern Europe, 152
Mediterranean area, 152
Mexico, 53–8, 62, 102
Michie, J., *see* Moss, B. and J. Michie
migration, *see* labour and migration
Milward, A., 12, 26, 34, 112
Minford, P., 100
Mitterand, F., 11, 13, 15–16, 70, 107, 114, 124, 174
Molle, M. and S. Boeckout, 147
Mollet, G., 108, 112
monetarism, *see* neo-liberalism
Monnet, J., 111
Monnier, L., 119, 122
moral hazard, 92, 101, 103
Moravcsik, A., 108, 114, 182
Moss, B., 3, 5, 7, 8, 112, 188
Moss, B. and J. Michie, 108, 110, 113
multispeed Europe, 22, 140
Murdoch, R., 21
Murray, A., 180–81

Napoleon, Bonaparte, 156
NATO, 15, 26–9, 142
negative integration, *see* European law and negative integration
Negri, A., 181
neo-liberalism
and European integration, 5, 7, 16–20, 31, 33, 38, 66, 68, 79–86, 98, 113, 152, 172–5, 184
and ordo-liberalism, 79–82, 99
see also ungovernability
Neunreither, K., 128
Neusüss, Chr., *see* Altvater, E., Blanke, B., and Chr. Neusüss
Neven, D. and C. Gouyette, 165
Niemeyer, O., 188
Nixon, R., 74
Nizamova, A., 150
Nsouli, S.M., Bisat, A. and O. Kanaan, 142

Oliver, P. and J.-P. Baché, 114
Olson, M., 111
organised crime, 155, 158–61, 166
see also Labour and moral panics and policing

Padoa-Schioppa, T., 87, 89, 90, 91, 92, 93, 96, 114, 120,
Peláez, E., *see* Holloway, J. and E. Peláez
Palmer, J., 10, 35
Parboni, R., 102
Peach, C. and G. Glebe, 165
Pearce, F. and M. Woodiwiss, 166
Pernin, A., 120
Petras, J. and S. Vieux, 35
Philip, A., 124
Picciotto, S. *see* Holloway, J. and S. Picciotto
Pinder, J., 115
Pivetti, M., 110
Pollin, R., *see* Baker, D., Epstein, G. and R. Pollin
Posen, A., 177
Poulantzas, N., 8
Prescott, E., *see* Kydland, F. and E. Prescott
prostitution, 161, 166

Radice, H., 181
Raymundie, O. and M. Debène, *see* M. Debène and O. Raymundie
Reagan, R., 30, 70
Redwood, J., 175
Regional Fund, 19, 88, 92, 118
regionalism, *see* convergence and divergence and regional differences
Rehfeld, U., *see* Deubner, Chr., Rehfeld, U., Schlupp, F. and G. Ziebura
Reich, R., 189
relationship between the economic and political, 5, 10, 15, 65–6, 79, 81, 83–4, 100–101, 180–81, 183
Reuvid, J., 166
Rhein, E., 142, 150–2
Ricardo, D., 109
Ricciardi, J., 103
Ridley, N., 14
Riley, F., 182, 187
Robinson, A., 172, 187
Robinson, J., 58
Rocard, M., 131
Roman, P., 153
Roosevelt, F.D., 83
Ross, G., 118, 125

Rouleau, E., 29
Rowthorn, B., 175, 181
Rukstad, M., 188

Saint-Martin, O., 122
Sala-i-Martin, X., *see* Barro, R. J. and X. Sala-i-Martin
Salesse, Y., 110, 117
Sandholtz, W., 78
Santer, J., 24
see also Coates, K. and J. Santer
Scheinberg, S., *see* Lindberg, L. and S. Scheinberg
Schengen, 160
Schlesinger, H., 177
Schlupp, F., *see* Deubner, Chr., Rehfeld, U., Schlupp, F. and G. Ziebura
Schmidt, H., 8, 13, 14, 87
Schmitt, C., 79, 83, 84, 100, 103
Schmitter, P., *see* Streeck, W. and P. Schmitter
Schöller, W., *see* Busch, K., Schöller, W. and W. Seelow
Schröder, G., 102
Schumpeter, J., 79, 102
Seelow, W., *see* Busch, K., Schöller W., and W. Seelow
Senf, B., 59
Shackleton, M., *see* Jacobs, F., Corbet, R. and M. Shackleton
Shapiro, J., *see* Eatwell, J., Ellman, M., Karlsson, M., Mario Nuti, D., and J. Shapiro
Sharp, M., 122
Shaw, E., 172
Shaw, J., 126
Shawki, A., *see* Geir J. and A. Shawki
Shelly, L., 166
Siegel, T., 59
Silvia, S., 125
Single Market, 107, 109–110, 114, 120–2, 125, 125, 127, 155, 171, 173
Single European Act (SEA), *see* Single Market
Smith, A., 4, 123
Smith, D., 103, 175
Smith, J., 172
Snake, 69
Snyder, F., 113, 123
Social Europe, 4, 7, 108, 118–20, 124–127, 130, 148, 173
Spaak Report, 112–13
Stabilty Pact, 19–20, 61, 64–5, 72, 95, 97–8
see also EMU and convergence criteria
state, *see* relationship between the economic and political
Stehmann, O., *see* Martin, S. and O. Stehmann
Stephens, P., 34
Stoiber, E., 23
Stoltenberg, G., 15
Streeck, W., 118, 125, 127
Streeck, W. and P. Schmitter, 129
subsidiarity, 86, 89, 91, 93–4, 96, 116, 125
Summer, L., 26
Summers, M. and L. Andor, 165
Swann, D., 49
Szyszczak, E., 116, 126

Taylor, P., 119
Thatcher, M., 13, 17, 21, 70, 71, 86, 111, 114, 155, 171–5, 186
Thirwell, T., 148
Thompson, H., 178–80
Thompson, G., *see* Hirst, P. and G. Thompson
Thomson, T., 166
Thygessen, N., *see* Gros, D. and N. Thygessen
Tietmeyer, H., 24, 25, 101
Timans, R., 159
Tinbergen, J., 115
Toniolo, G., 165
Tortella, G., 165
trafficking of
drugs, 155, 158, 162–3
women, 161–2
see also Labour and fortress Europe
Treaty of Amsterdam, 22, 127, 129, 172
Treaty of European Union (Maastricht Treaty), 10, 14–15, 18, 72, 115–116, 120, 122–3, 125, 127, 128, 131, 156, 158, 162, 170

Treaty of Rome, 12, 26, 108, 112, 113, 116, 117–18, 122, 123, 131, 156
Trichet, J-C., 24
Trosky, L., 131
Turkey, 142, 150, 155–7, 159

ungovernability, 80–82, 84, 180
see also neo-liberalism

value, *see* labour theory of value; exchange rate and appropriation of value
van Dormael, A., 183
Van Rompuy, P., *see* Abraham, F. and P. van Rompuy
van Paridon, C., 110
Verdun, A., 108, 127
Verheugen, J., 154
Verloren van Thematt, P., *see* Kapteyn, P. Gormley, L. and P. Verloren van Thematt
Verspagen, B., *see* Fagerberg, J. and B. Verspagen
Vieux, S., *see* Petra, J. and S. Vieux
von Mises, L., 80
Vredeling, 126, 128

Waigel, T., 19, 23, 61
Walker, P., 111, 131
Walter, A., 102
war
and European integration, 5, 8–9, 11, 12, 30, 96, 108, 109
and former Yugoslavia, 27, 29, 142, 153
Warburton, P., 102
Weiler, J., 116
Weiss, L., 20
Werner Plan, 68
Whalen, C., 57
Williams, J., Williams, K. and C. Haslam, 87, 90
see also Cutler, T., Haslam, C., Williams J. and K. Williams
Williams, K., *see* Williams J., Williams, K. and C. Haslam; *see also* Cutler, T., Haslam, C., Williams, J. and K. Williams
Williamson, J., 145
Wolf, M., 32, 188
Wolfreys, J., 35
Woodiwiss, M., *see* Pearce, F. and M. Woodiwiss
Wooley, J., 188
Wright., E.O., 131

Young, H., 173

Zapatista uprising, 55–8, 62, 102
Zelasko, P., 166
Ziebura, G., *see* Deubner Chr., Rehfeld, U., Schlupp, F. and G. Ziebura
Zuckerman, M.B., 35